Sailing with
Mohammed

A true yachting adventure in and around the Middle East

TONY FARRINGTON

NEW
HOLLAND

First published in 2005   New Holland Publishers (NZ) Ltd
Auckland • Sydney • London • Cape Town
218 Lake Road, Northcote, Auckland, New Zealand
14 Aquatic Drive, Frenchs Forest, NSW 2086, Australia
86 Edgware Road, London W2 2EA, United Kingdom
80 McKenzie Street, Cape Town 8001, South Africa

www.newhollandpublishers.co.nz

National Library of New Zealand Cataloguing-in-Publication Data

Farrington, Tony.
Sailing with Mohammed : a true yachting adventure in Asia and
the Middle East / Tony Farrington.
ISBN 1-86966-087-0
1. Farrington, Tony—Travel—Asia. 2. Antares II (Yacht) 3. Ocean
travel. 4. Seafaring life—Asia. 5. Yachting—Asia. I. Title.
910.45095—dc 22

Managing editor: Matt Turner
Editor: Anna Rogers
Design: Dexter Fry
Layout: Dee Murch
Map illustration: Sue Hall

10 9 8 7 6 5 4 3 2 1

Colour reproduction by PICA Digital, Singapore
Printed by Griffin Press, Australia

CONTENTS

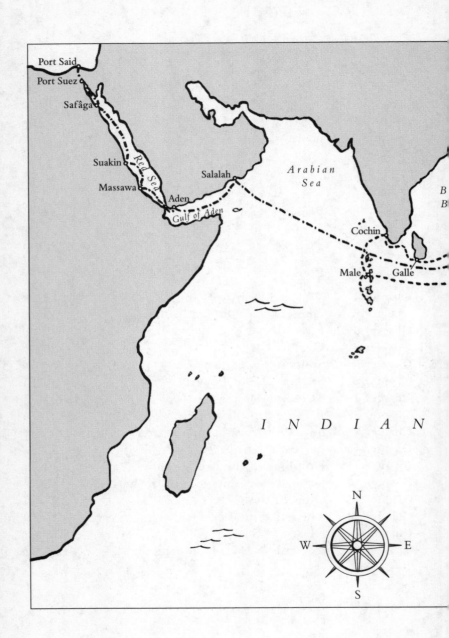

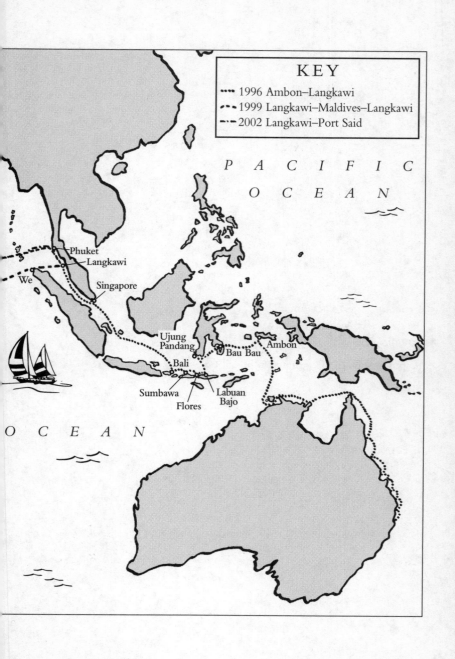

KEY
•••• 1996 Ambon–Langkawi
•–• 1999 Langkawi–Maldives–Langkawi
•–•– 2002 Langkawi–Port Said

P A C I F I C
O C E A N

Phuket
Langkawi
We
Singapore

Ujung
Pandang
Bali
Bau Bau
Ambon
Sumbawa
Flores
Labuan
Bajo

O C E A N

PREFACE

Misfortune led us to paradise. It happened in the closing stages of 1996 at Phuket, Thailand, just as we were preparing to sail our yacht *Antares II* to the Mediterranean.

Distracted by a conversation with my wife, Esmae, I lifted a bag of rubbish over the yacht's guardrail to drop it into a tender tethered alongside. Fortunately, I glanced down before I released my grasp on the bag's neck.

'Shit! The dinghy's gone,' I exclaimed.

'Stop having me on, I can see the painter from here,' Esmae responded.

'No, fair go, it's not here. It's been stolen!' I repeated incredulously.

I pulled up the rope that should have had a dinghy at the end of it. A shackle was the only evidence that something had once been tethered there. I was oddly relieved the painter was still attached to the deck: it confirmed that the dinghy's disappearance was not a result of poor seamanship. Many years before I had had to suffer the ignominy of watching a poorly secured tender drift away from my boat. With 200 yachts anchored around us, I could do without a

9

recurrence of such embarrassment.

Earlier in the morning we had fastened the dinghy to *Antares II* following a bumpy ride from Patong Beach where we had left it while we explored Baghli Street, one of Phuket's notorious nightspots. The evening before New Year's Eve, parties had raged in the scores of bars lining the street, a warm-up for the big event that would ring in 1997. Fascinated by the scantily clad, beautiful girls spilling out of bars and onto the street, as well as the topless transvestites shimmying on bar counters, the blaring music and unrestrained revelry, we had not returned to the boat until 3 a.m.

'The dinghy seemed secure enough when we got home,' I muttered, 'I can't understand what's happened to it.'

'You're right, it must have been stolen,' Esmae conceded.

'So why is the shackle still at the end of the painter?'

Suspiciously, I scrutinised the other boats anchored in the bay in anticipation of a spectacular party and fireworks display that would herald the new year. The tender was not with any of them.

The missing Aquapro dinghy was new, bought in Singapore only six weeks before. We aborted plans to return to town and spent the rest of the day searching for it. We visited other boats, alerted sailors to its disappearance via the radio and asked the Royal Thailand Police for assistance. There was no sign of it anywhere. Conspiracy theories abounded: some accused French sailors of stealing it; others blamed Australians; local Thai fishermen were the most popular scapegoats.

The piracy theory gained credibility when I met the crew of another New Zealand yacht, *Palma*, who had lost an Aquapro dinghy from almost exactly the same spot on the same night the year before. Someone suggested the pirates were divers who, under the cover of darkness, undid the shackle, replaced the bolt and floated out to sea with the tender.

'If it's locals, it's not the boat they're after, it's the motor,' one skipper in transit to the Red Sea announced confidently. 'If you're lucky you might get it back minus its engine.'

'Naw, it's scumbags who can't afford a good dinghy and need one to take to the Med. They'll be well on their way by now,' another suggested.

The only certainty was that unless we could quickly replace the dinghy we would not be continuing on to the Mediterranean.

The bay became bare as the days went by and yachts set sail for new adventures. Some headed to the Andaman Islands and Sri Lanka, on their way to the Maldives and Africa. Others plotted a course straight across the Indian Ocean to the Red Sea and the Mediterranean. A few struck out for the isolated Chagos archipelago. Our own hopes of heading west diminished daily.

For a while, we toyed with the possibility of sailing on without a tender. It was a foolish notion, as I discovered at Ko Rachi Yai, a beautiful little island a few hours' sailing from Phuket. The water there was so clear that, in the middle of the horseshoe bay, we watched the anchor settle on white sand seven metres below.

Tourists snorkelled along the island's fringing reef and, at the end of the compact little cove, we spied deckchairs, restaurants and souvenir shops.

'I'm going to swim ashore. Coming?' I invited Esmae. 'It's only a few hundred metres and we can look at the reef on the way.'

We donned our flippers and masks and slowly swam against an outgoing tide. Below us, a multitude of brightly coloured fish hovered over coral bleached bone white by currents warmed by El Niño. The swim convinced us it would be foolish to continue our voyage west without a dinghy. It had been taxing enough reaching shore in Ko Rachi Yai's gentle waters; it would be impossible in some of the stronger currents we would encounter on the way.

After tearful farewells with friends who continued their cruises across the Andaman Sea and into the Bay of Bengal, we set sail for Malaysia to search for a marina where we would await the arrival of a new dinghy.

A few kilometres north of a line on a chart where the waters of Thailand become those of Malaysia, we stopped at a dazzlingly

white sandy beach on the island of Tarutao. A cavernous, mountainous island, it was once a home for pirates who plundered boats
making journeys similar to ours. Without a dinghy, we could not
get ashore to enjoy the deserted beach, so we continued across the
border to the mystical duty-free port of Langkawi, where we could
save money by importing our new dinghy free of tariffs. Off
Langkawi, we searched for a nondescript little island called Rebak
where, we were told, we would find the haven we sought.

A small outcrop lying to the west of Langkawi's modern international airport, Rebak lay waiting to be discovered by international cruising yachts. A mangrove swamp that was the island's
heart had been dredged specifically to provide deep-keeled boats
with shelter from monsoons, no matter from which way the wind
blew. A stone breakwater had been built along a narrow entrance
to block the surge driven in by the south-west monsoon. Boats
could sit snug in even the worst of blows. Devoid of distinctive
landmarks, the entrance was hard to find.

As we entered a narrow channel that led to the harbour, jagged
rocks protruding close to our hull alarmed us. We worried about
the depths we would encounter as we crept along a short canal that
rounded a corner and widened into a bulbous lagoon. Surrounded
by hills adorned with tangled tropical rainforest, the lagoon was
alive with the drone of insects and the jabbering of monkeys.

'It looks like a great place to write a book,' Esmae observed,
'but I don't think there'll be much else to do here.'

Two enormous concrete fingers, each with pens for housing
boats, intruded like obscene abscesses upon the tiny harbour. They
looked even more abominable for being empty. Only three other
boats were there. Coincidentally, one, whose skipper had recently
succumbed to cancer, also bore the name *Antares*. His widow was
expected to return soon from Australia to take the yacht home.

We had the pick of the berths and Jim de Domville, the skipper
of *Beau Jeau*, a Canadian yacht, helped us with our lines. He spoke
enthusiastically about Rebak and explained he was recovering from

recent heart surgery. I suspected it had been a while since he had enjoyed conversation with another yachtsman.

'No one comes here 'cause they think it's too isolated. To get into the main village at Langkawi you have to take a ferry and then a taxi. It's supposed to be a resort,' he said, sweeping his hand in the direction of a large dark, thatch-roofed complex at the end of the pier. 'But there's no one there except the staff and a bunch of trainees. They're still waiting for guests to arrive.

'There's a restaurant where you get interesting meals and all the ice you want; it's free. You just help yourself. Electricity and water are free too,' he said, pointing to a pedestal at the end of the jetty that housed the facilities. 'It's as safe as houses here, very secure. There was some theft going on once but they caught the person doing it – one of the security guards – and there hasn't been a problem since. I think you'll enjoy it here, it's pretty hard to beat.'

Having introduced ourselves to the resort's staff, we set about exploring our new home. We were quickly seduced.

Delightful walkways meandered through lush gardens studded with unfamiliar tropical plants. The foliage ringed the bungalows, games rooms, restaurants and offices of the sprawling and luxurious tourist resort. A sparkling sapphire swimming pool snuggled under majestic coconut palms that swayed in a gentle sea breeze. From the pool, we gazed upon the tranquil waters of the Malacca Straits. In the distance, the low hills of Sumatra, Indonesia, smudged the horizon. Not only are the straits one of the world's oldest trading routes, but the number of pirates plundering passing ships rank them among the world's most perilous sea lanes. Fortunately, none of that danger was evident amid the tranquillity of Rebak.

Wide-eyed hornbills teetered in their roosts as they scraped cumbersome beaks on the bark of trees. Red kites, searching for food from the sea, swooped and spiralled on thermal currents. Brazen monkeys scurried into the cover of the forest as we explored walkways to a background of birds singing and water lapping on the shore. Intimidating monitor lizards crept from foliage and lumbered to the safety of the harbour's waters where carefree sea otters frolicked. Rebak appeared to be a tropical island paradise.

We had been at sea for eight taxing months, sailing from Brisbane in Australia through Indonesia to Singapore, Malaysia and Thailand. Although disappointed that we were unable to fulfil our ambition of sailing to the Mediterranean, we were ready for a rest, and Rebak offered the relaxation we needed.

Initially, Malaysia, a devoutly Muslim country, was intimidating, but when we visited the neighbouring island of Langkawi we met enchanting, humble, generous folk who made us very welcome.

We quickly discovered many other attractions that convinced us to use Rebak Island as a base for exploring Asia. Where else, for instance, could we afford to live at a luxury holiday resort, have a constant supply of duty-free wines and imported foods (including excellent New Zealand beef and lamb) and enjoy a tropical climate? On top of all this, we virtually had the place to ourselves.

Rebak became our base for five years. From there, we explored Asia, Islam and the Indian Ocean. It was there we returned to in *Antares II* from adventures in Thailand, Indonesia, Singapore, Sri Lanka, India and the Maldives.

Of course, the secret of our tropical hideaway eventually got out. Honeymooners from Korea and tourists from China and Europe arrived by the planeload. Flotillas of cruising yachts sheltered from monsoons until they could continue on to the Mediterranean, Africa, Japan or Australia. The spell was broken.

We weathered storms of political upheaval, cultural gaffes, economic crises and anti-Western sentiment following Israel's heavy-handed treatment of Palestinians and Osama bin Laden's attacks on New York and Washington DC. Believing we were fortunate to have enjoyed a unique time in a tropical paradise, we ignored government warnings of danger and lifted anchor to sail to the Mediterranean via the Red Sea four months after 9/11.

The accounts that follow are all true. Occasionally, a boat or a sailor's name has been changed for reasons that will be obvious.

14

CHAPTER 1

WHAT CHURCH ARE YOU?

'What, ah, gereja?' Cher glanced quizzically at her brother before impatiently thumbing through a tattered dictionary that translated Indonesian to English.

'Gereja,' she repeated, frustrated she could not find the correct word as Esmae peered over her shoulder. She scowled with concentration and licked her index finger to help turn the grubby pages.

'Ah, here!' Cher exclaimed excitedly, as if she had solved a complex puzzle. 'Gereja. Church. What … church … are … you?' she enquired slowly, struggling with our foreign language. Her black hair swept her shoulders as she tossed her head and smiled triumphantly, exposing perfect white teeth that glistened between full red lips.

Surprised by her forthrightness, and concerned the question could mask an ulterior motive, I contemplated a gap in the floor while considering a response.

'My sister, she asks what religion are you. We Muslim,' her brother, Jimmy, proclaimed.

Muslims regard all non-believers as infidels. Until now, we had

15

enjoyed the hospitality of Jimmy and his extended family, who had welcomed us warmly into their home and fed us a sweet made from red palm sugar and grated coconut wrapped in vine leaves, washed down with refreshing coconut milk. The answer to Cher's question could determine our continued relationship; in fact, our safety might well depend upon it. After all, we were surrounded by about 20 people in the house of a Muslim family we barely knew in an isolated Indonesian village in the Buton Strait. A machete with which Jimmy had deftly severed the tops of coconuts for our drinks lay at his feet. Through the crack in the floorboards an inquisitive goat strolled into view three metres below.

'My friend here, Francis,' Jimmy said, nodding towards a youth sitting beside him, 'he Christian.'

'I named after great saint, Francis Xavier, who brung church to Indonesia 500 year ago,' the youth declared proudly.

'You see. Here in Indonesia there is no problem. I Muslim. Francis Catholic. Other friends at university in Ambon, where I learn to be accountant, they are Buddhist and Hindu. Here in Indonesia, we all get on together. Religion no problem,' Jimmy assured us. 'My sister Cher, she ask what religion you?'

'I'm no religion.'

The expectant smile Jimmy wore while awaiting my response transfigured into puzzlement as he deciphered my words. His expression changed to one of shock as he comprehended them. Finally, he looked at me aghast, as if he had discovered he was entertaining Satan himself. He glanced at Francis and Cher, the only others in the room competent with English, as if seeking confirmation that he had misheard. Francis stared back stoically.

'What? You do not believe in God?' Jimmy finally whispered, incredulous.

'Oh no,' I quickly parried, 'I don't mean that.'

Jimmy, sitting in the lotus position on the floor, relaxed and slumped back a little.

'What I mean is that I don't have a name for my God. He's not

Buddhist or Christian or Hindu. I believe God is all these things, that all religions are equal. They all have the same God and it doesn't matter what He's called. You only have to sail out on the oceans to see there's definitely a God.'

As Jimmy considered my dogma, I glanced at Esmae, but she was preoccupied with the goat visible between the crack in the floorboards. I suspected that, just then, she considered it more intelligent than her husband.

'I not understanding you. What about the Prophet, may God rest his soul, what about Mohammed? What about Allah? Do you think Islam is equal with all religions?'

Esmae looked as if she wanted to squeeze through the crack in the floor to join the goat. My eyes searched the large room while I conjured up an answer. Except for the cane planters' chairs in which Esmae and I sat, the room was bare of furniture. The smiling mother of Jimmy and Cher gazed at us shyly from behind an oiled black coconut trunk, one of a number of pillars that supported a thatch roof. The other guests, dressed in a mixture of Western clothes and Muslim gowns and shawls, stared at us with bored expressions. Fortunately, Jimmy had not translated our conversation.

Cher was different from the others. She was about a year younger than Jimmy, probably about 18. Uncharacteristically precocious for a Muslim girl, she wore a pink-and-white checked sarong and a demure blouse. Her face was brightly painted with the exquisite skill Muslim women in Indonesia and Malaysia have acquired to enhance the beauty of the only part of their body they are permitted to display.

'I did not say that. Everyone knows Islam is a great religion. We have been in Indonesia only a few weeks. Before we came here, we were in Australia. In Australia and New Zealand, not much is known about Islam. Very few Muslims live there. We hope to learn a lot more about Islam during our stay in Indonesia.'

'That is good. You will meet many Muslim people and see many mosques. In Indonesia, we are very tolerant people. We have Pancasila democracy. You know Pancasila?'

Relieved the conversation appeared to be digressing from religion, Esmae and I shook our heads in unison.

'Pancasila goes back to first President Sukarno and continued by President Suharto. It has five rules. One is that everyone must believe in God. It not matter whether God is Buddha, the Prophet Christ, or whoever, everyone must believe. Although Allah is the only one true God and Mohammed, peace be upon him, is His prophet, government says we must all believe in God and be respectful of others' beliefs. We very tolerant of other people's gods,' Jimmy reiterated.

We had met Jimmy when he had paddled out to *Antares II* with a couple of other boys in a leaky dugout that was little more than a hollowed trunk of a coconut tree. They used jandals* to paddle their primitive craft, dipping them into the murky water with the rhythm of accomplished rowers.

'Hello Mister! What's your name?' A chorus greeted us when we appeared on deck. 'Where you from?'

'You have T-shirt?' Jimmy had inquired as he gripped the side of *Antares II*. The discarded jandals floated in ankle-deep water inside the dugout. 'You have cap?'

We produced a couple of caps and an old T-shirt for them to fight over.

'Magazine, I like magazine to learn English,' Jimmy demanded; his broad smile was disarming.

Antares II swung on anchor off a dilapidated jetty near the village of Lamboean Blanda on Buntung Island. Ashore, tall stands of coconut trees swayed in a gentle breeze. It was idyllic. Esmae produced a couple of women's magazines. Clinging to the side of the yacht with one hand, Jimmy flicked through them.

'You have *Playboy*?' he asked, apparently disappointed that the

---

* known more widely as 'flip-flops'

closest visions to those he lusted after were advertisements for brassieres and lingerie.

The other two boys, wearing only shorts that dripped wet from their excursion, were barely teenagers, much younger than Jimmy. They began making new demands: 'You have bonbons?'

We had arrived in Indonesia three weeks before at the tail of a flotilla participating in the 1996 yacht race from Darwin, Australia, to Ambon, the capital of the Indonesian Molucca Islands. The race was one of the last to be held because, after Suharto's demise three years later, the religious tolerance Jimmy boasted about dissipated almost immediately and religious intolerance spread through the Moluccas. Once associated with spices and romance, the Moluccas are now synonymous with murder, arson, looting and rape.

There was no sign of any of this when we arrived at Ambon. It is hard to believe that many of the villages, shops, churches and mosques we saw have since been razed. Christians and Muslims, who co-existed happily then, now have to be partitioned to keep them from killing each other. For many visitors, vulgarity, abuse and threats have replaced the friendly greetings and innocent demands for bonbons (sweets) and souvenirs. Today, a response to an inquiry about one's religion can provoke violence.

Evidently satisfied with his gifts, Jimmy asked: 'You like coconut? I give you coconut. My fudda has coconuts farm. I home from university to help harvest. You come to my house, number nine, and we have coconut.'

The usual shrill chorus of children merrily calling 'Hello Mister! What's your name?' greeted us as we made our way through the village.

The kids shrieked and laughed when I responded, 'Toe. Knee,' pointing to the appropriate body parts. A little girl attached herself to us as we walked along a dirt path bordered on one side by a single line of houses beyond which sprawled a tangled thicket of rainforest. She considered herself very fortunate to find us because we were real English-speaking people on whom she could practise

the language. Apart from visiting yachting folk, Westerners rarely
visited the isolated village, which could be reached only by boat.

'Me, I am Zareena,' she introduced herself as she skipped happily beside us, her little hand clutching Esmae's finger.

'My hobby,' she volunteered, 'I look after chickens.'

We passed a police station, which appeared to be the largest
building in the village, and a school. Small houses, ringed by neat
gardens of lush tropical foliage and colourful flowers, sat behind
picket fences. A few homeowners had struggled to create beds of
ornate shrubs that had been meticulously trimmed and shaped. The
houses were miniature replicas of elaborate façades their owners
had admired in prestigious foreign magazines, dream houses that
looked out of place among the other primitive ramshackle buildings. By the time we found number nine, a crowd of curious children and adults, all jabbering loudly, followed behind us.

Number nine was a traditional dwelling. Surrounded by
coconut palms, it stood high above the ground on stilts. A couple
of bicycles, three goats and piles of coconut kernels littered the
ground beneath the house. Shards of light penetrating through gaps
in a thatch roof and walls provided the only brightness in a room
made dingy by drawn shutters. There was neither electricity nor
gas and, because Muslims are forbidden from displaying images of
people or idols, the room was devoid of photographs and paintings.

Jimmy introduced his mother, a petite woman who smiled
warmly but could not understand a word we said. We wondered
whether she wore a brave face to disguise annoyance at her son's
impertinence in inviting foreigners to her home. We never met his
father, who remained outside toiling with the coconuts. However,
we met his uncle, his nephews, nieces, his friends and his vivacious
sister Cher.

Esmae told her Cher was the name of a famous American film
star and singer. Cher responded by posing and acting out the role
until a middle-aged man with a cruel pockmarked face entered the
room. Suddenly, she became subdued. 'This Ibrahim. Ibrahim, he's

my darling,' Cher announced coyly.

We assumed she was betrothed to him in an arranged marriage. Unable to converse because of the language barrier, he leered at us before noisily joining the others sitting on the floor.

Cher placed before us a plate of food wrapped in vine leaves. We ate with trepidation because crews from other boats had suffered stomach upsets from local fare. Jimmy slashed the tops off coconuts with a machete, drained them and gave us each a spoon with which to eat the delicious white flesh inside.

Cher admired a wide-brimmed blue hat Esmae wore to protect her from the harsh tropical sun. When we left we arranged to meet her and Jimmy at a waterfall where we would swim and give them both hats, but the arrival of the monsoon thwarted our plans. The rain bucketed down. We did not leave the boat and we sailed the next morning without seeing them again.

The deluge concealed the Buton Straits' beautiful coastline. Occasionally, when the rain eased, we glimpsed landfalls of lush forests climbing up steep cliffs below which nestled interesting villages. We wished we had seen more, but we could not dally. We had to maintain swift speed to sail the 4000 kilometres through the Indonesian archipelago to Malaysia. The Indonesians had issued us with only a two-month permit for the voyage and there was no chance of an extension.

The beams from our radar occasionally crept through the wet shroud to glimpse the coastline and potential hazards such as rocks, encroaching headlands and other craft. There were plenty of boats around: old wooden tuna fishing vessels with huge bamboo poles on their coach roofs for flicking fish out of the sea; little wooden dugouts in which people sat cross-legged, fishing in the rain; and huge Bugis prahus, handsome schooners powered by huge blue sails, ferrying cargo around the islands.

Even at sea, we could not escape from children calling, 'Hello Mister! What's your name?' We were ambushed in a most unexpected place: a canyon at the South Narrows, a tight squeeze through which we had to sail to reach our next destination, the historic port of Bau Bau, near the bottom of Butung, from where we would re-enter the Banda Sea and sail to Ujung Pandang, capital of Indonesia's largest island, Sulawesi.

The sea rushes through the narrow gap like a flooding river. Because sailing against its five-knot current is near impossible, boats anchor at the gorge's entrance to await a favourable flow. We met six other yachts there. Most of us towed lines for catching large fish, which legend incorrectly prescribed were abundant.

For most of the five-kilometre journey through the narrows, the canyon's towering walls rose vertically, too steep for anything but the most tenacious plants. Wherever there was a bay, however, cluttered wooden buildings clung to each other like a crowd cowering in awe of the soaring cliffs, and always the minaret of a mosque, or the spire of a church, rose as the centrepiece of the villagers' lives.

It was at the narrows that children launched their attacks. Dozens of naked boys rowed out in dilapidated dugouts. Blithely oblivious to the dangers they posed, they played chicken with the yachts, blocking our way. The current propelling us was so swift we would be unable to slow our boats to avoid collision if the children miscalculated their distance. As we careered past, we watched horrified while they dived from their unstable canoes. Swept downstream with the swift current, they disappeared from view. They emerged, chortling mischievously, behind lures they had attempted to steal from the fishing lines we towed. It was a uniquely peculiar and reckless sport. Fortunately, there were no mishaps.

Here again, the boys called 'Hello Mister!' and smiled broadly, displaying their sole possession – their teeth. The usual ritual started: 'What's your name, Mister?'

We'd tell them and they'd tell us their names.

'Bonbons! You have bonbons?' they cried as they approached the yacht to catch the handfuls of sweets we threw them.

Our course lay in the wake of a voyage an American yacht,

Arjumand, had undertaken the previous year when Connie and Ralph McNeil had sailed from Australia to Malaysia. They warned us to be careful at Bau Bau because thieves had used machetes and bolt cutters to break into a couple of boats while their owners were sightseeing ashore. Fortunately, apart from approaches by local fishermen selling squid, we were undisturbed.

Connie suggested we contact a Mr Rachmund, who was fluent in English and could arrange tours of the island, so we rowed ashore and enquired at a police station on the wharf. Perplexed, a surly man behind a counter talked to unseen people in an adjacent room. After debating our request in Bahasa, the local language, he responded: 'Ah, English guru.'

His demeanour improved as he unravelled the mystery of our request. He led us outside where he hailed a nearby becak (trishaw). He barked instructions at a wretched soul who, for a reward of a few worthless rupiah, pumped bicycle pedals to transport heavy passengers.

While he pedalled through Bau Bau's narrow streets, we sat back and relaxed in the carefree luxury of floating along at a speed of about a kilometre an hour. It was as if we had entered a timeless world devoid of rush and stress. Although there was little traffic, the town bustled with people who waved and yelled the usual chorus, 'Hello Mister!' The appellation applied to either sex. 'What's your name?'

Mr Rachmund was obviously very important. His name was emblazoned on an office on the main street. Unfortunately, he was not there.

'English guru?' We pointed at the sign as a small crowd gathered around us. 'Mr Rachmund, the English guru. Where can we find him?'

They smiled at us, not comprehending.

The becak driver had a noisy conversation then waved impatiently towards a youth who had stepped forward from the crowd. We suspected we should follow him. He led us down an alley bordered by slums. We gingerly stepped over a filthy pit, from which a stench of sewage, to which we never became accustomed, pervaded the air. Cardboard, paper, plastic wrappings and crumpled plastic drink bottles littered the ground. Inside a shack, badly in need of a facelift itself but obviously a beauty salon, women with their hair in curlers and mud on their faces tittered with embarrassment when we passed.

We found Rachmund in a small house behind a huge wall at the end of the alley. A tiny, plump, bespectacled decorous person wearing a sarong, he invited us into his home. Within minutes of our arrival children from nearby houses swarmed into the small room to see his unexpected visitors. Others lurked at the doorway and crammed their heads through windows.

'*Salamat pagi* [good morning],' Mr Rachmund began.

'*Salamat pagi,*' the children chorused in response.

'Good morning to you,' he addressed us in impeccable English. 'Welcome to my humble dwelling. How may I help you?'

We explained that friends had recommended we contact him to arrange a tour of the island.

'It would be my pleasure to show you around myself.' He smiled warmly and explained he would arrange for a van and driver to take us and other sailors on a tour. In the city, we should see produce markets and an historic fort built in the 15th century by Portuguese occupiers. Further away, we should visit a fishing village and a community renowned for artists who produced stunning ikat garments, a craft dating back more than two centuries.

As we toured he explained he had learned English at the University of Ujung Pandang, at Sulawesi. Now, he taught the language himself at Bau Bau's Muslim university.

Police had to rescue me outside the markets. While Esmae searched inside for spices, herbs and other exotic condiments, I recorded sights on a video camera. Children on their way to school mobbed me when they found they could view themselves on playback.

'Hey, Mister!' they shouted, standing before me and smiling broadly. 'Me! Me! Me!' they shrieked, jostling each other before the lens.

They grabbed the camera and clamped my wrist in a vice-like grip as they peered through the viewfinder like voyeurs at a key-hole. Pensive, they studied themselves moving in the camera, then grew boisterous again when their images disappeared and the picture panned onto a friend. Their excitement and din drew a multitude of others who scurried into the pressing throng that spilled over the road and impeded traffic. A truckload of police screeched to a halt at the end of the street. Fearing a riot, they blew shrill whistles, barked orders and menacingly raised rattans above their heads. The children scattered in all directions, leaving me alone with the policemen's black scowls.

Later, at the village famed for its ikat garments, we watched artists creating dyes from plants to colour yarn. Others drew intricate designs on cloth destined to cover men as sarongs, adorn women's heads as shawls, and wrap around the dead for burial.

Unexpectedly, a beautiful young Muslim woman, covered from head to toe in a powder blue abaya (overgarment), asked whether I had found the visit interesting. It was the first time an Indonesian woman had instigated a conversation with me. Usually, they remained reserved because precociousness earned chastisement, even punishment.

After engaging in light-hearted banter and enquiring where I was from, she proposed nervously: 'Would you like me for your wife?'

'I beg your pardon? I did not understand,' was all I could manage as she locked me in a firm stare.

'I would like to be your wife,' she suggested coyly.

Blushing with embarrassment, I felt uneasy, uncertain how to respond. She was probably the same age as Cher.

'Why?' I croaked.

She explained she was 19 and had done well at school, but there was no future for her on the island other than an arranged marriage followed by motherhood.

'We marry and you take me to your country. I go to university and become computer programmer,' she proffered.

'I'm sorry, I'm already married. That's my wife over there,' I explained, relieved to see Esmae emerge from inside the factory.

The girl fled before I obtained her name. Only later did I learn that proclaiming myself already married would not have lessened her sense of rejection because Indonesian men are permitted four wives. I pondered the depths of desperation that led such an attractive and intelligent woman to demean herself by proposing marriage to a middle-aged stranger from a foreign country, in order to escape the servile life preordained for her at Bau Bau.

Before we left Bau Bau, Rachmund dined aboard *Antares II* and suggested that when we arrived at Ujung Pandang we should contact his colleague Mr Muna, a tour guide who spoke fluent English.

Ujung Pandang, the capital city of Indonesia's largest island, is a grubby, banal little port. We relied on a dhoni to collect us from *Antares II* for a short trip to a dilapidated jetty, our entrance to the town. The ferry rolled and bucked like an ill-tempered mare as waves from a swell slapped her sides. Alighting and climbing aboard was precarious in turbulent conditions, which occurred with little warning when the monsoon's squalls swept over the harbour: you had to leap onto the wooden jetty after judging the precise moment the vessel would rise on a swell before plummeting below the wharf and crashing heavily against the piles that supported the rickety platform. A miscalculation could leave us straddling the boat's side, crushing a limb between the ferry and a pole encrusted with barnacles as sharp as scalpels. Several mishaps occurred, but fortunately no one was seriously injured.

Susan Brown, an Australian circumnavigating the world with her husband John, was an inspiration. John talked to her incessantly. When disembarking from the ferry, he would stand behind

Susan, his hands around her waist as she struggled nervously to maintain her footing on the violently moving boat.

'Right, right, the boat's coming up. Hold on. Hold on. Now! Jump now!' he commanded.

Susan usually obeyed but occasionally she froze, intimidated by the dory's angry motion. John would make light of her timidity and begin the rigmarole again. When she was safely on the jetty, he would take her arm and instruct: 'Okay, there's eleven steps to the top.' On reaching the street: 'There's quite a bit of traffic, it's pretty busy. Let's go now.' When traffic came to a standstill, they crossed the main boulevard, arm in arm, John raising his free hand to halt vehicles.

'Right, here's the kerb. Here we are now. Strewth, that was close,' he would tease. 'There's a shop here selling gold jewellery and watches. We don't want to stop there. Here comes a cigarette vendor. We don't need smokes. Oh, my word, there's a beaut sheila.'

'You keep your eyes off her and watch where you're going,' Susan chastised.

As they strolled like honeymooners, arms wrapped around one another, John seldom stopped talking: even at nightclubs, restaurants and karaoke bars, he maintained an incessant, animated low prattle. It was some time before we learned the reason for their behaviour: Susan was blind and John acted as her eyes.

Five years before they decided to sail the world aboard their yacht *Immanuel*, doctors at Sydney had removed a benign tumour from Susan's brain. After the operation, she could see only pinpricks of light. Shortly after losing her sight, Susan met John at a social function. They shared a good sense of humour, a desire for freedom and a love for the sea. They married in 1991, about the time they bought *Immanuel*.

Before setting out around the world, Susan trained at a gym three days a week. Twice a month they participated in yacht races on Sydney Harbour, learning about *Immanuel*'s idiosyncrasies and improving Susan's ability to master them. During these sea trials, they developed sailing techniques to which they still adhered: John steered, shouting instructions to Susan about sail trim, and she responded by winding winches to adjust a sail's setting.

Fully confident in each other, they worked well as a team. To enable Susan to steer *Immanuel*, they installed an electronic compass that not only used a voice prompt to indicate direction, but also emitted a series of electronic beeps if the yacht strayed off course. The sounds were designed to be easily recognisable for port or starboard headings. The pulses grew louder and faster the further *Immanuel* wandered from a predetermined course.

John placed Braille signs next to essential switches and equipment so Susan could easily recognise them. She protested she did not need to depend on such symbols because she knew the whereabouts of almost everything on board. By looking after provisions – stowing cans and packets of food and spare parts in hatches – she was aware of every nook and cranny. She cooked, cleaned, entertained and toured, just like crews on other yachts.

At sea, alone in the cockpit in the dark, Susan revelled in the conditions she sensed about her. The slight ocean swell and the warmth in the gentle trade wind blowing from the south-east made the sail through Indonesia a friendly one. Her other senses became acute when she maintained a watch while John slept below. She judged boat speed by *Immanuel*'s sound as the yacht sliced through the water.

She preferred standing watch on moonless nights when, even with her limited vision, she could still determine light reflected by stars. She became skilled at distinguishing between them and the white, red and green ships' beacons for which she remained alert while John slept in the saloon below.

Naturally, there had been scares, like a time in the Gulf of Carpentaria, at the top of Australia, when she panicked as a white light continued to bear down on *Immanuel*, a sure sign of collision.

'Come quick. A ship's about to hit us!' she shouted.

John scampered from the saloon to avert a disaster but was relieved to discover that Susan, then unfamiliar with night watches, had mistaken a rising moon for a ship. They collapsed in the cockpit laughing raucously with relief.

Their partnership was so successful aboard *Immanuel*, and ashore, that even friends often remained ignorant about Susan's impediment. As Susan told us, 'John worked at Cairns, on the Great Barrier Reef, for nine months. It wasn't 'til our last night, when we were leaving, that a friend said to him: "I didn't know Susan was blind. I thought you were really in love because you were always holding hands."'

John believed blindness had some advantages, particularly when travelling in bemos (vans used for buses) along Indonesia's narrow, crowded streets. While he sat white-knuckled in the back as the drivers recklessly darted in front of each other, apparently contemptuous of road rules and safety, Susan sat beside him, serenely oblivious to the chaos through which she was travelling. Walking on the street, though, was different. Bemos rarely stopped for pedestrians and the footpaths were uneven and potholed. Large open drains ran parallel to footpaths, a trap even for sighted pedestrians.

Susan and John managed much better than some sighted crews. An announcement over yacht radios that an Australian yawl, *My Way*, was about to arrive in the bay at Ujung Pandang brought everyone above decks. *My Way*, crewed by an entertaining and hospitable couple, Muzza (Murray) McCabe and his wife Flo, had won a well-deserved reputation for creating drama. Crews observing *My Way*'s arrival expected entertainment. They were not disappointed.

It was an unfortunate time to be entering the anchorage. The sun was too low to illuminate a coral reef that formed a breakwater a few metres beneath the water's surface. *My Way* approached the bay faster than was prudent, her course set to crash her onto the hidden danger fringing the bay.

I called *My Way* on the radio: 'Hi Muzza. You aware there's a reef out there?'

'Yeah. Where is it? It's pretty hard to see in this light.'

I gave him the GPS co-ordinates and *My Way* changed direction, slowed and searched for a deepwater channel that would enable her to enter the bay. Safely inside, Muzza cruised past eight other yachts that lay at anchor while he decided on a spot to drop his pick. He shouted at his wife, who straddled the anchor winch at the front of the boat, waiting for the order to drop it. Flo released a brake and the sound of the chain clattering towards the seabed echoed through the bay. Satisfied enough chain had run out, Muzza put the boat into reverse. The anchor chain remained slack as the pick skipped across the bottom.

'Haul it back up, Flo,' he shouted, his voice carrying across the water. 'It hasn't caught, we're gonna have to do it again.'

Flo used both hands to crank up the anchor, shouting abuse at her husband, ignorant that her vitriol was entertaining eavesdropping crews on surrounding boats.

After their third unsuccessful attempt at anchoring, Muzza discovered he had an audience.

'You bastards enjoying yourselves?' he shouted as he swept past the boats for another attempt at anchoring. 'Why don't you buy tickets?'

The show would have ended when, at last, *My Way* strained against her anchor and held firm. Unfortunately, the microphone on Muzza's radio had jammed open and we learned how he felt about the crew of every yacht in the bay. 'That bastard Farrington,' he echoed in the background, 'he shouldn't be out here. He knows nothing about sailing.'

Ujung Pandang had little to offer apart from a couple of good Chinese restaurants, reasonably interesting botanical gardens and a well-stocked market where hawkers washed vegetables in stagnant water lying at the bottom of a deep storm drain. Muna, our guide, suggested we travel by road into Sulawesi's central highlands, home of the Tanatoraja.

Between stubbing out cigarettes, Muna explained the Tanatoraja were one of the few Indonesian people not to embrace Islam. He suggested their resistance might stem from Islam's requirement for abstinence from pork and alcohol, both of which the Torajas enjoy immensely. 'Maybe for them it is too big a price for entering Paradise,' he speculated.

The Tanatoraja have woven their ancient beliefs into the brand of Christianity they follow: they fervently believe that their ancestors descended from the heavens to Torajaland's hilltops in huge ships. Muna promised they were one of the most interesting people in the whole Indonesian archipelago.

During the 500-kilometre drive to the highlands, we passed one intriguing sight after another. Every settlement, large and small, was clean and proud and reflected none of the squalid decay we had seen elsewhere. Flags adorned each village. Fences, painted in different colours, surrounded tidy homes. Along the side of the road, rice, coffee and cocoa beans, strewn like offerings, dried on mats. Beyond them, wild flowers bloomed. The government had provided the locals with seeds to plant to beautify the area for tourists embarking on the long drive to Torajaland. It was an unnecessary facelift – nature alone made it a splendid journey.

Beyond the flowers, over an expanse of plains, men and women toiled, up to their thighs in mud, in paddy fields so tranquil they mirrored the clouds and bush-clad mountains above them. Large buffalo, wallowing in mud pools, raised their heads to gaze lazily at huge butterflies dancing across the fields.

The countryside changed with every turn. As we climbed, rain-forests, tangles of tall trees and thick vines, devoured the plateau's gentle fields. Even here, on patches between trees, rice grew in orderly terraces hewn from steep mountainsides. Our van slowed for peasants who herded solitary buffalo and flocks of ducks along the narrow road. As the sun fell low over the forest, peasants washed oxen under waterfalls that cascaded beside the road, scrubbing their beasts with ferns plucked from the forest floor. In the highlands, buffalo are a prized possession, far too valuable to be subjugated to hard labour in the fields.

The mountains provided relief from the toll Ujung Pandang had taken on our senses. If squalor existed in the hill country, it was well camouflaged: we neither saw nor smelled it. The highlands provided welcome comfort as the sweet air cooled with each kilometre we climbed.

When we checked into a hotel, Esmae, who had gone ahead, alarmed a couple of porters when she dashed from the room shouting; 'A bath! A bath! We've got a bath!' The porters were mortified. They did not understand English and thought something was terribly wrong. Perhaps she had found a dead rat in the room! A monitor lizard? Maybe even a snake! Restricted to showering, occasionally with salt water, we had not experienced the luxury of soaking in a bath for many months. The porters stared at us stoically as we endeavoured to explain the outburst. A couple of American dollars placed in their palms made matters worse as they felt obliged to uncover the jinni (devil) that provoked such distress. No matter how hard we tried, we could not dissuade them from searching the closet, cupboards and bedside tables, even behind the curtains. Defeated, they looked at us oddly, shrugged and left the room, probably to warn their colleagues to be careful of the strange couple in room 303.

In the morning, we set about exploring Torajaland where, in the shadow of towering mountains, farming families live in houses shaped like boats which sit high above the ground on stilts as thick as elephants' legs. Their roofs swoop at each end like the raised prow and stern of an ancient Sumerian ship, similar to the reed boat in which Thor Heyerdahl had sailed in 1978. Each house faces north, toward the realm from which their ancestors came to settle on the hilltops. Elaborate engravings of stylised buffalo decorate gables, highlighting the hallowed position the animals enjoy within

Toraja culture. Tiers of the beasts' horns adorn entrances, the number displayed denoting an occupier's status.

Of all the Toraja's ceremonies, the most important are those that send the dead to Puya, the afterworld. The size of the rituals, the multitude attending them, the extravagance of the sacrifice and the lavishness of feasting all determine the fate of the dead and their descendants. The Tanatoraja fear misfortune will befall a family if it does not farewell its dead in a manner that will impress upon the gods the spirit's importance, thereby increasing its chances of interceding on their behalf when required. While we were in Torajaland, Muna arranged for us to attend the funeral of an 80-year-old man.

A Tanatoraja soul has to cross hundreds of mountains and valleys to reach the afterworld. Slaughtering buffalo and pigs eases the journey because a deceased's spirit can ride on the backs of the animals' souls. When they arrive, the size of the herd accompanying a spirit will confirm the status it enjoyed on earth.

Sacrificing insufficient animals, or having only a small gathering at a funeral, also causes considerable loss of face for the living, so Tanatoraja funerals are complex and prestigious events. They have survived the centuries, despite Christian, Muslim and government influence for curtailment of the slaughter of animals, which is the cornerstone of these ceremonies. The religious worry about the barbarism involved, but the government is concerned about the loss of wealth for families who possess little and measure their affluence by the stock they own. A buffalo can fetch several thousand rupiah, a small fortune for a peasant. But neither the government nor the churches have been able to diminish the Toraja's long-held beliefs; they now take their share in the form of tithes and taxes in a futile hope that the extra cost will deter the practice.

Because many families have members scattered around the world and the peasants do not have money to supply animals for slaughter, bodies can be kept for long periods before they are buried. The old man whose funeral we were to attend had been lying in state for three years.

Using traditional plants and techniques, the family had worked quickly to preserve the body. They had dressed it in clothes he had worn daily and placed the corpse in a coffin in a room reserved specifically for housing a suffering soul. To the bottom of the coffin they had attached a bamboo reed to capture fluids and odours exuded by the corpse. The reed channelled them outside through a hole in the floor.

News of the old man's demise had brought friends and relatives to the house. Rather than mourning his passing, they were jovial, anticipating the celebrations ahead and the abundance of buffalo and pigs to be slaughtered. They preferred to consider the old man terminally ill, rather than dead, although they knew he would never recover. His widow would fast until his funeral and place food and drink beside his casket three times a day. With other members of the family, she would pray, comfort and amuse him.

Scores of buffalo horns adorning the entrance to the deceased's house indicated the high position he had attained in society as, over the years, he amassed a fortune from rice fields. He used much of his money to educate his children who enjoyed positions at Ujung Pandang and faraway Jakarta.

A committee formed to plan the funeral had contacted relatives and friends scattered throughout the islands and set a tentative date for the burial, but obtaining approval from a large, well-educated and widely dispersed family had not been easy. Six months before the funeral, construction had begun on an arena in which the ceremony would be held. Because it was for a rich man, plenty of volunteers from surrounding villages had offered assistance. They knew construction would take many months, during which they would be well rewarded with pork, perhaps even buffalo. Scores of animals had been slaughtered over the period.

Builders set about erecting a village, constructed from bamboo, two storeys high, in a paddy field owned by the dead man. As the time for the funeral neared, construction was still incomplete so workmen toiled day and night to ensure it would be ready for receiving the body.

The procession taking the corpse from its home to the arena was a joyful occasion. It veered off the road and across rice paddies in which the family sang and jumped up and down, muddying themselves in the process. The revellers restrained themselves from kickboxing, which is also part of the tradition and has sometimes pitched villager against villager with fatal consequences.

The arena resembled a large sports stadium. Scores of tall thatch-roofed buildings, replicas of the curiously shaped Toraja houses, bordered the perimeter of a rectangular courtyard the size of a football field. As delicacies for sacrifices were paraded below, the buildings' high prows loomed over the quadrangle like the jaws of a herd of yawning hippopotami. Inside the 'mouths', people ate, drank and gossiped as they observed proceedings from privileged positions, like the select few in corporate boxes at sports events.

A death tower, a miniature of the buildings surrounding the field, housed a red-and-gold coffin containing the dead man, beside which sat his widow and close family. A wooden effigy of the deceased stood at the tower's entrance, observing the activity parading below. The statue portrayed him as a rotund, jovial man who appeared to approve of the fuss being made to propel his soul towards Puya.

We hid from the mid-morning sun in the shade of a corporate box while a group of beautiful young women danced gracefully on the field, apparently oblivious to the antics of a band of boys pampering pigs tethered to bamboo poles below the death tower. The girls moved their manicured hands and swayed their hips to a tune that told a story about the cycle of life and the old man's contribution within it. Their bare feet moved delicately upon trampled grass. Their voices were unheard, drowned by the commotion of 20 squealing pigs.

The pigs screeched as boys struggled to raise the heavy bamboo litters off the ground. Placing the poles on their shoulders, the boys ran from the arena, and the terrified animals, sensing their fates, increased the pitch of their pitiful whining. The six girls, doing their best amidst the pandemonium, continued their slow rhythmic undulating. Their painted faces and red-and-gold dresses contrasted starkly with a group, dressed for mourning, who meandered behind the pigs to join a throng of hundreds milling about outside, awaiting their turn to pay homage to the dead man and his family.

The bystanders scattered as the boys, labouring under the weight of their litters, stumbled and fell. The pigs' horrendous squeals terrified a buffalo that bellowed, broke its tether and escaped, running amok among scores of mourners. Horns down, desperate for freedom, the buffalo charged at the scattering throng. It trampled a couple who lost their footing. Others deftly leaped away from the charging horns just in time. The bid for freedom was short-lived when half a dozen men grabbed the buffalo and subdued it. Securely tethered, it was led, still bellowing, into the arena with a dozen other noisy beasts. Boys carrying as many pigs followed behind and laid them on their sides on the ground. A hush fell over the ground as mourners peered from the dimness of their accommodation to ascertain the nature and source of the offerings.

The old man's widow glanced down from the death tower to glimpse her grandchildren leading the latest procession of guests. Wearing traditional dress, they sported krises in golden scabbards around their waists. They led the new group of lamenters past the tower and into a hut reserved for receiving guests. Dozens of well-dressed affluent men and women, some carrying children, followed. Towards the front of the procession, behind the deceased's grandchildren, marched those who had provided the most valuable offerings. Dawdling at the rear, stooped with bowed heads, were those who provided only tokens.

Women followed a granddaughter into a hut reserved for them while boys took men to another area. As the guests sipped refreshments or chewed betel nuts, the dancing girls returned to centre stage. Surrounded by pigs and buffalo, they swayed like flowers next to a pole on which hung flyblown vital organs from beasts already slaughtered. Again, they sang praise of the old man's life.

Hundreds of swine were slaughtered during the three days of ceremonies. Butchers thrust sharpened bamboo stakes through the pigs' sides and into their hearts. The terrified animals, slowly bleeding to death, whined in agony. Satisfied the reeds had filled with sufficient blood, the butchers dismembered the animals while their limbs quivered in the butchers' hands. They mixed the meat with rice and added it to the blood in the bamboo that had pierced the pigs' hearts. It was cooked over fires and distributed to guests.

After receiving hundreds of visitors, the family set about selecting which buffalo would be sacrificed and which would be used for paying taxes and tithes. A man in the middle of the quadrangle, behaving like an auctioneer, led the discussion. It took many hours to debate the merits of each beast because agreement from the whole family was required.

After they had concurred, a man armed with a machete stepped forward. Beasts with spirits chosen to carry the deceased's soul to Puya were tethered. The executioner thrust his blade and slit their jugular with a movement as quick as a camera flash. The oldest buffalo, the one with the largest horns, was the first to fly to Puya. It fell to the ground, blood spurting from its neck. Its meat was pre-ordained to feed immediate family and important guests.

In contrast to their earlier behaviour, the family now wailed and threw themselves at the coffin during the procession to a wooden mausoleum that housed generations of their ancestors. They pledged to visit the grave over the years ahead to change the old man's clothes and comfort him.

Caring for the dead is a strong tradition in Torajaland. The countryside is dotted with graves and tombs, many hewn out of the steep rock face of mountains. Bamboo scaffolding is erected and bodies are pushed and pulled up mountainsides and laid to rest inside four-metre-high tombs that take about three years to create. Often, a deceased's effigy is placed outside the tomb, gazing down upon the rice paddies and the generations who follow. One hand is turned in prayer for the family, the other positioned to ward off evil. Peasants toil below, comfortable in the knowledge that their forebears watch over them.

On the way back to Ujung Pandang, Esmae and I bargained for a wooden statue, about a metre tall, that we considered would make a wonderful memento of the visit. The piece depicted a benevolent old man sitting in a chair and staring into space. The young girl selling it wanted an exorbitant amount. Everything purchased in Torajaland is subject to negotiation and her take-it-or-leave-it attitude perplexed us as she steadfastly refused to discuss a price.

To get negotiations under way, we asked Muna to interpret for us. He explained the girl was most upset about the prospect of selling the carving, which had been in her little shop for three years. It had brought many offers to which she had reacted the same way each time someone began to bargain. 'She says it is a *tau tau* (statue) of her grandfather. She considers it undignified to haggle over the price of such a great and kind man,' Muna explained.

The effigy's eyes followed us around the shop as we inspected other trinkets. Now that we knew whom it represented, we decided we could not bear to have it staring at us. We did not haggle any further and left the girl's grandfather where he belonged.

CHAPTER 2

DRAGONS AND OTHER MONSTERS

'The steering's gone!' I shouted as *Antares II*, out of control, changed the direction in which she headed.

Esmae had been on watch only a short time and I had just gone below to rest when the yacht began misbehaving. Disengaging the autopilot, I wrestled with the wheel. It felt limp in my hands. Turning it slowly, I groped like a blind man for a telltale sign that we were headed in the right direction on the gently rising oily sea. We lurched over on our opposite side and the boom swung lazily in the blackness of a starless night.

'It's spooky,' Esmae whispered.

'With the engine out, the last thing we need is for the steering to go as well,' I said, as Esmae scrambled to reset the sails.

I turned the helm the other way, waiting to feel it stiffen as water rushed against the rudder as the boat picked up speed. Still nothing. Then, without any reason, *Antares II* responded in the gentle breeze, rounded up and continued on the correct course. We reset the sails again.

Little had gone right since we had set out from Ujung Pandang. We had joined Kiwi boats, *Southern Voyager* and *Leeway*, both from

Picton, and John and Susan aboard *Immanuel*, to sail in convoy to the islands of Komodo to hunt for dragons, native giant lizards that grow up to four metres long. Rather than sail two consecutive nights, we agreed to stop at Taka Rewataya, a group of small islands on the way. We should have known better: the chart portrayed them as inhospitable.

When we arrived, we discovered a fringing reef kept us from anchoring in shallow water. We anchored deep, rolling uncomfortably in a swell that made cooking utensils, cutlery and crockery smash against each other in cupboards.

Tired after a 24-hour sail from Ujung Pandang, we had just fallen asleep when a muffled explosion awoke us. A second blast had us scrambling from our bunk and up on deck peering into the darkness. Beams from torches and spotlights danced on the reef where villagers were bombing coral to catch fish.

'I don't like it here,' Esmae admitted. 'They tried to board the boats further in and if they've got dynamite, they could use it for anything. I'll be glad to get out of here at first light.'

When dawn arrived, we said farewell to the other yachts as they motored away while we lamely awaited a breeze to fill our sails. We could not use the engine. On the way from Ujung Pandang, we had found it moving precariously on its cradle, likely to topple under load or in a violent swell. Close inspection revealed that three of the four thick bolts holding it in place on its mounts had sheared. Danny Clement, a young crew member aboard *Leeway*, had repositioned the engine on its mounts, warning they were safe only for entering an anchorage at a very slow speed.

When a breeze did come, it was gentle and from the wrong direction, right on our nose. Our only chance of reaching a port near Komodo, where we hoped to find an engineer to rebuild the mounts, was to sail across it. While the other boats in the flotilla switched on their motors and drove into the wind, we tacked across it, three hours one way, three hours the other, slowly inching toward our destination. The wind seldom blew from a direction that could assist us.

The waters in the Flores Sea suddenly plummet so deeply that the ocean floor does not register on a yacht's sounder; a little further on, the seabed is likely to reappear almost as quickly. The vast canyons create exceptional currents. At times, without breeze to propel us, the tide was so strong it pushed us backwards. Combined with the fickle wind, it made for slow progress. The other yachts took 15 hours to reach a landfall; we took 48.

On the second night of our struggle to reach Komodo, Esmae relieved my watch at two o'clock, just as she had the previous morning. Although we still had little wind, it was a better night. Stars twinkled above and we enjoyed a coffee together in the cockpit before I turned in. After only a brief period below, the boat's temperament changed, just as it had the previous evening.

'What's wrong with you, can't you hold a course?' I snapped as I reappeared in the cockpit, disengaged the autopilot and took control of the helm.

'I didn't do anything,' Esmae protested.

'You must have. This is the second time in two nights. What are you doing? Did you change course or trim sails?'

'No. I'd just got myself another coffee when, all of a sudden, the sails flogged as if they'd lost wind and the boat refused to respond.'

Antares II behaved as if she was inebriated. She wallowed and turned in circles three times, the sails flapping uncontrollably and the boom swinging dangerously across the decks each time she gybed.

'I'm going to risk turning on the motor to try to get us back on course,' I announced, concerned about the loss of control.

Gingerly, I pushed the throttle forward. The needle on the tachometer registered 2000 revolutions per minute, a speed at which we usually cruised at five knots. The boat still did not budge. The throttle nudged the power to 3000 revs, a force seldom used, even when cruising. I feared the unstable engine might collapse from its cradle under the strain and vibration.

'Shit! The propeller shaft must be damaged from the engine coming off its mounts,' I fretted.

'This is the last place I want to be disabled. There's nobody here to help us for miles,' Esmae said.

Gradually, as if struggling to free herself from a coiled spring, *Antares II* crept forward and we headed around to the correct course. Then suddenly, inexplicably, as if a tether had snapped, she moved at speed under full throttle.

We remained bewildered until several days later, when sailing around the islands of Komodo in daylight. The tide was so tempestuous in places it created huge whirlpools that spun the boat off its course. The moonless nights had been so black they had concealed the swirling waters of the vortex through which we had sailed. They had defeated the gentle breeze controlling *Antares II* and spun her around as if she were a cork caught in an eddy.

Because we had neither an engine nor wind, fickle breezes and currents took us well off course. Eventually, we anchored off a little village on a picturesque island, Labuan Bajo. We knew little about the harbour because it had not been on our itinerary, but high lush green islands surrounded it to provide a beautiful all-weather port accommodating local fishing boats, large prahus and small freighters.

A local restaurant owner, Harry, who learned English when practising his trade in Australia, introduced us to an artisan who fabricated new engine mounts.

'Ford, Toyota, Yamaha, Mercedes,' the engineer announced as he shook hands and grinned, displaying a set of nicotine-stained teeth.

I glared blankly at the stooped thin man in dirty overalls. Grease smeared his face.

'He thinks he talking with English to you,' Harry explained. 'That all he know, motor name. I tell him for you what you want. You tell me and I tell him, then he tell me and I tell you.'

Despite Harry's good intentions as interpreter, communication proved a tedious and challenging business.

The engineer turned out to be a craftsman. He introduced his son, explaining that, just as his father had taught him his craft, he was passing his knowledge on to his boy.

While waiting for the repairs to be completed, we whiled away our time getting to know the villagers. We discovered a special magic in encountering them early in the morning as the dawn stillness was fractured by a muezzin's gravel voice calling prayer time. Stooped old women, their heads covered by shawls, swept dirt paths outside their huts. Fishing boats returned with paltry catches. A chain gang of hungry men, covered from head to foot in dust, struggled to balance heavy bags of cement on their shoulders as, morning after morning, before it became too hot to work, they unloaded a beached freighter. The crude stalls opened to sell their meagre wares of sweet bread, eggs and cigarettes. Sombre girls, white shawls covering their heads, tried to control noisy little brothers who jabbered and kicked stones as they dawdled beside them to school. As they neared us, they happily chanted the national incantation: 'Hello Mister! What's your name?'

I repeated my mantra, 'Toe. Knee,' evoking the usual delightful laughter and the request for bonbons.

The repairs completed, we set out again in search of the fabled Komodo dragons. On the way, we continued to be in awe of Indonesia's beauty. We sailed past mountainous islands and active volcanoes belching steam and smoke. At day's end, we anchored off picturesque villages over which smoke spiralled skyward from cooking fires. Friendly people rowed out in their dugouts to greet us with a wave and a smile and asked for beer, cigarettes, sweets, pens, T-shirts and caps. At dusk, a black shroud blanketed brilliant sunsets as thousands of fruit bats filled the sky.

Over centuries, the elements have sculpted forbidding islands into bizarre shapes that fuel dark dreams. Some looked like dragons, others dinosaurs, and a couple had the heads and bodies of giants. One outcrop resembled a mermaid lying on her back, the bush-like long hair cascading over a voluptuous breast. In the eerie glow of dusk sparse trees and mountainous ridges became sinister mythological beasts. With the vortexes, and tides so strong, it is little wonder that sailors in ancient times conjured fearful images of leviathans and whirlpools that swallowed ships.

After cautiously making our way around reefs, we anchored off desolate Rinja Island, a national park where we hoped to find dragons. A ranger joined us as we crept through bush at six o'clock the following morning. Armed with only a bamboo reed, he narrated how, a few days previously, a large dragon had eaten a buffalo.

'Dragon very big. Has big jaws,' he explained, his hands opening and shutting to imitate a huge mouth, 'and teeth like shark. Runs very fast, much faster than you. Be very careful. Don't go too close.'

Scrawny scrub clung to rolling arid hills strewn with large rock outcrops that provided good camouflage for the ferocious lizards. We also kept a wary eye out for pythons lurking in the brown knee-high grass. We spotted plenty of interesting birds, families of monkeys and small herds of deer.

Unexpectedly, we came upon a large dragon, perhaps three metres long and weighing over 100 kilos, basking on a boulder in front of us. It balanced on stubby powerful legs, which were as thick as an elephant's. Each foot had five clawed toes sharp enough to tear a person to pieces, and an armour of spiny scales protected its massive body. With its thick tapered head raised and tilted toward the sun, the dragon seemed to wear a contented smile on its tight thin lips as it luxuriated in the warmth. Its yellow eyes glinted menacingly, following our cautious movements.

'He not hungry,' the ranger reassured us, 'see how big his belly. He already eaten.' Recklessly he set about prodding the brute with the bamboo reed. We were relieved it responded amicably and posed for photographs. Tired of being the centre of attention, it hissed, lifted its long thick tail and, bow-legged, lumbered further into the bush to escape our intrusion. Obviously, the ranger knew his dragons.

New dangers lurked underwater a few days later when two sharks stalked us as we snorkelled on a reef at Moyo, a national park off Sumbawa, further on in the Flores group of islands, where we anchored en route to Bali.

Much of the reef lay strewn over the sea floor like bleached and broken bones, evidence of the atrocities committed by local fishermen with greed in their eyes and dynamite in their hands. Luckily, the scars of their ugly vandalism were unable to totally disfigure the reef, which was one of the finest we had seen outside Fiji. Had it been in pristine condition, it would have been a rare jewel.

We swam with turtles whose lumbering awkwardness on land became gymnastic gracefulness under water. Hundreds of big-eyed trevally lazily circled in a beehive-shaped swarm 12 metres high and three metres wide. Blue parrotfish, their scales and fins etched pink, kept a wary eye on us, as did gropers, rays and translucent pipefish that mysteriously vanished at our approach. Black and yellow butterfly fish and angelfish with blue and yellow stripes darted among coral to which crimson sponges clung. The stinging tentacles of sea anemones undulated in the cool current. Molluscs bloomed like flowers in a garden. The owners of the Moyo resort had stopped the bombing and the reef was rejuvenating.

We introduced ourselves to the resort's British manager, who was not particularly hospitable.

'We don't welcome boat people. Our guests pay 600 American dollars a day to be here,' he explained. 'You chaps turn up in your tatty clothes and dive and snorkel and get it all for free. Naturally, our guests aren't too happy about that.'

His attitude was disappointing. Esmae intended remaining alone on *Antares II* for several days while I flew to Bali on business and to pick up guests. Because of the delay caused by the broken engine mounts, they would have to join us at Moyo Island. We asked him if hotel staff, whom we had found friendly, could keep an eye on things during my absence.

'Okay, I don't mind Esmae using the facilities while you're

away. But don't tell anyone how good the place is or that I'm making you welcome,' he insisted. 'Make out it's awful, because we don't want other yachts here.'

The next day, I accompanied him and six guests by luxury launch to the nearby island of Sumbawa which had a small airport from which the national carrier, Garuda, flew to Denpasar, Bali. The other passengers, a family of rich Americans and a New York stockbroker and his wife, were booked on connecting flights from Bali to Singapore and then on to the United States.

We patiently waited at the crowded little terminal while the manager welcomed a new group who would stay at the resort. Pandemonium followed an announcement that the flight, the only one of the day, was cancelled because the aircraft had burst a tyre when landing. A replacement would not be sent until the next morning. Then the stockbroker's wife realised, with a wail, that her bag had been stolen. Eventually, however, the manager crammed us into a bemo for an eight-hour journey to Lombok Island where the Americans would catch a flight to get them to Denpasar in time to make connections to Singapore and the States. After more problems, I reached Bali at one o'clock in the morning, following a five-hour ferry voyage.

I followed other passengers along a dirt track that led from the wharf to a parking lot for bemos. Hawkers swarmed over me like moths to a light, but I strode on purposefully, trying to determine where I was and how I should get to the hotel on the tourist strip at Kuta Beach. I shouldered my way through a throng milling about on a dirt square. The ferry passengers knew what to do: they loaded bags and goods onto dilapidated bemos. Dozens of minivans lurked on the perimeter of the dimly lit parking area like preying animals waiting for a Westerner to skin.

'Hello, Mister! Where you go, Mister?' Wisps of pubescent facial hair and a sparse moustache gave the youth a comical appearance. His persistence paid off when I realised I had no idea where I was. I told him the name of my hotel at Kuta.

'It very far. I take you there for 100,000 rupiahs,' he offered.

'That's outrageous!' I thundered. 'That's about 25 American dollars.'

A crowd of bemo drivers gathered around us as we haggled. The youth had a considerable advantage because he appeared to be the only Indonesian who spoke English. He also knew where we were and how far it was to Kuta. I did not have a strong hand for negotiating.

A short time after leaving the car park, I became alarmed when the bemo stopped in an unlit street and the young man demanded, 'You pay now.'

'I don't have any money,' I lied, fearing I was about to be robbed. 'I will get money at the hotel and pay you then.'

As it turned out, the youth was friendly. He sat beside me and chatted all the way, as if to make sure I did not leap from the bemo and abscond without paying the fare. We finally arrived at the hotel at three o'clock in the morning.

Later, I heard that the stockbroker's wife's bag was returned intact: not even the considerable amount of cash was missing.

CHAPTER 3

PIRATES!

'Pirates are scrambling the radio,' Muzza warned when we spoke to him early one morning as we sailed from Bali to Singapore on the last leg of our Indonesian odyssey. 'Listen to Channel 16. You can't get a word in because of the talking, whistling and singing going on. It's unreal. They're even farting on air! Channel 16 is supposed to be kept free for emergencies but you can never get on it. I reckon pirates are jamming it so we can't call for help if we're attacked.'

We put his fears down to paranoia that had gripped crews on many yachts since leaving Benoa, the inadequate port that is a boat's doorway to the holiday resort island of Bali. However, we understood why Muzza feared it was scrambled. Strange things occurred on the international emergency radio frequency, Channel 16. Day and night, it was cluttered with Indonesians singing, belching, talking, laughing and abusing each other. At night we had even heard long conversations in broken English that sounded like an Asian radio version of telephone sex.

'You have a banana?' a husky female voiced purred. 'I wanna banana.' Her suggestive tone evoked frenzied responses from numerous males we assumed to be Indonesian fishermen. They literally panted into their microphones.

While we sailed far out in the Java Sea, cruising between busy shipping lanes, *My Way* was many kilometres away, keeping close to islands near the mainland. Like several other yachties, Muzza was subjected to the bizarre attentions of local boats.

'Where are you, Muzza?' Esmae enquired.

'I'm not going to give my position any more because you never know who's listening. All I'll say is that I'm off Serutu Island.'

'Roger, Serutu Island,' Esmae confirmed, 'between Bali and Singapore. All well on board?'

'No, not really. We're bloody nervous. A freighter called us yesterday and asked us what the hell we're doing out here. He warned us not to give our position because pirates monitor the radio. The captain wouldn't divulge his co-ordinates for the same reason. It's too bloody risky. He said we're mad to be out here alone in pirate waters.'

'C'mon Muzza, if there are pirates out there, they're after cargoes and payrolls. They're not after us, we're only small fry.'

'Yeah? Well, you never know. I'm not taking any chances.'

The further we cruised in Indonesian waters the more nervous crews had become about the possibility of pirate attacks. We had all experienced frightening episodes. Twice, a large fast boat had appeared from nowhere and tailed us for six hours. When we changed course, it followed. When we tried sailing in a zigzag pattern, the mysterious vessel a kilometre behind did likewise. Fortunately, the boat eventually disappeared over the horizon and we never saw it again. Now we felt apprehensive every time a solitary boat approached. Often they sped toward us and, just as a collision appeared inevitable, veered away.

We had read that such antics were performed by fishermen trying to pass their bad luck across to us, and drew comfort from the explanation on numerous occasions. When we deliberately tried to pass behind Indonesian boats they usually ignored us. If, however, we cut across their bow, even at a considerable distance, we invariably invited pursuit. Perhaps rather naively, we bolstered our spirits by recalling we had always felt safe ashore in Indonesia. Why should the country's seafarers be any more threatening than those on land?

Unfortunately, benevolent thoughts do not erase the cold reality of history. Piracy re-emerged in South East Asia after the Vietnam War. The victims were mainly wretched refugees whose unstable boats were boarded by renegades who plundered anything of value. Before tossing their victims into the sea to drown, the pirates mercilessly pulled gold teeth and beat and raped women. Since then, piracy has steadily increased. More recently, several Asian societies have become dysfunctional as their economies have faltered and the subsequent poverty has bred a desperation that provokes fishermen, criminals and former members of the armed services to violence. At the same time, governments, struggling to meet fiscal responsibilities, have reduced sea patrols. Triads and other criminal syndicates have also discovered lucrative rewards from easy pickings at sea.

Before leaving Benoa, we heard several stories about boats being boarded while at anchor off isolated islands. A Pakistani freighter captain warned us to be vigilant, particularly at night. 'Every day at sunset I have pirate drill aboard my ship,' he revealed. 'The crew parade around the decks like soldiers carrying rifles.'

'How many guns do you have on board?' I asked.

'Oh no, we don't have any guns. If you have a gun, you have to be prepared to use it. If you draw a gun, you're likely to be shot dead by pirates because they're more ruthless than we are. They'll shoot first and ask questions later. When we have our pirate drills, my men have broomsticks over their shoulders so that, from a distance, they look like soldiers marching with rifles.' He laughed at his ingenuity. 'We hope that if pirates see us, they will think we're heavily armed and leave us alone.'

Now, between shipping lanes in the middle of the Java Sea, our vulnerability was stark. We drifted slowly on a light breeze while fleets of supertankers and massive container ships passed, determined to speed through this notorious area. The parade of ships continued during the night, moving with the swift monotonous regularity of traffic on a highway. They sailed in clusters, as if travelling in convoy, keeping close to thwart attacks. Beyond those on our port side, shards of lightning bombarded a cold glow from cities whose lights were hidden under a pall of smog.

During our five years in Asia, we saw piracy grow alarmingly. On one occasion, pirates struck very close to home, attacking a fishing boat only a few kilometres from our base at Rebak Island. The corsairs murdered two of its three crew before sailing away in it. The incident alerted Malaysia's maritime police to the fact that Rebak Island, with up to 200 foreign boats sheltering behind its jungle-draped hills, could provide booty for renegades. They tightened security at the marina and introduced nightly water patrols.

Despite an Indonesian, Malaysian and Japanese military presence, nearly 100 pirate attacks occur annually in Indonesia and in the Malacca Straits, regarded as the most dangerous stretch of ocean in the world. Although about 30 ships and several aircraft were supposed to be patrolling the area, we encountered neither navy vessels nor aircraft during voyages on the busy waterway. On one passage, we could not even interest the Malaysian authorities when we stumbled across a suspicious Indonesian freighter.

The incident occurred when we were only a few hours from the brooding monoliths that guard the entrance to mystical Langkawi. Because their unscalable cliffs and impenetrable jungles discourage exploration, the islands remain mysterious, inhabited by only battalions of squealing monkeys. Where cliffs have collapsed, perpendicular limestone walls tower hundreds of metres above the sea. When lit by the sun their veins ripple like ochre entombed in marble. Red eagles soar above their vertical crags, and in the cooler airs of dawn and twilight monkeys explore the shore, fossicking for crabs and fish stranded in rock pools. We intended to anchor in the emerald water beneath the imposing façades, to recover from a taxing five-day voyage from Singapore.

We had been especially vigilant in the Malacca Straits. Warnings were broadcast that, as we battled strong currents and unsettled weather, pirates working the channel had attacked three vessels. We grew apprehensive about a difficult task ahead: we must navigate past dangerous rocks that protrude from the islands. The night was so black the outcrops would be impossible to see.

Although we were still some hours from an anchorage, we mechanically set about a long-established routine for ending a passage. As if anticipating unexpected visitors, we worked in a frenzy to tidy the yacht, coiling ropes, filing discarded charts and making the cockpit and saloon uncluttered.

We toiled numbly, maintaining a careful watch for lights and hazards. Briefly, hovering off our port, I glimpsed a red sphere the size of a small coin. I dropped the rope coiled in my hand and squinted into the darkness. The light disappeared as we slid down a swell. We rose again and it was still there, burning menacingly. 'It's a flare! Someone must be in trouble.'

With no moon, and cloud hiding stars, we sailed in an abyss without an horizon. A blinking light, many kilometres to our starboard, was all that punctuated the void. The flare continued to glow like the tip of an inhaled cigarette until it slowly lost its incandescence. Three other flares penetrated the darkness in quick succession. We changed course to locate the source of the distress signals, which should be fired only when a vessel experiences serious difficulties.

We radioed the mainland to alert Malaysian authorities that a boat could be in trouble. No one answered Channel 16. The skipper of a yacht on a mooring outside Rebak Island rewarded our persistence by intercepting our call and undertaking to contact Langkawi's maritime police. He later told us that he too was unable to raise any interest.

After half an hour, another flare lit the darkness behind us and we realised we had gone too far. We turned back to search, sweeping the undulating water with a spotlight. After a while, the beam glanced on a target too obscure to identify in the darkness. We lost it at the bottom of a swell. We continued to illuminate the ocean for some time without success.

Suddenly, as if shaken from a magician's cape, we saw, trapped in the spotlight's golden, dappled haze, a crooked loft, perched three storeys high, teetering above patched wooden planks mottled by peeling paint. A cast of shadowy figures, their chests barrelled by bulky lifejackets, hollered and waved from decks that surrounded the edifice like balustrades and verandahs on a ramshackle colonial house. Suspended before us was an Indonesian cargo boat, about 18 metres long, of the type that ferries people and goods throughout the archipelago. An inflated life raft floated off its stern and another small craft lurked nearby.

'I don't know what to make of this,' I confessed. 'It's hard to tell whether there's a genuine problem.'

'Engine! Engine!' a crew member shouted. We interpreted it to mean the ship's engine had failed.

'How many people aboard?'

'Nine people.'

A phantom on a lower deck fired a rocket flare into the sky. Its red hue turned the boat into a surreal chamber from hell.

'Taxi!' the man called.

We presumed he was trying to explain he needed a ride. His limited English seemed to highlight his helplessness and made his position even more poignant.

'Langkawi!' he shouted, indicating the port to which they expected to be taken.

'Where you from?'

'Indonesia,' he confirmed.

A few fishing boats arrived on the scene and lay off, a safe distance away, probably sharing our concern that it could be a pirate ruse. Other crew shouted for help as we circled and checked them out under spotlights. We counted the number of planks above the waterline on the boat's side.

Rescuing them posed several dangers and we did not know what to do. Although they appeared genuinely frightened, we distrusted them. We feared that if we approached, or took them aboard, we might find ourselves under attack. We were not convinced the boat did not hide several more people beneath its decks.

Refugees and illegal immigrants were a more topical issue in Malaysia than pirates. Its government displayed little tolerance towards thousands of desperate people from Indonesia, the Philippines, Thailand and other Asian countries who illegally entered its borders. Australia's uncompromising policy of turning away boatloads of refugees, mainly Muslims, had recently captured headlines throughout Asia. Our arrival with a cargo of Indonesians could provide a weapon suitable for hitting back at Australia: the Malaysian government would not necessarily distinguish nationalities. We did not relish the possibility of becoming embroiled in an international incident.

Naturally, deciding whether to leave somebody, dead or alive, to the mercy of the sea is a torment. We continued to wrestle with the dilemma facing us; as we circled, their cries sounded pitiful.

The other fishing vessels attracted by the flares also held the boat in the beams of their spotlights. When we counted the thick planks remaining above the waterline, the total number was the same as it had been earlier, an indication that the boat was not sinking.

Deciding that the Indonesians' boat was seaworthy and weather and sea conditions were improving, we turned away and headed for an anchorage. As we motored away with heavy hearts, the Indonesians shouted and pleaded for help. We justified our decision with knowledge that we could not be confident they were genuine. If we took them aboard, we risked being attacked as we motored into the darkness. If they were genuine, and their boat was disabled by engine failure, it was stable and did not pose a threat to life. It was too heavy for us to tow. Although we were one of the first boats to arrive at the scene, several others remained after we had left. They would speak Bahasa, the language common to both Malays and Indonesians. Had the men been in the water, or on the life raft, or had their boat been listing, we would have unhesitatingly given them a hand.

Crews on many yachts carry arms to protect themselves against pirates. Although the temptation to arm ourselves was compelling, we decided to keep *Antares II* gun-free. We were not confident we would have the will to fire a weapon, even if we were confronted by camouflaged, balaclava-clad men wielding knives, swords, machetes and automatic rifles. Our brazen attackers would surely land a shot on a target before Esmae or I could. Our safety depended on a stern look, a gruff voice, good luck and common sense.

We envied Noel and Rebecca Mudgway, aboard *Southern Voyager*. Before leaving Picton, they applied Kiwi ingenuity by installing a transformer to feed 9000 volts through an electrified fence they attached to stanchions around their yacht. Each time they felt threatened by an approaching vessel, they activated a thin wire under the top lifeline that encircled the deck. When anchored in lonely bays and visiting other yachts, they relaxed in the knowledge that they would probably hear the painful shrieks of any intruder who tried to board their boat. They also slept easy with the reassurance that the fence was live throughout the night.

The only disadvantage was that they had to be extremely careful when they returned to *Southern Voyager*. Unless they disengaged the power, a hand absentmindedly curled around the wire, or a leg straddling it, could trigger an electric current severe enough to stun them. Noel overcame the danger by adapting an infrared remote control from a garage door to enable him to disengage the electrified fence before he climbed aboard.

During the years we sailed the Malacca Straits, we encountered hazards some considered much more threatening than pirates. Most daunting was the possibility of collision. With 600 ships traversing its currents daily, the narrow waterway is congested with all manner of vessels travelling at varying speeds.

A sluggish yacht, relying on trade winds for its speed and direction, can be as much of a menace in busy shipping lanes as a car stranded on a railway track. The perils are greatest at night when darkness distorts distance. On watch, crew have to be particularly attentive to ships' navigation lights to determine the direction in which they move. Local boats, often ignorant about the rules of the sea, can be particularly hazardous. They display a confusing array of lights that challenge decisions about holding a course.

Nerves of steel are required to maintain a course in the Malacca Straits. Ships often overtake so close that a fishing line could be thrown onto their decks. A loss of nerve can have dire consequences; even large ships collide.

Sailing outside the shipping lanes also demands caution, because occasionally ships stray from them. At times, visibility is severely reduced, particularly when the ocean is blanketed with heavy smog from bush fires ashore. If a person keeping watch on a ship's bridge is drowsy, or distracted, a yacht in an unexpected place may easily be missed. Several vessels have had narrow escapes.

The numerous hazards in the Malacca Straits are taken seriously. Responsible captains on merchant ships double watches. Many use powerful floodlights to illuminate decks so that intruders are easily seen. Spotlights frequently sweep bow and stern waves surging from ships as officers keeping watch scrutinise the surrounding water for fast-moving speedboats ferrying pirates. Extra care is taken to identify targets picked up by radar and to monitor their progress, particularly if they lie within a ship's track. As Muzza learned, little information is divulged about a ship's progress, its destination, crew numbers or cargo. Some captains have booty bags ready for turning over to pirates if they are boarded. They hope the renegades will flee with a few thousand dollars without inflicting injury on the crew.

Lightning is another hazard. Every night spectacular electrical storms play over the Malacca Straits as the sky seeks relief from an accumulation of moisture and energy created by the day's oppressive heat. Aboard a yacht, a battalion of metal appendages lure lightning like bayonets glinting in the sun.

Southern Voyager was hit one night. She reared like a mare stung by a wasp as tens of thousands of volts charged down her mast, blew out her electronics, popped her lights and set fire to an alternator. Noel was fortunate to escape with only a badly burned hand.

CYCLONE

Boiling scarlet nebulae churned at the base of a nugget of black cloud that scarred the horizon behind us. We had watched it evolve for the best part of an hour. At first light, we had spotted its anvil shape among a ribbon of billowy clouds that made the day dawn dark and gloomy. The anvil had spread like an enormous black hole that devoured surrounding cumulus. Gradually, it grew into an ugly solid mass of pent-up energy.

'Jeez, it looks like the gates of hell,' I remarked to Michael Dunlop who shared the watch with me as we studied the thunder-head.

'Yes, and we've just gone through them,' he chuckled.

We were three days from Phuket – three frustrating days in which we had found little wind except when squalls passed over us. So far, we had motored/sailed most of the way across the Andaman Sea, switching off the engine when the wind rose from five to 20 knots. *Antares II* revelled in the breeze, but it never lasted long. As soon as a squall dumped litres of water on us the wind dropped away completely, the sails flogged and the motor was on again.

Michael had bought our public relations and advertising business in 1995. The sale freed me to recuperate from ME (myalgic encephalomyelitis or chronic fatigue immune deficiency syndrome), which had depleted my professional drive. Selling the business had enabled me to follow my doctor's advice about changing my lifestyle to regain my health. I doubt he had in mind that I should take to the seas in search of exotic ports, but, although the debilitating illness continued to rob my energy, I was determined to overcome it.

An anonymous poem we found aboard *Antares II* captured the essence of my desire to sail across oceans. It became an inspiration:

> A small boy heard the ocean roar,
> 'There are secrets on my distant shore
> But beware my child the ship's bells wail,
> Wait not too long to start the sail.'
> So quickly come and go the years
> And a young adult stands on a beach – with fears;
> 'Come on, come on,' the ocean cussed,
> 'Time passes on, of sail you must.'
> Now it's business in middle-aged prime
> And maybe tomorrow there'll be time.
> Now it's too soon … It's raining today.
> Gone, all gone, years are eaten away.
>
> An old man looks out, still feeling the lure
> Yet he'll suffer the pain than go for the cure.
> The hair is white, the steps with care.
>
> So all too soon the secrets are buried
> Along with him and regrets he carried
> And it is not for loss of secrets he cried
> But rather because he'd never tried.

A friend had the poem laminated and we hung it on a wall in our bedroom; Esmae and I were determined not to end up with regrets.

We bought *Antares II*, a 15-metre Shannon Aegean ketch, in Auckland in 1993, specifically for ocean-going cruising. At the time, we owned a 13-metre William Gardner ketch and, although we enjoyed sailing her around the New Zealand coast, we did not consider her suitable for crossing oceans. We were not actively looking for a new yacht when Jeff Stone, a salesman at Orams ship brokers in Auckland, telephoned one damp Sunday morning. 'I think I've found that boat you're after,' he announced.

'What do you mean? I've already got one. I'm not after a boat.'

'You probably don't remember me. It must be two years ago when you gave me a brief to find a yacht for offshore cruising. I think I've found her for you.'

Vaguely, I recalled inspecting a couple of boats with him without finding anything suitable. It was a long time ago and I had forgotten about it.

Jeff reminded me that I had given him a long list of requirements, outlining my ideal boat as being a ketch with a full keel and an aft cabin and centre cockpit. Equipment I insisted upon included a generator, water maker, radar and a dozen other accessories and features I regarded as essential.

As soon as we saw her sitting on the hardstand at Gulf Harbour Marina, north of Auckland, we knew *Antares II* was our ideal boat. She was a good-looking vessel, of traditional style without being ornate. She was practical and built for safety. Her keel, which ran three-quarters of her length, was 2.13 metres deep: that would give her stability in big seas and encourage her to roll upright if, heaven forbid, we ever turned turtle. She was a little over four metres wide, her belly bulging like a pregnant horse, which promised a roomy saloon. She was long and sturdy and rigged with thick stainless steel cable strong enough to hold her masts in place in the most violent conditions. All her gear, including winches, was heavy duty; she was well equipped for rough weather. Below decks, heavily lacquered holly and teak were enhanced with a patina that reflected a maturity and grace well beyond her six years.

A grate at the bottom of the companionway stairs over which we could stand to discard wet weather gear was the only feature missing from my list. We had wanted a grille in which water from our gear would drain into a bilge rather than onto the floor which, when wet, would become slippery and dangerous in heavy seas.

Her owners, John and Stephanie Pew, from Florida, had sailed from Alaska to New Zealand with two small children aboard. When they sold *Antares II* they intended building a larger boat in which they would sail back to Alaska.

The timing could not have been worse. We already owned a yacht and we had only recently concluded a couple of costly business deals that had drained our cash. We were also frantically busy, working with Michael Fay's consortium to buy New Zealand Railways, which the government had decided to privatise. We had worked with Michael before when he put a syndicate together to challenge for the 1987 America's Cup. It was then that I first experienced the thrill of yachting, which spurred my ambition to sail the world. Ironically, negotiations to buy *Antares II* lasted much longer than it took to clinch the deal to buy the Railways. Fortunately, the yacht was only a fraction of the price.

Since buying Consultus, our public relations and advertising business, Michael Dunlop and his partner Glenys Coughlan had sailed with us on a number of occasions. Their last voyage had been in Indonesia where they enjoyed calm seas and night watches under balmy star-studded skies as we sailed from Moyo Island to Bali.

During a brief visit to New Zealand in 1998, Esmae had enticed Michael and Glenys to join us on a 1700-kilometre voyage to Sri Lanka, promising them idyllic armchair sailing with a steady 15-knot trade wind caressing our beam. During the past two years, yachts making the passage across the Bay of Bengal on their way to Africa and the Red Sea had relished such conditions. We had also studied pilot books and weather patterns: the chances of striking bad conditions in February were rare.

Before we set sail on 27 January 1999, yachts already in the Bay of Bengal reported running into more squalls than usual, probably because of a low-pressure system hovering over the area. We considered delaying our passage, but our guests had tight schedules and had to return to work. We estimated it would take three days to cross the Andaman Sea to the Bay of Bengal, by which time we expected the low-pressure system to have dissipated or moved on. Unfortunately, it did not. It hovered over the Andaman Islands, spitting out bullets of bad weather that continued to unsettle yachts ahead of us. It was confusing: some complained about the weather; others sailed in the magical conditions we sought.

I predicted the elusive trade wind would fill our sails after we passed the Nicobar Islands. The Indian government controls this cluster of hilly outcrops and, at the time, prohibited yachts from anchoring off them. Those who had stopped there in previous years had been detained by military police. The travellers' bible, the Lonely Planet guidebook, says that not too long ago cannibals inhabited some of the islands. If we had to hide from a tropical storm, the Nicobars did not sound particularly hospitable. India also controls the Andaman Islands, about 480 kilometres to the north of the Nicobars. Here, too, are primitive settlements where foreigners are not permitted to tread.

The two groups of islands comprise an outer edge of a basin that forms the Bay of Bengal whose vast power shapes the shores of Myanmar (Burma), Bangladesh, India and Sri Lanka. We decided to enter the Bay of Bengal by sailing through the Sombrero Channel, a 50-kilometre stretch of water about eight kilometres wide that flows between the Nicobars' craggy islands. The channel has a reputation for being boisterous, but it provided our shortest route. The islands are like a breakwater separating the Andaman Sea from the Bay of Bengal. Currents have to squeeze through, tightly compressing energy into a force that can slow an opposing boat's progress, or even push it backwards. The current is not the only impediment. When the wind blows against shallow water streaming between the Nicobars, the sea rises as if to fight it. But it is too heavy and it collapses in a sudden fury of white spume that slams into a boat and halts her progress. If the sea really rages, it can topple her.

As we approached the islands, we struggled to make headway. For a long time, the Nicobars were only a black outline that we occasionally glimpsed through an early morning pall of cloud.

'The gods aren't with us today,' I announced to Michael. 'We had hoped to have the current and the wind behind us coming through here, but we've got neither.'

Esmae was below for the scheduled morning radio broadcast. 'I'm not getting anything worthwhile about the weather,' she complained. 'There's a trough about, but I think it's well below us. No one seems to know much about what's happening here, although Ross on *Gemini* reckons we should strike good weather in 24 hours because he was hit by lots of squalls but now seems to be out of them.'

'We don't have too many choices, anyway,' I said. 'We're not allowed to anchor off the islands and it's too far to go back to Thailand. The north-east monsoon is usually as regular as clockwork, so I think we've got to get it soon.'

Michael and I left the cockpit to shorten the mainsail so it would be safer if we were hit by a squall we spotted ahead. The dense cloudbank still hovered behind us like a border post separating the Andaman Sea from the Nicobar Islands. It disappeared when the squall seized us just as we entered shallow water that we knew could become dangerous when wind opposed the current's flow. Torrential rain tumbled from the squall with such fury it flattened the boiling sea and reduced the danger. Since we were not taking sea over our decks I opened valves to divert the rain into our tanks rather than let it spill overboard.

The rain was a bonus. The generator that ran the desalinator was inoperable because, halfway across the Andaman Sea, a rubber exhaust elbow had perished and spilled water into the engine room when the motor ran. The elbow was about the only spare I did not have on board; we would not be able to operate the generator again until I could buy a replacement part in Sri Lanka. Filling the tanks with rain would avoid rationing water.

After a while inside the squall the sails flogged annoyingly as the wind died completely. Even without the wind the rain continued to fall so hard it blocked our vision and we motored in a white-out as thick as fog. Little changed during the next 24 hours and we sailed from one squall to another. When it did not rain, the sky remained angry and threatening.

The next morning, Glenys was the first to mention that the fresh water tasted brackish. The contamination became more noticeable as the day progressed, until the taste became vile. Fortunately, we had spare water stowed in plastic drums on deck.

Esmae came up from the radio with alarming news: 'They're warning of a cyclone. I heard it on Rowdy's Net.' (Rowdy ran a radio network popular with licensed amateur radio operators.) 'He says a weather report from Guam warns that the low has formed into a depression and could become a cyclone, a hurricane,' she continued.

'Holy hell! We're not supposed to get cyclones out here in February. What's our Inmarsat weather report say?' I demanded.

'Fifteen to 20-knot winds from the north-east with occasional thunder storms. That's all they ever say. I don't think they change it, they repeat the same message day after day,' Esmae complained.

'Guam's a long way away. They can't be right.'

'They get their weather from the American navy. I'll believe them more than the forecasts we get from New Delhi.'

It was not shaping up to be a good day. I went below to carry out routine checks in the engine room. Black water slopped about high in the bilge. I switched on pumps to dump it overboard but after 15 minutes there was still no sign of it subsiding. The wind had come up again and was right on our bow. As we leaned to our starboard side, the water appeared to have risen higher than it had been before. Propelled by the rocking of the boat, it splashed and slopped and slurped loudly. When *Antares II* briefly lay still I heard a much more disconcerting sound: water trickling into the bilge with the speed of a running tap. 'Shit! We're taking on water,' I barked, and grabbed a torch to search within the hull's dark caverns for the source of the flow.

Noise from the seepage continued but I could not see where where the water was entering. I went from the engine room to the saloon and the forward cabin and peered into hatches, but I saw nothing. Under a locker in the floor of the aft cabin, below where the propeller shaft connected to the transmission, water flowed at an alarming rate. I called Esmae.

'I don't want to scare the others,' I confided, 'but water is gushing into the bilge. I think we've got a leak somewhere. It seems to be coming from our cabin. I need you to help me find it.'

'Oh, God! We're heading into a cyclone and we've sprung a leak! What are you going to do?' Esmae demanded.

'We've got to find out where it is and how bad it is before I'll know what to do,' I snapped.

'Could it be connected to the contaminated water? Could sea water be getting into our water system?'

'I can't see how. The fresh water is stored in sealed tanks.'

'Could they be leaking into the bilge?'

'I don't think so. I want to see if the stern gland is leaking.'

The water flowing under the propeller shaft had indicated that the most likely culprit was the stern gland, a sleeve in which greased hemp is packed around the shaft to block water entering from outside. It had been repacked in Thailand before we set out but stern glands can give constant trouble. However, this time it was performing as it should.

The beam from the torch illuminated a steady flow of water running down the side of the boat on the opposite side to which she heeled. Its steady volume alarmed us both. When we dismantled a cupboard beside the bed we discovered the source of the water was in the lazarette, a small stowage compartment at the back of the boat. Michael helped to empty the locker of ropes, diving tanks and a storm sail we decided to stow in the cockpit for use in atrocious weather. Peering into the locker, we saw a broken hosepipe through which the bilge water should have drained onto the sea. The pump was doing no more than recycling bilge water that, instead of going overboard, spilled into the lazarette and ran under our bed and back into the sump. I assumed that people in Thailand working on the boat's stern had snapped the pipe when standing on it. Fixing it was easy.

Obtaining accurate weather information was almost impossible. We could not locate the cyclone's position because nobody supplied its latitude and longitude. Weather faxes could provide diagrams of conditions but nobody sailing the Bay of Bengal could receive a transmission; nor was anything available on high frequency radio. Inmarsat C, which received text messages directly from satellites, kept telling us we were sailing in ideal conditions of 15 knots of wind from behind us. Its only warning was for occasional thunderstorms. Whoever provided the satellite's knowledge was right about the electrical storms, but wrong about the weather.

Antares II heeled over and bucked about in high seas as the wind blew from west-south-west, not the north-east, where it should have been. A plague of squalls, spinning toward us like baby cyclones, battered us from varying angles with winds gusting to 38 knots.

Antares II came alive to confront the challenges the squalls hurled at her. She creaked and clattered in protest as the reefed mainsail and headsail strained to contain gale-force wind. She heeled precariously, as if trying to throw us off balance. Her rigging screamed. Plumes of water crashed over her and poured along her decks.

Each squall had its own personality. Sometimes we felt exhilarated as gusts pummelled us from behind and we rode waves as if on a surfboard. Others attacked us head-on and would have knocked us down had too much sail been showing. Eventually, the squalls folded around us like a dense shroud and dumped a torrent of water on us. Inside them, it was relatively calm and we wallowed on an eerie, oily, windless ocean swell that rose and fell with a heavy sigh. Denuded of whitecaps, a squall's core could be beguilingly tranquil, until a menacing streak of lightning ripped through the cloud, slicing the sky in a jagged line before plunging into the sea. To determine its distance from us, we counted the seconds between each flash and the rumble of its thunder. Each second denoted a mile. If lightning struck *Antares II*, we would, at best, lose our electronics; at worst we could lose lives.

The squalls were relentless. They were so intense they dotted the radar screen and we had to determine whether its beams detected bullets of weather or distant ships moving toward us. No ships were out there. The storms became easy to distinguish: blips on the screen grew into fluffy smudges that underwent a further metamorphosis into ominous weapons poised for attack. Over four days we must have encountered well over 200 of them. Occasionally, if we changed our course, we out-ran them.

We envied boats ahead announcing on the radio that they were near Galle, the Sri Lankan harbour in which we would find safety and shelter. We also envied others behind us anchored snugly at the Andaman Islands, Sumatra and Langkawi. They followed our progress while waiting for the weather to improve before setting sail themselves. A couple of boats had experienced problems: a non-functioning GPS and a torn mainsail. Compared with them, we hadn't experienced anything too serious.

None of us admitted being afraid but few crews would escape being apprehensive with a cyclone forming somewhere nearby. I was probably more aware than most about what could happen if the tempest crossed our path. My mind filled with memories of interviews I had conducted for my book *Rescue in the Pacific*, in which survivors had recounted their ordeals when caught by a weather bomb while sailing from New Zealand to Tonga in 1994 – a storm that, at the time, ranked as one of the worst to hit a fleet of yachts since the infamous 1979 Fastnet Race.

Our morale plummeted when Esmae picked up from the radio that chances of the depression developing into a cyclone had increased. We scoured the ocean for towering dense columns of clouds and other signs that we could be entering a cyclone. The barometer was down and the squalls and gales made us fear that perhaps we were already in the cyclone's grip. The urgency in the voices of other cruisers in the vicinity increased our awareness of the danger we faced.

We prepared for the worst. We secured hatches and portholes, making them watertight so they would not leak or be sucked open if we pitch-poled in a cyclone's gigantic seas. We double-checked the lashing on the dinghy and made sure everything above deck was secure. Life jackets were hauled out of a locker. We showed Michael and Glenys how to activate the electronic positioning beacon (EPIRB) that would alert rescuers to our position if we became disabled and required assistance. We retrieved a parachute sea anchor from a locker. In the lazarette, we stowed long warps for trailing in the water behind us to slow the boat when surfing at speed down gigantic waves. We agreed we would wear harnesses, even in the cockpit, a precaution we took only on rough nights or in extreme conditions. Being tethered would prevent us from being washed away if enormous waves pounded *Antares II*. In the saloon, we placed a grab bag full of essentials that would be required if we fled in the life raft. As we made our storm preparations, I tried to reassure the crew that *Antares II* was a very sound boat with a thick hull and strong rigging; she was, in fact, a lifeboat.

The winds did not scare me – we sail comfortably in 50 knots – but anticipation of the building sea did. In the Pacific storm, winds of more than 70 knots had created a 15-metre swell which made yachts unmanageable so that they slid sideways down waves. The crest of foam at the top of gigantic breakers had acted like a huge baseball mitt, picking up the little boats and rolling them over or catapulting them end over end.

My apprehension was not relieved when Bill Choice, a Texan whose boat was called *First Choice*, alerted us on the radio to another danger lurking on the ocean. Although she was 320 kilometres ahead of us, *First Choice* had experienced similar weather. Bill recounted that a few hours previously he had seen something similar to an explosion in the water off his port bow. Urgently, he tacked away. He stared incredulously at the monster forming only a few kilometres from him. It was a huge waterspout, spinning towards them like a tornado.

'It shot up water at a 45-degree angle and it was probably 100 feet across. It was real compact and concentrated, sucking the water right up out of the waves. It spun at an incredible speed. It's hard to explain how fast it was slinging this water around,' Bill announced on the radio. He had turned to get away from it but it seemed to get closer and looked like it was coming at them. It passed not more than two boat lengths to their port side.

'I think if it had hit us, it would have taken our rig down. The force of the thing was incredible,' Bill recalled.

'It was building and the water was getting higher the longer it was building. I think it must have been 300 feet high. It went zooming right on by and we were just awestruck by this thing.'

Throughout the day, we dug into reference books to learn more about northern hemisphere cyclones and prepared ourselves for the worst.

Eric and Cynthia Lockeyear, aboard *Rozinante* (named after Don Quixote's horse), from Hong Kong, were sailing to the north of us and had winds of 35 knots and torrential rain. Esmae picked them up on radio and they admitted that they, too, had been lulled into a false sense of security by the forecasts.

Eric plotted the storm's progress from information he received on a radio net run by Trevor Winer, South African owner of an

American registered yacht, *Gallivant*. Trevor lay snug at Port Blair, at the Andaman Islands, waiting for the weather to improve before setting out for India. When we contacted him, he confirmed there was a cyclone in the Bay of Bengal. It had a name: Cyclone Deb. 'If it's any consolation, it's the first cyclone they've had in the area during the month of February for 22 years,' he said.

Weather reports from the other boats in the Bay of Bengal enabled Eric to ascertain that he was probably in the worst position of us all, right in the cyclone's most dangerous sector. With the wind coming over our port bow, we calculated we were sailing into the safest quarter in the south-west. We hoped we were right.

'It's moving so very quickly we're going to go through the eye,' Eric said. 'We've hardened up on starboard, as closely as we can comfortably get to the wind, and that's put us on a course due north.'

We monitored each other's progress every four hours. *Rozinante* was a fast boat and managed to outrun the worst of the weather. Aboard *Antares II*, we continued to race toward the safe sector, scanning the horizon for signs of towering cloud columns and other evidence that we were in the cyclone.

'Christ! We've just received a Pan Pan over the Inmarsat,' Esmae announced when we were three nights from Galle Harbour. 'It's warning us of 50-knot winds and further deteriorating conditions.'

We were sailing at eight degrees and decided to alter course and head towards the equator where we expected the wind would be lighter. Cyclones do not usually form below seven degrees, so we concluded that although it might add several kilometres to our passage, it should be much safer further south.

After we altered course we were surprised to find ourselves sailing outside the band of squalls. The radar detected them constantly forming 48 kilometres ahead but, instead of coming toward us, they moved to our starboard. We watched them skimming across the ocean a few kilometres off our beam, not presenting any threat at all. They continued to roll by in their scores, as if staying strictly in their allotted lanes on a highway. The pattern remained much the same for three days until the wind unexpectedly disappeared completely and we motored all the way to Galle. While dropping our mainsail at the entrance to the outer harbour, the gentle north-easterly trade wind Esmae had promised Michael and Glenys began to blow.

We had arrived too late to enter Galle Harbour. At dusk, the navy secured a huge net across the port's mouth to stop Tamil Tigers from sneaking inside in the dark. Naturally, it kept everyone else out as well. It did not matter, we were happy to swing on anchor, rolling on a swell, outside the breakwater. Quaffing champagne to celebrate the end of the passage, we enjoyed the beauty of the sun's last rays splashing a golden hue over quaint white buildings left by the Portuguese who had arrived in gunboats in the 16th century.

Landfalls are always wonderful. The sense of achievement is often bewildering. For Esmae, landfalls are a time for celebration, an occasion for a party; I prefer to sit in a quiet corner and let the emotions wash over me like an ocean swell. But there was no time for quiet contemplation tonight. Tonight, we would definitely celebrate.

CHAPTER 5

SHOTS IN SRI LANKA

Esmae had produced a duck into which she had rubbed spices, herbs, chillies and garlic. While it cooked to a crisp tantalising masterpiece, she dissected a pineapple that she drowned in coconut milk through which she laced gentle curry. As it sizzled in the galley, her creation teased our senses.

The sensual aromas of our feast must have wafted into Galle Harbour's naval base. It was not long until the drone of a motor interrupted our revelry and competed with Maria Callas singing Puccini on the stereo. Soon, a spotlight blinded us.

'Who are you?' demanded a shape in the dark.

'We're the sailing boat *Antares II*. We radioed port control about our arrival and they said we have to wait out here 'til morning.'

'What is your last port?'

'Phuket, Thailand.'

'How many of you?'

'Four.'

Esmae prodded me. I read her mind: as a deterrent, she would have preferred me to inflate the number of crew.

Our interrogator was a swarthy middle-aged man whose sweat-stained shirt was unbuttoned to his waist where a gun holster protruded. A gawky youth beside him cradled an automatic rifle that pointed in our direction.

'We inspect boat,' the man announced.

'No you won't, we're having dinner,' Esmae protested. 'Who are you? We don't even know who you are.'

'I'm navy.'

'You can inspect the boat tomorrow morning before we go in,' she insisted.

He did not look official. Neither he nor the youth beside him wore uniforms. We could not make out who else was in the boat or how many there were.

'You have beer?' the man asked.

Michael brought four beers from below. Before we gave them to our visitor, he instructed us about the procedure for entering the harbour.

'You call agent, Don Windsor, and he get navy and customs to see you when you arrive.'

'We've already spoken to him on the radio.'

'Good. You not go into the harbour until navy inspect boat.'

At eight o'clock the next morning, we motored closer to the harbour entrance and circled about until a gunboat with half a dozen crew crunched against our side. Four armed, uniformed men wearing heavy black boots jumped aboard. Two set about searching every nook and cranny; they pulled out drawers and inspected the engine room and floor hatches. Another asked questions similar to those posed by our nocturnal visitor. The other went through a pile of women's magazines, closely scrutinising advertisements in which scantily dressed young women advertised lingerie. He seemed disappointed they were not *Playboy*.

Outside, a sailor donned an aqualung and dived under the yacht to make sure Tamil Tigers had not attached mines to the hull during the night. Satisfied we were not gunrunners, and that there was nothing on board that could be activated by radio after we entered the harbour, they asked for beer and cigarettes. We paid our dues and they left disappointed with the size of the gift.

About 15 other yachts lay in the harbour. An Australian we knew from Rebak rowed out and offered to secure our bow and stern lines to buoys that held the yachts in an intricate pattern. With ropes attached to yachts running in all directions, the boats resembled insects caught in a spider's web.

'Customs will be out to see you,' he said. 'Watch 'em, they're a bunch of thieving dingoes. You have to go and see immigration and they'll probably send you out with customs, 'cause they don't have their own boat and they'll need you to take them to and fro.

'They want lists of everything that's dutiable. Smokes. Booze. You know, the usual. List everything, even bottles that are half full 'cause if you don't they'll do you. They're a corrupt bunch of bastards.'

'What do they expect you to give them?'

'Depends on the mood they're in, or how big your boat is, I think. They took a dozen beers, a couple of bottles of wine and a carton of smokes from me. One bloke lost a whole carton of Johnnie Walker to them. Before you see any of them, you've got to get a clearing agent to do the paperwork. Most of us have used Don Windsor, but there are others.'

We didn't like the Windsors when we found a gang of them lounging about in a cramped air-conditioned office. Don Windsor, who had set up the agency, was long dead and his sons now ran the business. They chattered among themselves, uninterested in us.

Don Windsor had evidently been a businessman who built his reputation by being helpful and professional. He stared disapprovingly at his sons from a photograph on a wall. A commendation from an American ambassador hung nearby, recording the United States government's appreciation of the assistance Don Windsor had provided to a procession of sailors who had used his services over the years. A framed cartoon, yellow with age, hung on a wall like a mission statement. It showed Don Windsor holding a yacht in his cupped hands. The words '10 per cent' adorned the mainsail, indicating the amount he wheedled out of visiting yachtsmen who crossed his threshold to ask for advice and assistance.

One of the sons gruffly instructed us to take a bundle of paper he had processed to immigration. He demanded US$170 for a permit that would expire after a month.

'If they ask you for extra money, don't give any,' he snarled. 'Then customs will inspect your boat.'

A plain-clothes customs officer ordered me back to my boat where I would wait until he arrived after inspecting other vessels.

'Come on, Es, let's go,' I said.

'No, Cap-i-tain, they not go,' he ordered, pointing at Esmae, Glenys and Michael. 'Just you go and wait for me. Madam and the others will wait here.'

It dawned on me later that he preferred to have me on the yacht alone so there would be no witnesses to the intimidation that would take place.

The skipper of another yacht brought the surly official and his plump smiling colleague to *Antares II* after they had processed, or rather plundered, his boat.

'Good luck,' he said, raising his eyes in exasperation, as the pair climbed aboard *Antares II*.

'Good morning, Cap-i-tain. Welcome to Sri Lanka,' the officer said with mock sincerity. 'Sri Lanka is a very poor country where we work long hours for hardly enough money to buy food for our children. Now, I want to be your friends. I want to help you so you have a good time here with no problems.'

'That's kind of you,' I mumbled suspiciously.

'Yes. I help you, you help me. Now, you have list for me?'

His sly eyes studied the inventory of wine, spirits, beers, soft drinks and cigarettes. 'This is an accurate list? There is nothing else?'

I shook my head.

'Sign this,' he commanded.

I quickly scanned the document he thrust before me that listed prohibited items and the consequences of making a false declaration.

'Now we search your boat,' he said.

We went below. The plump man had not uttered a word since boarding. He slumped onto a settee in the saloon and left the inspection to his colleague who was beginning to perspire in the heat below decks.

'You have *Playboy*, *Penthouse*?' he enquired as he thumbed through the pile of women's magazines.

I shook my head.

'Let me see the alcohol,' he demanded.

We had provisioned with enough drinks to last us until we returned to Malaysia in about four months. I showed him the cupboards in which they were stowed and he ticked them off against the inventory.

'Ah-ha, Cap-i-tain, I cannot find everything on this list,' he said triumphantly.

We compared the bottles now littering the saloon with the inventory. Two bottles of spirits were missing.

'We must have made a mistake,' I admitted.

'Oh, Cap-i-tain, a mistake is very serious trouble,' he gleefully announced. 'Read the paper you signed.'

The plump man smirked as I read the declaration.

'It's not a problem,' I suggested. 'It's not as if I've understated what we have. I made an innocent mistake and listed too much, things that we must have drunk before we arrived.'

'I am sorry, Cap-i-tain, but it is a problem. It's a big problem. You are in very serious trouble,' he emphasised. 'You signed a false declaration. That is a criminal offence. I am going to have to take you ashore where you will be arrested for signing a false declaration. You will have to appear in court. Unfortunately, our courts are crowded and very slow. It will cost you much money to wait here for your hearing because you will not be allowed to leave Sri

Lanka until you have been judged. You might not even leave before the monsoon.'

'That's ridiculous. I haven't done anything wrong. It's not as if I've tried to smuggle anything into the country. All I've done is overstate how much grog is on board. Surely that's not an offence. It's not as if I'm trying to smuggle in booze I didn't declare.'

'Maybe not, but you *have* done wrong. You signed a false declaration.'

I scowled at him and he gloated at his victory as he started to select bottles of wine and spirits for himself.

'I want to be your friend,' he said. 'Taking you to court will involve a lot of paperwork and take a lot of time. Today is my day off and I only came out here to help you so you can go ashore and have fun. When I finish here I will take my wife and children for a picnic.

'You are a successful man,' he continued. 'You have a nice expensive boat that is bigger than my house. Maybe you have gifts for me and my friend,' he suggested, nodding in the direction of the man smirking on the settee.

'What do you want?' I asked hoarsely, defeated.

He helped himself to half a dozen bottles of wine, bottles of spirits and cans of beer.

'Where is bag?' he demanded when he had completed his plunder.

'I beg your pardon?'

'Do you have bag?'

'No,' I responded.

Let him carry his loot so everyone can see his dishonesty, I thought. However, he was incorrigible. The prospect of carrying his booty without cover did not deter him from further blackmail.

'My children would like gifts too. You have Coca-Cola?'

He took some cans and helped himself to chocolates and sweets that we had aboard for giving to children. He still had not finished.

'You have T-shirts? Caps?'

I denied having any on board, claiming to have given them away in Thailand. He and his friend loaded their loot into my dinghy and I took them ashore.

'Cap-i-tain, you're my friend. Any problems, you just come and see me,' he warmly invited, pumping my hand and smiling when we reached the dock.

Another agent, a stocky man with smiling eyes, had attached himself to the trio awaiting my arrival.

'Tony, this is Marlin,' Esmae said as she introduced us. 'He's arranging for us to have an authentic Sri Lankan dinner at Galle's oldest hotel. He's also booking a car to take Michael and Glen to the airport at Colombo to catch their plane tomorrow morning.'

Marlin disarmed me with a warm and friendly smile that displayed a row of perfect white teeth.

'How much do you charge for your services?' I asked, still reeling from my experience with customs.

'Nothing. I do it as a friend,' he said still beaming. 'If you think I do good, you give me gift before you sail. If I not do good, I don't deserve anything.'

Marlin more than made up for the unpleasant experience with customs. He introduced us to good restaurants that served excellent cuisine and he scoured Galle to track down an elbow for the exhaust on our generator.

'There is only one of these in all of Galle,' he revealed as he studied the old perished elbow he had hawked through the town to explain the part he sought. 'Because there is only one, it will cost much money.'

'How much?'

'I don't know. How much you pay?'

'I don't know. I'll come and have a look at it first,' I suggested.

'No, you cannot come, we can see it only at night.'

'What do you mean?'

'It is on another motor,' he revealed sheepishly.

'What? You intend stealing it from someone else's engine?'

'Do you want it or not?' he asked impatiently.

'Not if you've got to steal it.'

'Good, I didn't want to get it for you that way, either,' he said.

Marlin solved the problem by introducing me to an elderly engineer who beat red hot metal into shape in a stormwater drain beside a shack. Working with hot coals and bellows, he created a perfect bronze replica of the rubber elbow. With a piece of rubber from a bicycle tyre inner tube for a gasket, the sculpture was still working faultlessly when I replaced it with an authentic piece many kilometres later in the Maldives.

'Why do they call you Marlin?' I asked one day.

'They call me after fish because 15 years ago, when I was young man, I used to swim out to meet yachts when they arrive. I take their ropes and tie them to buoys. Then they ask me to clean their boats and do other work. Because they say I swim like fish, they call me Marlin,' he said proudly.

'I wish you had swum to us the other day – you might have made things easier when we checked in.'

He laughed. 'I was only 23 years old then. I was hungry and determined to find work. I couldn't swim out there today.'

Marlin accompanied us down dark alleys to buy rice, eggs, food and spices we would never have found on our own. He accompanied us to produce markets where we bought fruit and vegetables and fish and chickens that were killed and plucked before our eyes. He sternly reprimanded beggars and touts who pounced on us and he haggled with shopkeepers he claimed were trying to cheat us.

We explored Galle in a tuktuk, a three-wheeled vehicle that is little more than a motorcycle with a cab attached. To a cacophony of impatient car horns we fought for right-of-way with carts pulled by donkeys, with noisy two-stroke motorcycles on which whole families balanced, and with wizened, bare-chested old men and gummy women wearing saris who precariously pushed extra-large burdens on bicycles. Beyond them, in a haze created by heat and dust, stood once-grand buildings erected by the British. Monsoons and relentless sun have stripped paint and stamped ugly black mould upon the edifices that were once the pride of the empire.

Early one morning Marlin put us on a third-class train for a wonderful journey to Colombo, Sri Lanka's capital. We travelled, at a sedate pace, in carriages reminiscent of a bygone era. Outside, the leaves of thickets of rubber trees, coconut palms and other brilliant green foliage, polished by dew, glistened in shafts of sunlight. The train clattered over bridges above slow muddy rivers in which fully clothed women bathed and gossiped as they did their laundry. The train slowed to a crawl when passing slums built so close to the railway that we could have touched their cardboard box walls. As we neared bustling stations, we chugged past ramshackle homes and shops outside which men and women, busily preparing for their day, ignored us. They washed and shaved and spat toothpaste onto the ground as they cleaned their teeth with pieces of bamboo dipped into tin mugs of dirty water. Inquisitive children in immaculate uniforms waved and shouted and flashed enchanting smiles as they wandered to school. Even though it was early morning, boys shouted and yelled excitedly as they played cricket, Sri Lanka's national game, on a scrap of barren dirt.

The civil war with the Tamil Tigers had turned Colombo into a city under siege. Armed guards in camouflage uniforms manned roadblocks and hovered behind mottled sandbags that formed fortifications outside strategic buildings and government departments. The soldiers, poised for an attack at any moment, looked ill at ease.

Tight security protected the route to the airport, which we travelled by taxi to meet our daughter, Justine, who was flying in from London to sail to India with us. Soldiers stopped us at roadblocks and pointed guns through the taxi's windows. They searched the boot and under seats and glove compartments. Justine's plane was late, so we paid a considerable amount to sit in a waiting area where mosquitoes ravaged us.

Even though it was dilapidated, Colombo's rambling Galle Face Hotel still reflected the grandeur of the 1920s, when British

colonials had strutted the globe as if they had inherited it.
Developers were keen to upgrade the hotel into a complex incor-
porating a shopping mall, similar to the way in which Raffles
Hotel, Singapore, has been preserved. As with most projects in Sri
Lanka, the civil war had delayed their dreams.

Staying there was a treat. Our room was large but old and dusty.
The bed was hard and the floorboards, covered with a worn Indian
rug, creaked under our tread. From our room, we looked over the
Indian Ocean. At dusk, families thronged the beach, promenaded
up and down a sandy stretch and bought food from hawkers.

Inside the hotel, we walked along arched whitewashed corridors
and reclined in deep cane chairs while enjoying sundowners in a
lounge beside an empty pool. The atmosphere was reminiscent of
a slower, more genteel era. At a table under a large ceiling fan that
had kept patrons cool since Victorian times, curries for dinner
simmered in bains-marie.

The following day, we set out from Colombo to tour as much
of the island as we could. We were disappointed that, because
Tamil Tigers controlled much of northern Sri Lanka, tourists were
prohibited from visiting there. The north boasts much of the country's most beautiful scenery.

George, our guide and driver, proudly explained in impeccable
English that he was a Burgher, a Sri Lankan of Dutch ancestry,
whose roots went back five centuries. Initially, we assessed him to
be a gentle man who was at peace with himself. Several times,
when he saw a snake slithering on the road, he swerved to avoid
running over it. On one occasion, he stopped to pick up a large
butterfly that glanced the side of the car and insisted we keep it in
the vehicle until it had recovered enough to be set free.

Surprisingly, his concern for life did not extend to humans. If
they dared to block his way, he furiously honked his horn, forcing
pedestrians to flee and cyclists to wobble off the road, fighting to
maintain their balance. He ploughed across pedestrian crossings
outside schools where scores of children strolled. Clearly, he con-

sidered the narrow rutted roads to be *his* domain, because he was a professional driver, and heaven help anyone who got in his way. Many of the jalopies rattling along were, like much about Sri Lanka, also from a bygone era – Morris Minors, Hillmans, baby Austins. The narrowness of the roads did not deter George from taking risks, and when trucks and buses slowed our progress he thought nothing of passing them on bends.

Still savouring the safe enjoyment of the railway journey from Galle to Colombo, we decided to leave George and travel through the highlands by train. We chugged up steep tracks hacked out of mountainsides that plummeted into valleys hundreds of metres below. Every centimetre of ground was cultivated. Crops, tea and coffee grew in neat rows. In the distance brightly dressed women picked leaves off tea bushes. Hawkers boarded the train at every station and rushed through carriages loudly offering spicy food and drinks to passengers snoozing in their seats.

In the highlands, George waited for us at the tiny Nuwara Eliya railway station. He explained with a flourish, as his hands swept a vast expanse of rustic beauty below, that a reason for the country's ailing economy was that no one went hungry. 'Look at it,' he demanded as we stood amidst fertile mountains and valleys, 'all the food we could ever wish for. We might have poverty, but no one goes hungry in Sri Lanka because they can help themselves to food off the land. People don't have to work to eat.'

After the sweltering heat at sea level, Nuwara Eliya, or Little England, at an altitude of 1884 metres, was refreshingly cold. The area is aptly named. Lying at the heart of the tea country, the town resembles a piece of the Lake District with its Victorian buildings, cascading waterfalls, beautiful gardens and crisp, sweet-smelling mountain air. It is a complete contrast to the dusty decay and pandemonium of Galle.

We stayed at the Hill Club, a quaint hotel that was once a club for the genteel folk managing tea plantations. Dark wood panelling made our cramped room dingy and reminiscent of boarding school accommodation; heating was sparse and air conditioning unheard of. Tradition prevailed: to keep us warm at night we were each given a hot water bottle.

From the hill country, we travelled to the 1800-year-old ruins of settlements in the ancient city of Polonnaruwa. The inhabitants had built vast dams and ingenious sluicing mechanisms to control the height and flow of water needed to irrigate hundreds of hectares in the dry central region where they grew rice and vegetables. They are still being used today. The same people carved huge statues of Buddha in the sides of granite hills, the ruins of which are still visible.

At Sigiriya, north of the centre of Sri Lankan culture, Kandy, we climbed 2000 steps to the top of a huge rock on which a Sri Lankan king had housed his fortress 1500 years ago. The castle and surrounding water gardens are an incredible engineering and architectural feat.

The climb up the mountainside was a daunting challenge and we dallied about whether to undertake such a demanding trek. George assured us it would be worth the effort and, to give us encouragement, he arranged for a guide to accompany us. Our chaperon turned out to be 75 years old. We suspected George was telling us that if an old man could manage the climb, we should be able to sprint up the mountainside.

As we slowly trudged towards the summit, the guide pointed to large dams and vents that, during the monsoon, filled with water as rain flowed down the mountain into subterranean caverns. Those early engineers' calculations were so precise that, when in flood, water spouted from the holes like geysers in a thermal wonderland. We pondered what had happened to transform the country to the backward state it is in today.

As a reward for climbing the rock, I was presented with a certificate to say I qualified as a member of a Senior Citizens' Club eligible only to those 55 and over who had accomplished this challenging feat. Not wanting to be outdone, Esmae lied about her age so that she also received a certificate. It is the only occasion on which I have known her to increase her age.

We ran into roadblocks everywhere. The military were present even at the remote Yalla Game Resort where we spent our last couple of days before returning to Galle Harbour. The game park skirts the coast on the south-east corner of the country. An army camp had set up on the beach to protect migrant fishermen trying to eke out an existence. Probably more important, they were also charged with keeping tourists safe from Tamil Tigers who had infiltrated the area. An attack on tourists would have a significant adverse impact on the economy. In the park, we rode safari in an open jeep and saw an abundance of animals and birds. We were even lucky to spy elusive elephant.

Galle Harbour was far from a happy place with visiting yachtsmen. While we were away touring, a German catamaran was given only a few hours to leave after the skipper refused to pay bribes. Others grumbled about being refused fuel because they would not pay bribes demanded by officials. A senior policeman quizzed one couple about their sex life.

The harbour's unsavoury side did not deter merchant vessels from stopping there. Galle was a busy little port. During our stay, dozens of boats discharged their cargoes. Several large freighters from China worked around the clock unloading hundreds of tons of cement. Loud rumblings came from deep within the ships' bowels and their waterlines rose as cranes on their decks scooped out the heavy load and disgorged bagged cement onto trucks that appeared to be remnants of the 1930s. We were intrigued about what they intended to do with the cement because we had seen no signs of new construction anywhere.

Workmen unloading the cargo toiled in frightful conditions. At the end of their shifts, covered from head to toe with grey dust, they wandered down to the water's edge near our anchorage. Undeterred by the garbage and oil polluting the water, they washed themselves and their clothes in the sea.

Even in the harbour, we could not hide from the poverty that gnawed at our consciences. Apparently ashamed by their plight, desperately poor men hid within a clump of coconut trees and spied on sailors as they alighted at the dinghy dock to go ashore. Every time a plastic bag was dumped in an unlit incinerator next to an ablution block, they darted out to inspect its contents, hoping to discover a treasure that could make life a little easier.

Neither could we hide from the danger of our situation: we were visiting a country gripped by a bloody civil war. Security was rigid and armed soldiers and seamen patrolled night and day. Because Galle was a navy base, warships came and went. Every night, until we became immune to them, explosions from depth charges disturbed our sleep when the navy dropped dynamite in the harbour's waters to discourage Tamil Tigers from sneaking in and attaching mines to warships. Each time a bomb was detonated, it sounded as if it had cracked open our hull. Fish were the only victims of the bombing. Each morning, fishermen in primitive dugout canoes trawled nets through the harbour to scoop up fish stunned by the blasts.

Before we were due to sail, Marlin invited Bill and Maggie Choice and Esmae and me to dine at his home. His wife prepared a sumptuous banquet of spicy food that included several curries, fish and vegetables. The fragrances and tastes were wonderfully exotic, but we could not relax over dinner because Marlin's wife and extended family stood around watching us dine. As is their custom, they would not eat until we had finished our meals.

At the end of the evening, just as we were discussing the country's political situation, there was a muffled thud of an explosion. Initially, no one took much notice. We had almost become blasé about nightly blasts.

'Do you normally feel the depth charges in the harbour?' Esmae asked. The house was some distance from the water.

'Sometimes,' Marlin reassured her.

Four more explosions followed in rapid succession. The reports sounded very loud and close. Alarmed, Marlin and his family deserted us and rushed outside to determine the cause of the commotion.

'What do we do now?' Bill asked as we sat alone at the table.

'Let's wait and see if they come back,' Maggie suggested.

We heard the noise of people running along an alleyway next to the house.

After some minutes, Marlin still had not returned and we decided to venture outside to discover what was happening. Marlin reappeared to tell us that neighbours had identified the explosions as hand grenades that had detonated close to their houses. He thought it prudent for us to return to our yachts as quickly as possible.

Marlin escorted us through a labyrinth of narrow winding lanes, lit only by fireflies darting about in the darkness. People, anxious to discover the cause of the explosions, lurked in silence in shadows outside every house. Eventually, we arrived at a road leading to the entrance of the navy base. Pandemonium reigned. A line of armed soldiers nervously patrolled a checkpoint 50 metres from the barrier arm at which security officers processed those entering the base. Behind it, huge wooden doors, like the impenetrable gates of a medieval castle, had been drawn closed against the possibility of invasion. They blocked our way back to our yachts.

'Shit, I haven't got my security pass on me, I left it on the boat,' I admitted.

The others confessed they too had forgotten to bring the passes necessary for entry to the naval base. Guards frequently tried to wheedle cigarettes from us when we passed through the checkpoint. Having no passes tonight could cost us dearly.

Sentries, usually asleep at their posts at this time of night, were alert and nervous as they patrolled, rifles at the ready, outside the huge barriers. As we approached, they blocked our entrance. One stepped forward and requested our passes.

At that moment, a small door in the barriers swung open and a group of naval men, armed with automatic rifles, dashed out. The urgency with which the men ran into the darkness intensified the sentries' fear. They became too preoccupied with imagined dangers lurking in the darkness beyond us to worry about our passes.

'Go! Go now!' Bill yelled and we ran through the small door as naval men, their rifles ready to repel Tamil Tigers, rushed past in the opposite direction and disappeared into the darkness towards the sound of the explosions.

The pandemonium continued inside the base as officers shouted orders to spectres running aimlessly around in the night.

'I haven't seen anything like this since Vietnam,' Bill said. 'I think we'd better get back to our boats quick smart.'

As we untangled lines holding our tenders at the dinghy jetty, we were startled by a clattering similar to the sound of the boots of a distant army on the run.

'It's magazines being loaded,' Bill said, pointing to two frigates at a wharf close by.

'Christ, I hope they don't mistake us for Tamil Tigers,' I said, fumbling with the lines.

As if in answer, a shot rang out over our heads. We fired our engines and sped across the water towards the security of our yachts, hoping no nervous trigger-happy ratings would take pot-shots at us. A blaze of light lit the harbour as beams from anti-aircraft spotlights swept the water. They found us and held us in their grip. We feared more bullets might whistle over us, but no more shots were fired.

A few days later, after paying an exorbitant bribe customs officials demanded for diesel to top up our fuel tanks, we sailed for Cochin, India.

CHAPTER 6

SAILING SEAS OF POVERTY

Gradually, the speck on the horizon grew larger. Soon it would be upon us. Over recent days, messages from satellites gliding high above had warned ships in the Indian Ocean to be vigilant for a speeding boat of Somali pirates who had attacked and robbed vessels much larger than our 15-metre yacht. I suggested that Esmae and Justine should go below and cover themselves. Skimpily dressed women wearing only a swimsuit and a bikini could add to our troubles if evil hearts possessed the mysterious boat hurtling toward us. The determination of its course and its speed added to our apprehension; it was certainly much faster than any of the scores of fishing boats we had encountered since leaving Galle a couple of days before.

We had no idea where the nearest vessel might be if we needed help. Certainly, none was in sight. I eased the throttle forward to nudge the engine to 3000 revs in anticipation of lifting our boat's speed to seven knots but the current was against us: it confined our speed to a mere five knots. Outrunning them would be impossible.

Esmae and Justine, now draped in sarongs and T-shirts, emerged from below. The boat was closer now. It was about seven metres

89

long and afforded its occupants no protection from a merciless sun.

'They look like Somalis to me,' Esmae observed nervously.

'I doubt it, we're a long way from Somalia. I think they're from Sri Lanka or India,' I suggested, afraid they could be Tamil Tigers.

'No, they're definitely African,' she said.

'Well, if they are, they're a long way from home.'

I suggested that Justine, a tall, attractive blonde, should keep out of sight. Reluctantly, she disappeared down the companionway, suggesting I was paranoid.

Wearing tattered rags, the crew in the pursuing boat were dishevelled and unkempt. They waved vigorously at us, indicating we should slow down.

'We're not stopping or letting them on board,' I muttered as I left the cockpit and gesticulated and shouted to the strangers that they should keep away from the yacht. Esmae began shouting too.

'Go away, you can't come alongside,' I commanded as they slowed beside us.

Three of them stood up and yelled in an unfamiliar language.

Their boat was unlike others we had encountered off Sri Lanka's coast. Two 40-horsepower outboard motors propelled it at speeds much greater than fishermen required. We saw no fishing gear in her open hull.

Although we could not understand a word they said, it was obvious that they wanted us to stop and allow them to come alongside. I was relieved they had not brandished weapons and hoped they harboured the same qualms as Indonesians, who told us they knew from television that most American yachts should be feared because they were armed and crewed by people with a penchant for violence. They did not distinguish between nationalities, believing that the crews of all yachts hailed from the States and were extraordinarily wealthy.

Justine re-emerged to see a stocky crew member with a mass of curly hair raising a pewter jug toward the sky. The fingers of his free hand moved to indicate water falling and he shook his head as he shouted, repeating his message several times.

'They need water, Dad. He's trying to tell us they've run out of water and there hasn't been any rain. Let them come alongside,' she pleaded.

'No!' I was adamant. 'No one comes on this boat unless I'm sure they're genuine. I don't believe them.'

'They're thirsty, Dad, we've got to help them. We've got plenty of water. How can you deny it to them?'

It was true. We could supply an abundance of water because, in one of the miracles of modern technology, our desalinator could convert 130 litres of salt water into fresh drinkable liquid in a single hour.

'Come on, Dad, we've got to help them. How would you feel if we were out of water and they wouldn't help you?' Justine cajoled.

All five men in the boat, which kept pace a few metres off our port side, proffered water vessels to reinforce their predicament. Their appearance fuelled my suspicions: none looked emaciated. On the contrary, their bodies were lean and muscular. If they were genuine, they could not have been without water for long.

'Go away!' I demanded, thrusting my hands forward as if trying to push them out of our lives. 'I can't help you. Go away!'

'Dad, you can't,' Justine pleaded.

'You can't,' Esmae joined in.

Ignoring the rebuke, I climbed back into the cockpit, disengaged the autopilot and swung the yacht away from the forlorn group as they stood in their dilapidated boat gaping at us. Fortunately, they did not pursue us. As I endured the rancour of those aboard *Antares II*, the strangers, still shouting, turned about and headed back in the direction from which they had come.

Until the confrontation it had been a wonderful day. As we motored/sailed on a calm sea under a blue sky with warm sun caressing our bodies, all boded well for our passage across the Gulf of Mannar which separates Sri Lanka from India. It is not always so tranquil: the gulf is notorious for the brutality of its gales.

Since sailing from Galle Harbour, we had enjoyed good weather. Initially, we were tempted to sail directly from Galle to Cape Cormorin, the southernmost tip of India, which is the shortest route. However, following advice from sailors who had traversed the waters before us, we set a course to cross the gulf further north, along the coast near the port of Chilaw, an historic town where tourists wander among ancient ruins and temples. It was a tough call. The route took us more than 180 kilometres out of our way. On more than one occasion, particularly at night, I was tempted to change direction and sprint across the gulf. Fortunately, the wisdom of Esmae, our navigator, prevailed.

Sailing along the coast at night presented a variety of dangers we could have avoided further out at sea. Large freighters and tankers passed close to us, miraculously avoiding colliding with the scores of wooden fishing boats that lurked in the darkness, invisible even to the ever-watchful electronic eyes of radar. We had to be constantly alert.

Justine had the most eventful watch. While she was training a torch on the mainsail a small bundle of fur dropped from the sky and landed on her foot. Her shriek brought Esmae and me bolting from our berth to see what had alarmed her. The intruder quivering on the deck was an ugly little bat that had somehow managed to stray 20 kilometres out to sea.

It looked an evil little critter, small enough to fit in the palm of my hand, its tiny wrinkled face like that of a discarded foetus. It had a tight, mean mouth and slits for eyes. Esmae suggested Justine should scoop it from the deck in a cloth and return it to the night. Gingerly, Justine gathered it in a rag and held it over the side of the boat until darkness devoured it. Its pathetic squeals and screwed-up little face troubled her for hours as she pondered whether it had managed to fly to safety, or fluttered onto the water to become a meal for a predator lurking in the deep.

As we held our course to Chilaw, *Antares II* leaned into a gentle coastal breeze and we enjoyed cruising at a pleasant six knots as we passed a pall of smog that blanketed Colombo.

But Esmae and Justine refused to let me forget the incident with the strange boat. Their contemptuous looks left me in no doubt about the odium in which I was held. I retreated to the foredeck and sulked alone in the friendly sun. I reflected on how cheap life could be in Asia. Had the three years we had spent there really changed my values to such an extent that I could leave desperate men in the middle of the ocean?

'They're probably dead,' Justine proclaimed when she joined me. 'How could you do that, Dad?'

'For God's sake, give it a break,' I replied tersely. 'They'll be okay. It's only about 100 kilometres to Sri Lanka and India's not far away. They could go to either country for water if they're desperate.'

'They might not have enough fuel.'

'I'm sure they have. They didn't ask us for fuel, did they? They'll have plenty. If they're desperate for water, they'll be able to get some. It was too dangerous to let them come alongside with only us on board. Anything could have happened.'

Despite my reassurances, the callousness of my decision continued to trouble me and the forlorn look in the men's eyes as I turned the yacht away haunts me to this day.

The sun sank into the ocean in a blaze of orange, leaving us alone in a black moonless void. But the night sea was far from barren. Lights glowed and darted all around us as hundreds of little fishing craft began their toil, laying their nets and hauling them in. Others drifted aimlessly with fires glowing brightly so they could jig inquisitive squid lured to the surface by the illumination.

'Those guys wouldn't have died of thirst. Just look at that,' I said relieved, as I swept my hand in a large arc to emphasise the vastness of the fishing fleet. 'If they needed water they could have got it from any of those boats.'

We were never alone again as we rounded the Horn of India,

Cape Cormorin, into the Arabian Sea and made our way along Southern India's Malabar Coast toward our destination of Cochin, India's oldest port. Hundreds of boats, ranging from heavy steel fishing trawlers to precarious overcrowded dhows crudely sculpted from tree trunks and propelled by wooden paddles and patched sackcloth sails, drifted on the water 16 kilometres off the coast. Oblivious to the dangers of a fickle sea, their occupants strove to feed themselves by stalking fish in waters that had long ago been plundered of their prizes.

Fish can be scarce in Asian waters. We had trawled a heavy line behind us all the way from Sri Lanka. Only once, off Cape Comorin, did we hear the joyful sound that told us we had caught a fish: the clatter of screws inside a Coke can attached to a bungy on the end of a fishing line. The commotion shot adrenalin into our veins and charged us with energy.

Before dashing below, Esmae thrust the throttle into neutral to slow the boat to reduce drag on the line. Justine grabbed the line and, hand over hand, pulled its load toward the centre of the boat. I scrambled to a backstay to unclip a gaff.

'It's heavy. It's a good one,' Justine beamed, flinching as the nylon rope slipped and burnt her hands.

'Careful, don't lose it,' I cautioned.

'Look at that! It's a big one. It's a beaut,' I shouted, glimpsing a long silver streak flash near the surface a boat length from where Justine struggled with its weight.

'I don't think I can get it in, it's too heavy.'

'Don't lose it,' I pleaded.

'Take your time,' Esmae suggested as she rejoined us with a bottle of gin.

'I should have worn gloves,' Justine muttered as she palmed wire trace attached to the end of the nylon rope that only the sharpest of teeth or heaviest of fish could snap.

The fish splashed beside the boat. I raised the gaff and plunged it into the water, deftly twisting it so the hook would stab the fish.

Missed! The gaff's hook struck the fish at the wrong angle and harmlessly patted its side, alerting it to the new danger. The fish twisted and tried frantically to escape.

'Hurry! I don't think I can hold it much longer.'

The gaff struck the struggling fish again. This time the lance pierced its side and blood rippled along the black stripes on its silver body as I hoisted it on board.

'A wahoo!' I declared as it thrashed the deck, spraying blood everywhere. The lure disappeared behind teeth as sharp as stilettos and lodged down the fish's throat. 'You wouldn't want to get in the way of those teeth,' I said, cautiously slipping a hand behind a gill and turning the creature onto its side.

Justine clung to the wire trace to ensure her catch did not escape as Esmae knelt over it, aiming the nozzle of an old deodorant bottle filled with gin at its gaping mouth. A jet of alcohol shot between the fish's teeth as she pumped the cap. She pumped twice more, spraying alcohol between its gills, and the fish's violent threshing subdued into a quiver as it succumbed to the ethanol.

'That's much more humane than beating it to death with a stick,' Esmae said, satisfied with her handiwork.

'Less messy too,' Justine observed.

'You know the rule on the boat, the first one goes back to Tangaroa,' I reminded them.

It was a canon to which we had adhered religiously since sailing in New Zealand, where it is believed that sacrificing the first catch to the Maori God of the Sea brings good luck. Usually, the fish is returned to the sea alive.

'Not this time. It's the first decent fish we've caught since Australia,' Esmae reminded us.

'She's right, Dad.'

'We've trawled a line most of the way from Indonesia to India without so much as a nibble. Now we've got a fish that would take pride of place on a wall of any trophy room and you want to give it away. You need your head read. You've got to be joking,' Esmae protested.

I was, but I was not prepared to concede that yet. 'We're losing our values,' I muttered as I opened the fish's mouth to remove the lure before setting about cleaning the deck.

The wahoo would have fetched a pretty price in any of the villages veiled in a sultry heat haze off our starboard. Instead, it provided sushimi and sushi for lunch and steaks for the freezer.

Fish were not the only prey locals stalked that afternoon. Many appeared to consider us a more reliable catch than anything below the water. As soon as we loomed out of the smog, they frantically pulled up their nets and lines and chased us, begging, as usual, for food, clothes, beer and cigarettes. We had expected to encounter beggars on India's streets, but not here, out at sea. Some fishermen disarmed us with dazzling smiles and good humour while others intimidated us with black looks and sneers. All wore rags, the uniform of the wretchedly poor.

Initially, we responded to their pleas by tossing a packet of cigarettes, a can of beer or corned beef or fish their way. Our gestures were not always gratefully received and elicited cries for more. Outstretched hands on overcrowded boats competed for our attention and we quickly realised our meagre offering could never satisfy the demand for food. After throwing tins of food to the first few boats, we waved, smiled and gesticulated to others that approached, indicating we had nothing to offer. During the day, we turned away dozens of boats, their crews departing with frowns of disappointment.

Without a breeze for relief we sweltered in the 32°C temperatures and dripped in humidity of over 70 per cent. Sails flogged and the motor droned as we slowly made our way toward Cochin. It was so calm we set a dinner table in the cockpit and washed down succulent wahoo steaks with a crisp New Zealand sauvignon blanc that Esmae had stumbled upon in a treasure trove at Langkawi a couple of months earlier.

In the dark, avoiding collision with the clutter of small boats

ABOVE *Antares II* under full sail in the Timor Sea.

RIGHT Susan Brown, determined not to allow her blindness to inhibit her from sailing with husband John. The two Australians circumnavigated the world in their yacht *Immanuel*.

LEFT *Antares II* at anchor in Indonesia.

BOTTOM LEFT The architecture of the Tanatoraja symbolizes spaceships in which, according to their mythology, their ancestors travelled to Indonesia's highlands.

RIGHT Buffalo horns denote status in Torajaland – this was obviously the home of a very important family.

BELOW The Tanatoraja place effigies of their ancestors on mountainsides to protect descendants.

LEFT A 'thumbs up' from Michael Dunlop and Esmae after beating a cyclone in the Bay of Bengal, and ...

BOTTOM LEFT 'High fives' by Glenys Coughlan and Tony celebrating surviving the traumas of sailing to Sri Lanka.

RIGHT Picking tea in the Sri Lankan highlands.

BELOW Spice market at ancient Kochi, Cochin, India, where aromas remain as piquant as when King Solomon obtained spices there.

ABOVE Chinese fishing nets – a unique method of fishing introduced to Cochin centuries ago.

BELOW Phang Nga Bay. The best Thailand has to offer is in the water.

ABOVE You never know who
– or what – you will meet
on Thailand's beaches.

LEFT Californians Ralph and
Connie McNeil. Ralph ran
'mechanical clinics' to help
sailors at sea.

RIGHT Justin with yet another fish.

BELOW Justine, Justin and Esmae repairing the mainsail in the Arabian Sea.

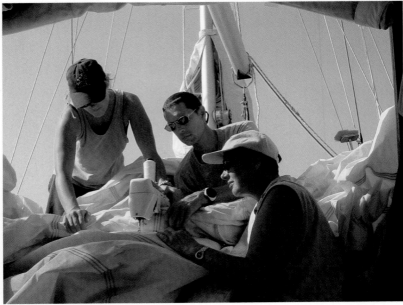

required immense concentration and we doubled up our watches in the belief that four eyes were safer than two. We cautiously wove through hundreds, perhaps even thousands, of little boats, many unlit. Others confused us by displaying nonsensical beacons and navigation lights. Merchant vessels that strayed from shipping lanes to our port had no qualms about holding a steady course as they sped toward Cochin with reckless disregard for the little craft around them.

'I wonder how many of them don't make it back to shore?' Justine pondered.

'I wonder if anyone cares?' Esmae responded.

In the distance, toward shore, lightning lit the murk and etched the shapes of gathering clouds, signalling another hazard with which the fragile fishing boats might have to contend.

The glow of towns on the mainland only occasionally penetrated the fog that taxed our navigation skills as we craned our necks searching for lights our chart said we should detect on the distant shore. As a precaution against collision, Esmae ensconced herself in front of our radar to determine the position and direction of the scores of green blips that lit the screen. Each bright dot represented a vessel of some description. Every half-hour, she marked on a chart the position we received from satellites via our global positioning system (GPS). This marvel of technology accurately places us within a couple of metres of a spot on the ocean. By deciphering its information and calculating it on a chart, it tells us about our progress and our whereabouts, thereby forewarning us of such hazards as rocks, wrecks or shallows. Unlike radar, however, it could not help us avoid the hundreds of fishing boats that surrounded us like a picket fence. To dodge them Justine and I rotated watches in the cockpit and on the bow, straining to make out pinpricks of light and shadows looming out of the darkness.

'We're heading for shore,' I called from the cockpit where I watched the depth sounder trace the seabed rapidly rising as we approached the lights of a large town.

'We can't be,' Esmae responded, 'we're a good 20 kilometres off the coast. I can see an outline of the land on radar.'

'Well, I tell you I can see a town ahead of us. It's lit up like a Christmas tree and the depth has risen several metres in the last few minutes.'

'It can't have, it's not possible. I'll check the chart again.'

'Be quick about it because I don't like this one bit. I think we should head further out to sea.'

'No, not yet, I don't want to get into those shipping lanes.'

Pulses from the depth sounder's sonar bounced from our keel to the seabed and back again and converted into figures on a screen that showed we continued to head into shallow water. The droning of the engine changed pitch abruptly as I pulled the throttle back.

'According to the GPS we're just south of Crocodile Rock. It does go a bit shallow but there's nothing to worry about, we'll have plenty of water under us. We're too far from land for a town to be near. How's it look now?'

The glow in the darkness ahead was brighter than anything we had seen since leaving Sri Lanka. As the boat slowed, I noticed the lights were slowly moving. 'It must be an enormous fishing fleet,' I admitted sheepishly.

I increased the boat's speed again and, as we motored toward the lights, the depth continued to decrease before levelling off to remain at a constant 30 metres. We motored into a glowing curtain of haze through which the flickering lights were transfigured into boats that loomed out of the yellow fog. Their shapes were weirdly distorted in the golden shroud, as if they had tumbled from a cartoonist's fertile mind. Some had high prows, others listed precariously to one side, exposing an acne of barnacles on their hulls as they glided close by; dhows with crooked tree branches for masts lay low in the water ahead, as if awaiting collision, but serenely drifted away only centimetres from our bow. On one occasion, we stood still, as if taking a salute, while a flotilla of 30 boats with tall crooked superstructures passed before us. All identical, they chugged along one after another, only a few metres between them, each resembling *Toot*, the little tugboat in the children's story.

The insipid light of a bleak dawn exposed the boats for what they were – craft with noisy motors and harsh lines and dirty sides and decks piled high with black nets. Some roared up beside us, encroaching closely on our space and then turned quickly away, as if hoping to douse us with spray. We waved, they shouted and we indicated we had nothing for them.

St Peter met us when we arrived at Cochin. His master pointed to where we should anchor and ordered us to wait until customs, police and immigration appeared to approve our entrance into the pearly gates that took the form of splendid waterfront buildings that housed the port authority. Beyond them beckoned the new city of Cochin, a complete contrast to the charming historic town of old Kochi we spied further across the water. Over the coming weeks these cities, full of contradictions, would challenge our values, our courage and our tolerance.

The first test came as we patiently awaited the bureaucrats. Even though we could not leave the yacht to go ashore until formalities were completed, nobody was in a hurry to check us in. We did not mind. *Antares II* swung on anchor opposite the port authority building, a beautiful mixture of colonial and modern architecture whose centrepiece was a benevolent clocktower that could have been transposed from an English village. After the stresses of the passage from Sri Lanka, sitting with a drink and soaking up the atmosphere of such an exotic port was a wonderful reward.

A long boat carrying two men, one rowing while the other sat at its stern, came alongside. An elderly gentleman with hard eyes and tousled, thinning dark hair, wearing a grubby dhoti, proudly introduced himself: 'I am Ali. I am a boat boy.

'I am looking after boats for thirty years,' he explained, his head bobbing and shaking peculiarly, as he spoke. 'I get you anything you want: food, water, fuel – anything. You need boat cleaned, I clean. You go touring, I sleep in cockpit and protect boat from robbers. You need to be very careful here and not leave boat alone.'

Producing a plastic bag, Ali pulled out a dozen tatty letters in which previous visitors extolled his virtues and the services he offered. He sat in the lotus position, proudly erect, as we studied the testimonials. As he spoke, his head continued to wobble from side to side and he toyed with a grey moustache that still contained a few strands of the dark hair of his youth.

'You need to change money?' he enquired expectantly. 'I can do for you while you wait here.'

I gave him some American dollars and his friend rowed him ashore.

Ali's reputation was sound. We had been told in Malaysia to use him when we arrived at Cochin and assured that, like most Muslims we encountered, he was trustworthy. Sure enough, he returned with a bundle of grubby rupees. Surprisingly, he declined payment for his efforts and I suspected he had made a handsome profit on the exchange rate. When I checked later, I discovered he had converted the currency at the market rate. I was puzzled that he had not made a profit from the transaction until I recalled the Koran forbade Muslims from usury.

The names of boats and ferries chugging past intrigued us: each was dedicated to a saint. One called *St Anthony* went by, another named *St John*, a *St Paul* and so on.

We surmised the appellation on the harbourmaster's vessel clearly registered his authority: *St Peter* was the head honcho. Although we hoped Peter and his apostles would display beatific tolerance, kindness and honesty when they checked our papers and approved our stay, we prepared ourselves for corruption.

ST PETER'S MASTER

St Peter's master stood at attention behind a desk that came up to his waist. His bowed head revealed thinning, oily, grey hair. He clasped his hands in the shape of a steeple in front of his chest. Dirt lay black under his fingernails. His lips, quivering beneath a grey moustache, emitted the sounds of prayer: 'Hail Mary, full of grace, the Lord is with thee; blessed is the fruit of thy womb ...'

Wooden slat shutters, which he would close against the searing afternoon sun, had been flung open for ventilation. *Antares II*, framed in a tall arch window, made a curious sight as she rode the tide. A wreath of weed and flowers, washed down the Periyar River that carries debris into the harbour on every ebbing flow, enveloped the yacht so thickly she appeared to be aground in a field of yellow daisies. Away in the distance, the ramshackle buildings of ancient Kochi clung precariously to the banks of a yawning basin around which the harbour has evolved over centuries. The beauty of her waterways and the charm of her antiquated façades capture the imagination. It is little wonder poets have crowned her with accolades – Queen of the Arabian Sea, Venice of India.

St Peter's master appeared oblivious to my presence as I patiently waited for his prayers to end. Eventually, he blessed himself and gently kissed a crucifix attached to black rosary beads.

Still ignoring me, he pulled a handkerchief from his pocket and vigorously polished the top of his already gleaming desk. He paused, admired his handiwork and, with a flourish, noisily pulled out a drawer from which he produced three rubber stamps and a tin containing an inkpad. He delicately placed the instruments of his power in the middle of his bare desk as if they were keys to the Kingdom of Heaven. He fussed over them for a few seconds, ensuring they were correctly positioned.

'Now, tell me, what it is I can do for you?'

'I'm running out of water and I want to take the boat out past the fairway buoy to use my water maker. I need your permission to leave the harbour.'

'I do not understand. What is this water maker?'

'It enables me to turn salt water into fresh water,' I explained.

He gave me a quizzical glance, as if determining whether I had produced a far-fetched story to disguise a sinister motive for leaving the anchorage.

'You turn salt water into fresh water?' he asked incredulously.

'Yes.'

'I have not heard of this. Our Lord Jesus Christ,' he reverently bowed his head, 'turned water into wine, but I have not heard of man turning salt water into fresh water.'

'Well, nor had I until a few years ago. It's one of the miracles of modern technology. My water maker does that. I'm almost out of water and I need to go out of the harbour to make some.'

'Why not make it here?' He pointed to the yacht visible through the window.

'There's too much oil and silt in the harbour. It'll damage the water maker. I need your permission to go out,' I repeated.

He ruminated for a few moments. Deciding the request was too unusual for him to grant, he announced, 'No. No, it is not me you must see. It is the general foreman. He must see you.'

'When can I see him?'

'He comes in at 10.30. He has tea at 11 o'clock. From noon until 3.30, he is at lunch. He goes home at 4.30. So, you will come back and see him at,' he glanced at his wristwatch, 'perhaps, 10.30? Later if you wish.'

His expressionless eyes fixed on mine as his head wobbled in the peculiar side-to-side motion many Indians use in conversation. His motive for disclosing his superior's work hours was unclear. Did he intend to impress upon me the foreman's importance, as reflected by his genteel hours, or to portray him as a lazy bounder who left the real toil to his underling?

'I'll wait outside until he arrives,' I offered, happy to explore the imposing building that housed hundreds of bureaucrats who could, with the thump of a rubber stamp, decide our fate.

'Keep out of the sun,' he advised, 'even now, at a quarter past nine in the morning, it can be very hot and your fair skin will quickly burn.'

The harbour administration building was a quaint, whitewashed, sprawling Victorian warren. The cramped offices contained many more workers than the British colonials, who had designed it, had ever intended. A tattoo of typewriter keys clattered from rooms in which women clad in colourful saris pounded antiquated Remingtons. When the documents were completed, men aspiring to appear important carefully uplifted them, page by page. They swaggered, like despots, along spacious verandahs to seek approval of the texts from their superiors who, befitting their station, occupied larger, less populated chambers. After obtaining a signature, the messengers wandered back to the typists who split the many duplicates and filed them in tattered manila folders that bulged from ceiling-high cupboards running the length of the rooms.

On a previous visit, *St Peter*'s master had proudly extolled the port authority's significance for employment. It held 5000 bureaucrats who worked in conditions similar to those in his building. Computerisation would devastate the workforce by exposing massive inefficiencies and stealing thousands of jobs. Such an upheaval would have destabilising political ramifications in a country with more than its share of poverty and unemployment. It was not surprising technology was kept at bay.

St Peter's master extracted a wire tray from a dusty cabinet that resembled a chicken coop. He sat erect at his desk, shuffling papers in a futile attempt to appear busy. At a desk beside him, the general foreman, a plump, pallid, unhealthy-looking man in a dirty cream open-necked shirt, lounged back in a chair in deep contemplation. He peered, mesmerised, like a psychic searching for secrets, into a plastic paperweight globe perched in the middle of his desk.

'This is a very difficult business,' he announced profoundly. 'You know that to leave the harbour you must get permission of the police and customs before I can permit it?'

'I've already seen them and they say it's okay, if you agree.'

He rubbed his chin as he considered the request.

'It is very difficult,' he emphasised again. 'I cannot give you authority for this. You must get permission from the Conservation Department.'

I was astonished. Outside his window, almost within spitting distance, *Antares II* swung on anchor in possibly the vilest, most putrid water in the world. Aghast, we had watched the Periyar River wash a baby's grotesquely bloated corpse past us the previous morning. On another occasion, a dead horse, its entrails streaming from a gash in its side, nudged the yacht's hull. Bloated goat carcases, encased in stinking effluent and rotting vegetation, had also floated by.

The dolphins that inhabited the anchorage satisfied their ravenous appetites by grazing on a smorgasbord of decomposing rubbish. Watching a dolphin struggling to crush a plastic hairbrush in its beak-shaped mouth was almost as upsetting as discovering the baby's corpse. Other dolphins had grappled with plastic bags and bottles.

A large sign proclaiming 'POLLUTION CONTROL' adorned

St Peter, the port authority's antiquated wooden dory. We despaired each time she chugged past because her crew was oblivious to the horrors contaminating the harbour. To learn there was also a Conservation Department almost beggared belief.

'The Conservation Department,' I mused. 'How do I go about that?'

'You write them a letter. Tell them you have talked with me,' he proposed generously. 'They'll give you permission, but it will take three or four days.'

'Three or four days!' I thundered. 'I need to go out tomorrow. I'm almost out of water. Don't you understand?'

'Yes, Mr Tony, I do understand very well. But that is how long it will take and nothing can change that,' he scolded. 'Why don't you buy some water from the barges that go past your boat? You can always get water from them.'

It would be inappropriate to explain we did not trust the quality of Cochin's drinking water. India is notorious for the debilitating effect its water has on Western visitors. We feared we would court trouble if we filled our tanks from a barge. As it was, we could use our tanks only for washing because rain taken on in the Bay of Bengal still contaminated them. Drinking water was stowed in plastic drums on deck.

'Is there nothing you can do?' I pleaded.

'If you were going out of the harbour for sea trials, that would be a different matter. It would be not be so difficult. But you want to take sea water to change to fresh water. I am sorry, that is definitely a matter for the Conservation Department.'

'Well, I have been working on my engine,' I uttered quickly, grasping at a life buoy he had cast. 'I do need to go out for sea trials. Can you help me with that?'

'You have seen customs and police?'

I nodded.

'No problem then,' he announced with a smile as he produced a paper from a drawer. He wrote on it and passed it to *St Peter*'s master who checked it carefully before pounding it with a stamp. He handed it back to the general foreman who studied it again, as if suspicious that his colleague may have added something that should not be there.

'Your permit to go out of the harbour tomorrow,' he announced triumphantly as he passed it across the desk. He glanced at his wristwatch. 'Time for tea. Would you care to join us?'

Before being assassinated by a terrorist bomb in 1991, Indian Prime Minister Rajiv Gandhi admitted in a television interview that bureaucracy was the main legacy the British had bequeathed his country. He was right. India, probably more than any other jewel in the old British Empire, succeeds at imitating its former rulers in many ways, but none better than the way it runs its government. Thickets of unbending petty regulations cover minions' backs and obstruct progress and independence in decisions.

The port authority building stands like a beacon at the head of Willingdon Island, which the British built in the 1930s from silt dredged to deepen Cochin Harbour. In colonial days, Willingdon Island was a prime address. Glimpses of its former glory are still evident when you stroll along dusty avenues to catch a ferry to the modern city of Cochin. Grand houses and charming bungalows nestle behind high fences in lanes lined with rain trees the British had planted to shade them from the blistering sun. The dwellings are testimony to the deterioration that has taken place since the British left over 50 years ago. Fences hide unkempt grounds and buildings that have fallen into disrepair. Mould, a scourge of the tropics, smears the walls of the once prestigious dwellings, from which paint flakes like dandruff.

As with the ferries on the harbour, the houses confirmed that the island's residents emulated the class consciousness of the British. None were named after saints, but plaques on gates and mailboxes proclaimed the residents' names and status. The more important a resident's professional position, the bigger the house.

Discrimination of another type was evident at the ferry station, where throngs of passengers queued for tickets. Men patiently stood in a long line before a grilled opening polished with the sweat of thousands of hands. At another window, shy tittering women, hiding self-consciously behind colourful shawls, bought their passes. Because fewer females ventured out alone, even in daytime, long queues did not form at their counter. But, heaven help any impatient male with the effrontery to use the women's area: he would recoil from the lash of scorn dispensed by a bureaucrat lurking in shadows behind the grilled window. We used the system to advantage, avoiding queuing by having Justine or Esmae purchase tickets.

Surprisingly, although the ferry held us captive during a 20-minute trip, no one pestered us for money. It was a different situation, however, after we alighted at a terminus on the mainland. Chaos reigned in the large square outside, which teemed with a seething tide of noisy wretches and animals. Women wearing brightly coloured saris balanced snotty-nosed babies on their hips. Dribbling, flabby grey cows hindered progress as they inspected the ground for scraps of food. Children in neat school uniforms that, despite the dust and squalor, remained miraculously clean, excitedly darted around a forest of legs. Others, in ragged clothes, stared at them forlornly. Mangy dogs eyed us with menace as they licked their sores. Hawkers thrust baskets of vegetables, chapattis and cigarettes expectantly before us. 'You buy? You buy?' Bells on bicycles clanged as perspiring men, balancing enormous loads, fought for a passage through the sea of humanity. A crowd gathered before a shack, held together with posters of Indian heart-throbs, from which screeched loud Bollywood music. Nearby, psychics and astrologers offered other dreams, as did gamblers shouting odds on anything the foolishly desperate imagined might fill their pockets. Crows cawed. Scrawny rickshaw men offered their sweat and muscles for exorbitant prices. Sly taxi drivers demanded to know where we were going. Hopeful beggars in grey rags tugged at our clothes and blocked our way by thrusting empty tin mugs under our noses.

Vanquished, they spat on the ground, and yelled and shrieked to those around them that we had offered no alms.

Before arriving in India, we thought our earlier experiences in Asia had made us streetwise and hardened. We knew, for instance, that some women in Thailand rented the babies they cradled on their laps to generate pity while they begged on Bangkok's impersonal streets. George, our tour guide in Sri Lanka, had explained that for many people begging was a necessity for spiritual growth. We had been warned that many of India's beggars were actually not destitute: seeking alms was a profession offering rich rewards.

Whether these assumptions were true was of little consequence. One could not escape the reality of the pain suffered by those milling about the square. The desperation in their sunken eyes mirrored a hopelessness passed down through countless generations. It was etched in the parchment skin wrapped around protruding cheekbones and mouths of rotting teeth. Stripped of dignity, prematurely aged, they wore their poverty on their backs in tattered rags. Some leaned on crooked staffs; others squatted on the ground, holding out trembling, gnarled hands in anticipation that we would share the good fortune bestowed upon us. Some, who could not see us because they had no eyes, muttered loudly and incomprehensibly to arrest our attention as we passed. Others, without limbs to thrust toward us, stared with such intensity that their pleading blocked our way like a physical barrier.

Always, we set out on our excursions with rupees in our pockets, but we never had enough. Laden with guilt, we trudged the city's hot, dusty, unattractive streets, depressed by the magnitude of its poverty. Aware that eye contact with a passer-by could trigger an outstretched hand knotted with pain, we avoided looking at the wretches. We were surprised that, despite the poverty, Cochin's bureaucrats, untainted by the appalling corruption we found in Sri Lanka, carried themselves with pride. Perhaps it reflected the spirituality they had attained.

Esmae has a passion for India. She experiences it through the senses of a cordon bleu chef, the eyes of a photographer and the appreciation of a collector who loves a bargain. She sees beyond squalor and poverty; she glimpses dramatic light, shade and colour. Oblivious to the risk, she roams crowded alleys hunting for spices and oils and the secret ingredients of Indian cooking. She has no shame when haggling for rugs, antiquities and jewellery.

It was with dismay that I waved goodbye at Cochin Airport early one misty morning as she and Justine set out to explore northern India. Between them, they carried only two small backpacks that I knew would never hold all the treasures they would discover during their adventure. With the commitment of the recently converted, Esmae proclaimed she was *backpacking* with her daughter; there would be no need for a larger bag.

We had visited northern India some years before and I had no desire to visit there again. It had been too distressing. The north housed battalions of beggars who were much more demanding than those in the south. There, we *had* encountered corruption, along with bad food that caused ill health and more heat, dust and frustrations than anyone needs while on holiday. My despair was not confined to India's people. Animals suffered too. Bears, so haggard and worn that their coats hung like cloaks on an anorexic, did not even strain on their leashes as they followed their owners along New Delhi's boulevards. Chimpanzees sometimes offered a little more fight, only to be beaten into submission. Elephants, majestic and proud in the wild, meekly responded to whippings as they carried their burdens through the city. They were sights not to be witnessed again.

Antares II swung on her anchor outside the Taj Malabar Hotel, reputedly one of the finest in Cochin. While Esmae and Justine were away, the Taj fussed over me, providing its finest cuisine for less than I could prepare a meal on the yacht. Every evening, in the last shadows of twilight, I rowed across a swift current to alight at a jetty under a pagoda, an entrance to the hotel's lush gardens.

Dusk at the anchorage was entrancing. Stillness spilled over the water, as if the enormous country paused to watch the sun slip away. Dolphins tumbled lazily through an oily mauve sea on which antiquated dhows wallowed; the dhows' primitive lateen sails, stitched from patched sacking and torn plastic wrapping, waited expectantly for a zephyr to rouse the exhausted boatmen from their rest. Across the harbour, the sun burnished old Kochi's ramshackle buildings that leaned precariously toward the bay, like herds of grotesquely misshapen animals poised to drink at a waterhole.

After a final flicker of flame, the sun disappeared. The dolphins vanished, the water rippled gently as the tide shuddered and the port slowly stirred to life. Tired wizened dhow-men dipped bamboo poles and propelled their craft, laden with heavy sacks of rice, through the shallows close to shore. Fishing boats, listing under the weight of their loads as they entered the harbour, were followed by gulls, a reincarnation of beggars ashore, petitioning for a share of the fishermen's good fortune. The boats lumbered past ferrymen who never tired of rowing passengers across the wide, swift-flowing estuary, breaking their backs for the prize of a rupee a ride. Red and green lights to lead ships out to sea glowed like jewels as brightly lit tugboats guided sparkling passenger liners and dowdy freighters into the night.

None of their tables would boast delights as fine as the Taj set before me: spicy Kerala chicken curry, gentle biryani rice that radiated the colour of the sun, tender lamb submerged in rich creamy gosh, sweet Kerala prawn curry – topped off with apple pie and ice cream.

Darkness did not provide relief from the debilitating heat that made even mosquitoes travel at half speed. Alone on *Antares II*, I slept with hatches and portholes wide open. Netting covered them to keep out insects, the only intruders with which I anticipated having to contend.

I was wrong. One night, a noise disturbed my sleep and I cautiously made my way to the pilothouse from where I spotted a shadowy figure moving stealthily across the stern.

'What are you doing?' I demanded.

'Hello!' he responded as he leapt over the side.

'What do you want?' I called.

It was too late. His dugout disappeared in the darkness.

'Pirates!' I cursed, realising the reason for the visit.

Robbers, intent on pillaging anything they could find on deck, had climbed aboard *Antares II*, right beside where I was sleeping. The bump of their dugout nudging the yacht's hull disturbed me as they clambered aboard. A search in the morning revealed they were interrupted before they could pilfer anything of value. Fortunately, a dinghy anchor was the only piece of equipment missing.

When I recounted the incident to the crew of a British ketch anchored beside me, the skipper announced that thieves had also boarded his vessel, climbing through hatches while the crew slept. Moving about like spectres, they had silently taken whatever they fancied. The crew awoke in the morning to discover backpacks, clothes, money and other valuables stolen.

'They took my papa,' a Russian sailor lamented.

The skipper laughed at my quizzical expression.

'It's true. He kept his father's ashes in a brass shell case that he hung around his neck. He'd taken it off for the night and put it on top of a locker beside his bunk. The thieves took it from the cabinet, right next to his head. He didn't hear a thing,' he said. 'You shouldn't drink so much vodka before you go to bed, Boris, then you'd be awake to protect us and you'd still be looking after your old man,' he teased.

'Although it pisses me off, I can't get too annoyed with them. I'd probably do the same myself in their situation,' he continued seriously. 'The poor bastards have got nothing. They're desperate for money and food.'

'Yes, but they took Papa,' the Russian reminded us. 'He no good to them. I want Papa back.'

'They'll find a use for him, I bet. Your old man has probably been mixed with gunpowder by now. That should wake him up.' He laughed. 'They have a use for everything, no matter what it is. If it can be recycled, they'll use it.'

A ferryman who rowed our boatman, Ali, to and fro confirmed the truth of this. Occasionally, when passing *Antares II*, Mustafa would ask whether he could take our garbage ashore. Usually, I declined: it was a demeaning chore I preferred to undertake myself.

One day he forthrightly asked, 'Why you not want me to take rubbish?'

His youthful honest face smiled as I explained.

'I not mind. Next time you call me when I pass by and I take rubbish. It is of no problem. You have watch for me?'

Shocked that he should demand such a gift, I sternly assured him I did not have a wristwatch for him. He looked crestfallen.

Reflecting on the incident after he rowed away, I recalled disposing of a couple of spent, cheap, salt-encrusted wristwatches a few days previously. I wondered how he knew about them. They were buried deep in a plastic rubbish bag dumped ashore at a jetty at which ferrymen picked up passengers. Rusted tins of food, expiry dates long past, were also in the bag. They were old and corroded and could pose a health hazard to anyone eating their contents.

Somebody probably *had* eaten the contents because, on a subsequent visit, I discovered the bag had been slit open and only useless trash lay scattered about the site. Only now did I realise that the ferrymen took a keen interest when I disposed of the garbage. Usually they squatted, or sat cross-legged, their crumpled dhotis tucked between their legs, smoking and playing draughts, using bottle tops for pawns. When unobserved, they must have scavenged for loot they would either keep for themselves or sell on the black market. Everything had a value here, including sump oil drained from the yacht's motor and tins of hardened varnish and paint. They, too, quickly disappeared from the dump.

The desperate plight of the ferrymen filled me with shame. Outwardly happy, they smiled and joked with us whenever we passed. They were proud men to be admired for their strength and determination to work. Unfortunately, as with the beggars, there were so many of them that I had to accept the inevitability of their lot.

Once, in ancient times, the city of Kochi was the trading centre of Asia. Positioned strategically on the Arabian Sea, on the south-western coast of the Indian subcontinent, it lured merchants from the distant lands of Europe, Arabia, Persia and China. They made arduous journeys to Kochi by land and sea to buy spices – cardamom, cinnamon, vanilla, nutmeg, betel nut and pepper.

Strolling through Kochi's maze of narrow alleys is to take an adventure into the past. Shirtless men, so lean their ribs protrude from their skin, push and pull heavily laden handcarts. Brightly coloured trucks block the alleys, which were never intended for anything larger than carts pulled by donkeys or buffalo. Vividly painted with pictures of gods, trees, rivers and mountains, the trucks, like the ferries, are named after saints. Stone buildings designed by former occupiers, Portuguese and Dutch, line the streets. Here, in the diffuse light inside, nostrils twitch and senses quiver under assault by tantalising fragrances of the same perfumes, oils and bales of colourful spices and grains that brought traders from throughout the ancient world.

Further down the town, opposite the end where birds roost on ropes that make the old Chinese fishing contraptions creak and groan, exists another relic of antiquity: Jew Town. Here, it is claimed, King Solomon obtained spices. Jews have lived here since the first century AD. Their synagogue, one of the world's oldest, still stands, although its congregation now numbers only a few dozen. The floor of the synagogue displays another link with antiquity: porcelain tiles brought from China many centuries ago, perhaps by the great Chinese explorer Zheng He.

Legend holds that Jewish trickery secured the tiles for the synagogue. They were intended for the palace of a great rajah, a devout Hindu, who discarded them after hearing that the Chinese made their porcelain from a secret formula involving cow's blood. A Jewish trader, who coveted the decorative tiles for his synagogue, allegedly spread the fallacy.

Kochi has survived the trickery, rivalry and jealousies of the centuries better than most, and her people accept each other's religious beliefs and practices. Jews, for instance, have lived in harmony with others at Kochi since shortly after the birth of Christ, without enduring any of the bloody pogroms encountered elsewhere in the world. The Star of David and artefacts from Roman Catholic and Coptic churches are displayed alongside various Hindu goddesses. A muezzin's guttural call to the faithful competes with drums and chanting from a Hindu temple that, in turn, argues with the strains of hymns from Christian churches. Kochi is an island of tolerance in the troubled Arabian Sea.

While I uncovered treasures in the old city, Esmae and Justine explored the north. Unbelievably, they had been unable to find a travel agency in Cochin to arrange their expedition into the heartland. The closest was evidently at Mumbai (Bombay), more than 1000 kilometres up the coast. When they arrived there, however, locating an agent proved almost as difficult. Early one evening, at the recommendation of the manager of the hotel at which they stayed, they groped along a couple of flights of dimly lit, rickety, wooden stairs in a building that should have been condemned. The steps creaked and sagged underfoot, garbage and rat droppings littered their way and an acrid stench of urine pervaded the air. They were tempted to flee, but driven by curiosity, they persisted and, sitting behind a small table in a filthy cubicle, found a lean little man who claimed to be a travel agent.

It took three days to complete the arrangements, during which they parted with US$2,500 for an adventure that would involve travelling by air, road and rail to some of India's most remote places. As the itinerary evolved, each new demand for extra money to cover costs made Esmae fear they could be victims of a swindle.

While waiting for their itinerary to be arranged, they explored the city's busy marine drive. From a café nearby, they watched a mesmerising sunset. The dry season's dust magnified the orb as it sank beyond the horizon, the tiny particles distorting the sun's colours to provide a display of spectacular beauty. The darkness that followed did not remain empty for long. Sparkling lights and neon bejewelled the shanties and streets, belying the squalor exposed only a short time before by the sun. Exotic and enticing aromas wafted from the transformed buildings and hawkers' carts.

Esmae and Justine were drawn to popular Chowpatty Beach, where hundreds of locals played at the water's edge and promenaded along the foreshore. The illusion did not last for long: plastic, excrement and filthy flotsam littered the shore. As the only Westerners there, they became the evening's big attraction. Throngs of people surrounded them.

'Where you from?' women asked. 'Where's your husband?' They could not believe mother and daughter were so far from home without chaperones. 'How did you get here?'

'I give you good time,' unsavoury men offered, suspecting, because of pornography they see on the Internet and on videos, that all Western women are immoral.

'You want massage? I give you good massage,' said young boys. Groups of girls wanted nothing more than to practise their English.

At the Gateway of India, the city's most prominent landmark, where they stayed for three days waiting for their travel arrangements to be finalised, they watched a young beggar on a skateboard weaving in and out of heavy traffic to solicit motorists. She squatted on the board, cradling a baby in her arms, and used her legs to propel herself through the traffic. Another child, only a toddler, ran beside her. When the vehicles became gridlocked, she selected a target, sped toward it and, hand outstretched, pleadingly stared at the car's occupants. They seldom refused.

Street vendors plagued Justine. Ignoring her protests, they slipped ankle bracelets around her legs and demanded she pay for them. On one occasion, after ridding herself of the pests, she noticed that a sad little girl in a stained floral dress followed her.

'My mudda in hospital with new baby,' the urchin volunteered, her big brown eyes innocent and sad.

'Oh, that's nice,' Justine responded genuinely. 'Is it a boy or a girl?'

The urchin stared blankly, evidently not comprehending the question.

'Do you have a little brother or a little sister?' Justine asked slowly.

The girl ignored the question. 'I show you round Colaba. I know many places.' She skipped merrily beside them, chattering away about her mother and the new baby, apparently excited about the prospect of a sibling in the home. 'We need milk for baby. My mudda not have money for milk. Baby will die.' The girl began to cry.

Pitying her, Justine and Esmae took her to a shop and bought the biggest can of milk powder. Without any expression of gratitude, the girl ran off, clutching the heavy parcel under an arm. They felt good until an Indian told them later the girl would have gone to another shop and sold the milk powder; they were probably victims of a child confidence trickster.

By the time they reached Jaipur, Rajasthan, in northern India, Esmae had already found it difficult to fit everything into her backpack. She and Justine decided that, because clothes cost only a pittance, they would save space by discarding their dirty laundry and replacing it with cheap garments bought in bazaars.

A distraught middle-aged woman rushed up to them as they returned to their hotel after sightseeing.

'Memsahib, you must help me,' she pleaded, before they could enter their lodgings, 'I am in very much trouble.'

Neither Esmae nor Justine could understand her heavily accented English. They suggested she should stop crying and take her time.

'Boss, he says he dismiss me because I steal from you,' she said tearfully.

They feared the worst, wondering what was missing from their room.

'What did you take?' Justine demanded.

'I didn't mean to steal from you,' she wept, kneeling before them at the entrance of the hotel.

'Get up and tell us about it,' Esmae coaxed, embarrassed. A porter dressed in a warrior's uniform approached but Esmae shooed him away, assuring him the woman was causing no trouble.

'I clean your room. I have worked at hotel for two years and never have problem. Today I clean your room after you out and I find old clothes in waste bin. I think you not want them, so I take them for myself.

'When I leave hotel to go home, they search my bags and find your clothes inside. Boss, he call me a thief and says he will call police and they send me to jail for robbing tourist and getting hotel bad name. I try to tell him you don't want clothes, but he not listen to me. I tell him lie. I tell him you give me clothes,' she sobbed. 'I am sorry, I should not told lies and stolen from you. I'm sorry.' She wailed loudly in despair.

'Don't worry, you can have the clothes, we didn't want them. I'll tell your boss I gave them to you,' Justine promised.

'Oh, thank you madam, thank you very very much.'

The woman was reinstated after the misunderstanding was rectified.

After touring the northern region of India in an old chauffeur-driven car, Esmae and Justine visited the Taj Mahal. From there they went to New Delhi where they caught a train for a three-day journey through central India and back to Cochin.

Aboard *Antares II*, I was having problems of my own. A plastic bag was blocking the generator's raw water strainer. Without sea water pumping through the generator, there was no power for the refrigerator, freezer and other essentials. I asked Ali the boatman to arrange for someone to dive under the yacht to remove the obstruction.

Some hours later, Ali arrived at the yacht with a middle-aged man and a teenage boy. After listening expressionlessly to my tale of woe, the man proudly told me, 'I am diver. This is my son. He too is diver. We will get aqualung and look under your boat to find problem.'

'It's not a big deal, it's only a piece of plastic in an inlet hole. I can show you where it is and it will take only 30 seconds to get out. All he will need is a snorkel and mask,' I suggested, 'he doesn't need full scuba gear.'

'Oh no, sir, it is not that simple. There could be many things wrong. I am navy diver and I have dived under many ships in Cochin. Whenever there is a problem underwater they ask me to fix it because I am so experienced. This may, as you say, be small problem, but it may also be very big problem.'

I asked how much it would cost.

'At the very least, sir, 200 American dollars,' he announced without flinching.

'I beg your pardon?' I ventured hoarsely. The price was preposterous and more than many Indians earned in a year.

'I will have to supply the wetsuit and other gear and bring a compressor out for filling the tank,' he explained.

'Get off my boat! You are a robber and I won't have robbers on my boat. Ali, take him away, I don't want to set eyes on him ever again. He is a thief!'

The man protested that his work was of the highest quality and he could reduce his price if I wished to reconsider.

'Get off! Get off before I throw you off!' I shouted.

After they departed, I used a snorkel to free the plastic myself. The water was so brackish that visibility was reduced to only a few centimetres and I groped about until I felt the plastic and pulled it out of the hole. Although I was back on board *Antares II* within a minute of entering the water, my skin burned as if I had been swimming in an acid bath.

The streets of Cochin were quiet at 3 a.m. when I took a taxi to the station to meet the train bringing my crew from New Delhi. It was already nine hours late. Outside the station entrance, hooded trishaws stood in a neat line, awaiting the onslaught of impatient office workers who, in a couple of hours, would stride from trains. Their weary drivers slept at obtuse angles on the trishaw seats, their long sinewy legs sprawled out on handlebars.

The scene inside the station was bizarre: the concourse resembled a mausoleum in which lay dozens of mummies. Scores of homeless, swathed in cocoons of dirty rags, huddled together as they slept on the cold marble floor. The only activity occurred in a distant corner where a couple of men boiled water on a brazier for tea they might drink or sell to others. Coughs, snores, grunts and wheezing echoed in the cavernous room.

A sleepy official, resting behind a cubbyhole through which he sold tickets, informed me that the train was still three hours away. He directed me to the platform at which it should eventually arrive.

The wretches occupying the station stirred as vapid light crept through the rafters. Beggars searched between railway sleepers for scraps of food for breakfast: a discarded chapatti, half a rotten orange. Boys selling newspapers shouted headlines. Men lugging stainless steel urns yelled 'Chi! Chi!' as they sold tepid tea mixed with herbs. Waves of humanity swept onto the platforms and noisily boarded and left dirty crowded carriages with grime-encrusted windows through which I occasionally glimpsed morose men and women balanced on wooden planks.

When the New Delhi train finally slid into the station Esmae rushed toward me. 'You've got no money. Tell them you've got no money,' were her first words.

A plump man, stomach tumbling over his belt, puffed behind her as he struggled with two heavy suitcases. Esmae introduced him as the senior guard who had looked after them admirably during their journey. He smiled and shook my hand enthusiastically.

'There is a little problem,' he whispered slyly. 'Madam must pay an extra 20,000 rupees for her ticket because the price of the fare went up since she bought her ticket in Mumbai. Unfortunately,' he gave me a knowing glance, 'she has spent all her money and does not have the extra available.'

The guard shouted at two porters who struggled with more baggage and dumped them at our feet. Justine, also laden with bags, arrived behind them. Esmae stood behind the guard shaking her head, indicating I should not pay the disputed amount.

'How can you charge more than the tickets were bought for?' I enquired.

'It was a mistake, sir. The man who sold the tickets could not have been aware that fares were about to go up.'

'I don't see why my wife should pay more than the original price.'

'Oh, but she must, sir, because she has enjoyed our fine service all the way from New Delhi at much less than she should have paid. Now, if you could just give me the extra 20,000 rupees, all will be well.'

'I don't have that much with me. Because there are thieves and pickpockets all over the place, I never travel with more than a few rupees on me. Perhaps we should go and see the stationmaster and fix up the problem with him. I can bring the money to him later.'

'Oh no, sir, that will not do,' he protested urgently. 'He is only a regional worker and will not know anything about the new ticket prices. He will be of no help whatsoever.'

The argument continued until a whistle blew and the train inched forward. The guard, hurling insults at us, leapt onto the steps of a carriage before it was too late.

CHAPTER 8

A HAVEN FOR TERRORISTS

A wall of white water crashed over the bow as *Antares II* slid down a wave in the middle of the Indian Ocean. It lifted Justine off the bowsprit and flung her high into the air. Angrily, it wrapped itself around her and fought to rip her from the grip of a lifeline that tethered her to the deck. She disappeared from view.

'God,' I beseeched from the safety of the cockpit as I fought to control the wheel, 'let her be all right.'

Devouring Justine did not satisfy the wave. It pummelled Esmae, who grimly wrestled with a genoa, our largest headsail, which tore from her grip as it inflated like a balloon when slivers of a 50-knot gale sneaked under it. The wave rushed over the decks, crashing into the windows of the pilothouse. As it disintegrated in ripples on the glass Justine reappeared, drenched and clinging desperately to the bowsprit.

Esmae glared in the direction of the pilothouse, damning me for having them out there on deck, for again jeopardising their lives in the treacherous Indian Ocean, for ever having taken them sailing in the first place. It added to my moroseness. *I* should have been the one out on deck wrestling with the sail that lashed like a whip each time the wind flicked it. But I could not. Fever racked me. I was so weak I could barely handle the helm.

Earlier, as the storm intensified, Justine had furled the headsail to reduce the amount of canvas but the cable winding it in had jammed and, only partially furled, the huge genoa now flogged dangerously. There was no alternative but to unwind it and wrestle it to the deck, a hazardous task in violent conditions. The wind grew stronger as they fought to free it and the sea churned with waves over 8 metres high.

Dropping the genoa in calm conditions was difficult enough; there was always a risk of it spilling over the side and under the boat. In a storm, with crew struggling for balance as the yacht rode waves like a roller-coaster and the wind wrenched the cloth from their hands, it could be disastrous. If the sail fell into the ocean and filled with water, they would have to cut it free and hope it would drift away. At worst, it could immobilise *Antares II* by wrapping around the rudder and tangling in the propeller.

Desperate to control the flogging sail, they repeatedly fought to lower it down the stay to which it was attached at the bow. Each time, the gale stole it from them until, at the bottom of a trough where the wind was not so strong, it collapsed half in the boat and half over the side. They scrambled to haul it in and, panting for breath, threw themselves on top of it while they regained their strength and considered how to protect it from the storm.

They shouted instructions but the wind devoured their words. 'I can't hear you,' I called. 'What do you want?'

It was no good. They could not hear me either.

Esmae pointed to the forward hatch that opened into a companionway entering the front cabin. They indicated impatiently that I should open it for them to shove the sail inside.

The autopilot, the computer that automatically steers the boat, had groaned and protested as it struggled to hold a course in the mountainous seas. We had disengaged it and steered by hand to keep *Antares II* running with the waves before their white crests broke over us. If the autopilot failed and we skewered broadside to the sea, we risked rolling over as we scudded down the swells.

Reset, the autopilot promised to behave as the boat lifted high on a rising swell and sped down the other side. As I moved below, I trembled from the cold caused by my fever and dripped, not from the water outside, but from perspiration generated by a temperature that was over 40°C.

The hatch felt much heavier than usual as I struggled to prise it open. Justine pulled it free just as another wave crashed over them. Water cascaded inside, dousing everything, including bedding on a bunk in the forward cabin. Kneeling to protect themselves against the force of the sea and the yacht's violent, unpredictable motion, they struggled to squeeze 20 square metres of soggy, heavy cloth through the narrow hatch. They pushed it into the opening while I pulled it inside as the boat, without a headsail to propel it forward, bucked and rolled aimlessly like a crippled bird that had lost a wing. Finally, with all the genoa inside, I firmly sealed the hatch cover to protect against intrusion by the sea. Water that had entered with the sail made the floors as slippery and dangerous as a skating rink.

We were six days out from the Maldives where, after leaving Cochin, we had dived and snorkelled. Although disappointingly bleached by El Niño's warm waters, the reefs teemed with spectacular fish. We had anchored in sparkling clear water at numerous atolls that protruded only a few metres above the sea. After evolving over thousands of years, conveniently forming a habitat suitable for humans, the islands may be only an epochal second away from oblivion. Doomsayers predict their disappearance over the next 20 years as they vanish under rising seas caused by global warming.

The Maldives was a distinct contrast to Cochin. Not only was it clean, and its waters clear, but hospitable officials welcomed us with a minimum of formalities. It is a devoutly Muslim country. The government, while encouraging tourism on which the economy depends for foreign currency, determinedly safeguards the faithful from the corrupting practices of infidels from the West. To secure a permit to cruise among the country's 1000 islands, we had to agree not to visit villages or entertain locals aboard our yacht. We had to observe a nightly curfew and any gifts for villagers had to be approved by customs. Officials warned that a strict dress code prohibited women from wearing scanty clothing or bathing topless. Breaching the regulations would incur a US$5,000 fine.

With a breeze and currents at our back, we enjoyed some of our best sailing as we headed to the capital, Male. Each afternoon, with the sun high enough to illuminate a passage through the reefs, we cautiously made our way between rocky caverns, avoiding tall heads of sharp coral that could ram a hole in our side if we scraped against them. At the end of each exhilarating sail, we dropped anchor off exotic atolls ringed with necklaces of white sand and coconut palms.

Usually, we had to settle for anchoring on rock 30 metres below us. Often, it took several attempts before the pick would snag an outcrop strong enough to hold our 29 tonnes secure against a stealthy wind that might creep into the lagoon in darkness and attempt to blow us onto the nearby reef. In the morning, it took patience and luck to free the anchor.

As a precaution against the difficulties of anchoring off coral reefs, before leaving Thailand we installed a new Maxwell windlass for lifting our 30-kilogram anchor. Unfortunately, it failed to perform the task for which it was designed and a couple of times we had to haul the anchor, and more than 50 metres of heavy chain, by hand.

Distinctive buildings dominated each atoll. Beyond the beaches there stood either a hotel, if it was a resort island, or a mosque, if it housed a fishing village. Male's whitewashed buildings, in a labyrinth of cobbled lanes, glowed gold, pink and mauve in a setting sun. The dwellings, constructed from coral, were held together with mortar mixed with white sand from surrounding islands.

With appropriate Muslim modesty, fully clothed women and girls splashed about in the sea, mindful that they were forbidden to tempt men by exposing their flesh. Males, on the other hand, played half-naked nearby. Five times a day activity in the bustling town slowed as muezzins' voices blared from loudspeakers, calling the faithful to prayer. Shops shut their doors, banks closed their counters and even at the fish market negotiations stopped until prayers were completed.

At one outlying island we ignored the ban on mixing with locals when we met a group of teenage boys who took us snorkelling in crystal waters off their reef. We swam with angelfish, butterfly fish, triggerfish, parrotfish, turtles, manta rays and sharks. In the evening, they took us fishing for red snapper. The angling was not much good, but their entertainment more than compensated. In the moonlight, to a beat on a drum carved from coconut wood and covered with the hide of a manta ray, they serenaded us with folk songs and nursery rhymes.

The next day, they borrowed a village dhoni (dory) and chugged into an emerald lagoon. The warmth of their genuine friendship and humility touched us. From a mound of sand they made a dining table near the water's edge and decorated it with leaves and debris scavenged from the white sand. On broad banana leaves, they served succulent fish grilled over a fire they had prepared from driftwood. We ate by ripping the thick flesh apart with our hands. Because of their hospitality, we lingered at the island longer than we had intended. We were sorry to leave our young friends whose companionship had made their island the highlight of our Maldives odyssey.

The tranquillity of the atolls was a distant memory now as we headed back to our base at Rebak. On the southern edges of the Bay of Bengal, the weather again behaved obscenely out of character. The storm had held us captive for four days and it showed no signs of abating. The south-west monsoon should have settled in and provided a comfortable ride back to the other side of the Indian Ocean. Instead, the wind raged in confusion, blowing from behind for short periods but then swinging to the front of us, forcing *Antares II* to sail uncomfortably on her side so that we moved about the boat clumsily, scuttling along like crabs out of water.

Ill health compounded our discomfort. Since leaving India, we had all suffered fevers and kidney and chest infections. A German physician on a catamaran 1000 kilometres away talked to us each morning on our high-frequency radio. He diagnosed our symptoms and prescribed the medicines we should take for relief.

Yachting folk are, by nature, a self-reliant bunch. Alone on vast empty seas several days from civilisation, they have to fend for themselves. In such circumstances, contact with another human being provides considerable comfort. An authoritative, reassuring voice on a radio, even if it is coming from the other side of an ocean, can make a crew's spirits soar. The good doctor had such a voice. A dozen patients travelled the airwaves daily to reach his surgery for free consultations. Listening to their complaints was almost a tonic in itself, making us realise we could be much worse off. He dispensed advice for dealing with ailments ranging from haemorrhaging to common colds to infections caused by grazing skin on coral. No matter how bad we felt, we left the consultation with hope that our ailments would soon pass.

Our friend Ralph McNeil aboard *Arjumand* ran a clinic of a different kind. A retired aircraft engineer, Ralph explained how to repair myriad mechanical failures that could cripple a boat and jeopardise a crew's well-being out on these lonely waters. With patience similar to the doctor's, he elicited information about faults in water pumps, gearboxes, engines and a host of other equipment. With the precision of a surgeon, he talked less knowledgeable sailors through the process of stripping and rebuilding their gear. At times, the wisdom dispensed by both clinics could make the difference between life and death.

Ralph and his wife Connie had left the Maldives five days ahead of us. They reported enduring only occasional squalls, certainly nothing like the atrocious conditions we encountered.

While I lay on my bunk shivering and too ill to contribute

further to battling the storm, Esmae steered the boat by hand to avoid being toppled by the violent seas that buffeted us day after day. Engulfed by a swell, *Antares II* would sit heavily and wallow uncertainly, baffled as to which way she should travel on the confused currents and fluctuating wind. She would sink into the swell until, attacked by a seething comber that lifted her like a surfboard, she would flee before the wave's foaming crest. Esmae would feel her motion through the helm and instinctively guide her down into the trough below. Each wave's character was different and demanded its own unique response. Hour after hour Esmae steered the boat into the night until she could no longer stand and Justine would take over, trying to outrun the surf in total darkness. Their ordeal lasted for six harrowing days. Each time I approached the wheel I was ordered below with instructions that I should get well quickly because they would need my knowledge and strength should anything go wrong.

As we neared Sumatra, we faced another peril. Sumatra's headland was a beacon at a major shipping junction. From here, scores of freighters and tankers entered and departed the Malacca Straits, the narrow ribbon of water between Indonesia and Malaysia that is one of the world's busiest shipping lanes. With vessels impatient to reach their destination, cluttered shipping lanes can be extremely hazardous for a small yacht, particularly when stormy weather reduces visibility. Already we had spied rapidly moving ships looming, too close for comfort, out of a gloomy horizon.

Conditions were not good aboard *Antares II*. Exhaustion was not our only problem: we had several pieces of broken gear. Pounding seas had ripped a red navigation light off our bow, which meant that in darkness approaching ships would be unable to determine our direction. The furling mechanism for the headsail remained jammed. A couple of days before, the gale had shredded the mainsail. Using a small mizzen and a staysail, we made inconstant speed. When catching the gale on the crest of waves, we sailed well until we lost the wind and wallowed uncomfortably in troughs deep at the bottom of each swell. We were steering by hand because the autopilot could not manage the storm conditions. Another problem threatened to cause considerable discomfort: the genoa we had forced down the hatch blocked access to a locker where our supply of toilet paper was stored. We were running low.

'We should stop over at the island of We, there's supposed to be a good anchorage there,' Justine suggested. 'We can rest and repair the sails.'

'I don't know. It's part of Aceh, which is in the middle of a civil war. Aceh is said to be the birthplace of Muslim fundamentalism. Not many boats go there because it's a hotbed of terrorists fighting for Aceh's independence from the rest of the country. Hundreds have been murdered in recent years,' I explained.

'We need the rest,' said Esmae. 'A couple of boats stopped there on the way across and seemed to get on okay. Why don't we stick our nose into the harbour and have a look?'

We had fond memories of sailing through Indonesia four years before. People at most of the islands at which we had anchored had been friendly and hospitable. Since then, Indonesia's mood had changed dramatically. The government's strongman, President Suharto, had been forced to step down in disgrace after ruling the country for more than 30 years. Rebellion, bloodshed and economic catastrophe had accompanied his abdication.

Conflict in Aceh had intensified as freedom fighters stepped up activity to attain their goal of secession from Indonesia. Dozens had died as armed gangs of both soldiers and terrorists had murdered, kidnapped, raped, pillaged and plundered. We had not heard of Westerners being attacked, but the guerrillas had kidnapped wealthy Indonesians and civil servants and released them only after receiving ransoms.

We had been at sea for 10 days, most of them in storm conditions. We were exhausted, ill and struggling with broken gear. From the rolling sea off the island, the distant landscape seemed to offer peace and tranquillity. As we motored into Sebang, We's deep-water port, it was difficult to imagine violence lurking in its picturesque wooded hills and gentle bays.

We anchored off a jetty in a harbour that housed clusters of dilapidated shacks. Nearby, a couple of dozen people with parcels wrapped in sarongs queued to board an old wooden ferry that appeared barely seaworthy. A sleek modern fishing boat and an intimidating grey navy frigate lay against a sea wall at the harbour's side. After a while, a bunch of untidy, unshaven men came alongside *Antares II*. Some, in blue and brown uniforms, were armed.

'Hello, Mister. What's your name?' The slightly built young man with long hair and wearing jeans explained he was Aziz, a ship's agent. Upon learning we did not have a cruising permit, he said international convention would be followed and we would be granted only a short period to carry out repairs. He would influence the authorities to allow us to stay as long as possible. 'Perhaps, if you have some beer and cigarettes, it would help.'

We grudgingly turned over beers and packets of cigarettes for the party of police, customs, immigration and military officials crowded into the cockpit.

'How many days you stay?' asked an elderly man in a brown uniform unbuttoned to the middle of his chest.

'One week. I'd like to stay a week.'

'That is a problem,' he laughed. 'You need permit for one week, but you don't have. You stay only 24 hours.'

'We need longer than that to fix the boat.'

'You have more cigarettes and beers?' Aziz suggested that such gifts could buy more time.

'I didn't think Muslims drank alcohol,' Justine reprimanded.

'There are three kinds of Muslims: good Muslims, bad Muslims and ugly Muslims. You know which ones you got?'

Over smiling nondescript faces, a dozen eyes and ears strained to learn the answer. Uncertain how many understood English, we declined to play the game.

'You not so lucky. You have bad ones and ugly ones.' Aziz

chortled at his joke.

Raucous laughter erupted among the others after a man, whom we suspected to be a police officer, repeated Aziz's comments in their native tongue.

After we handed out more beers and cigarettes, they agreed to extend our visit to 72 hours, the maximum they could allow. Reluctantly, we acceded to a request to surrender our passports, which they assured us would be returned at the end of our stay.

Aziz remained on board as the others, weaving merrily from the effects of the alcohol, climbed into their dhoni and headed for shore. We probed our visitor about the political situation on the island.

'Here is not so bad. But in Banda Aceh, since Suharto went,' he noisily cleared his throat and spat over the side of the boat, 'there is more lawlessness than ever. Look at this,' he said, sweeping the harbour with his eyes. 'We could have a great marina here for you and your friends, to bring tourists for diving and fishing and swimming. It could be a great port because it is a gateway to the world. Once, there was a casino here and visitors came from far away. Now there is nothing. No one cares about us. Suharto took our oil and gas. He robbed us of our wealth and never gave anything back. He and his friends got rich while we stay poor.'

He cleared his throat and spat over the side again.

'Maybe things will improve with the election,' Aziz said, referring to a pending plebiscite, the first since Suharto had stepped down. 'But I don't think so. Here in Aceh we've been struggling for independence for over 200 years. They won't give it to us now, Jakarta needs our minerals.'

Aziz's candour surprised us. Perhaps the alcohol had undermined the reserve that typified his people. However, he was right to be sceptical. Before falling victim to European powers' lust for worldwide dominance, Aceh had been an independent kingdom whose influence reached across the Malacca Straits. Arab traders had brought Islam to Aceh more than 1300 years ago. From here, over the centuries, its teachings spread through neighbouring Malaysia and the 13,000 islands that comprise modern Indonesia, the world's largest Muslim country.

Aceh's geographic position had made the kingdom vital to the ambitions of a succession of European powers – Portuguese, Spanish, Dutch and British – who, from the 16th century, fought to possess her. The Japanese had also occupied Aceh during the Second World War.

The Dutch reneged on a promise of independence in 1871 and their deceit cost them dearly. The Acehnese engaged them for more than 60 years in the longest war ever fought by the Dutch, who lost 10,000 troops in the process. After the Dutch left and Indonesia became a republic, Acehnese considered they were still under occupation when a government based in Java included Aceh in its policy of unifying the 360 tribal groups living in the Indonesian archipelago.

'The struggle has been long and hard,' Aziz said whimsically. 'Many mothers have lost sons. Many have disappeared and never been seen again. No one knows whether they are dead or alive. Habbie (Suharto's successor) is letting East Timor choose whether they want to stay with Indonesia or be independent. Why won't he let Aceh? I'll tell you why, it's because of our minerals.'

Aziz took us to a dilapidated Chinese restaurant for dinner. Over our meal, a nervous waitress attributed her command of English to education she received in Australia. She whispered that her studies had ended abruptly after Indonesia's economy collapsed the previous year in a monetary crisis that gripped South East Asia.

'Ah, it not good here. It very dangerous. I scared to go out in dark. Ah, you know, they attack Chinese, burn our shops. Rape us. I very afraid what will happen. At moment it quiet here, but tomorrow?' She shrugged dejectedly. 'I want go back to Australia. It very good there.'

The waitress fled when a man with the appearance of a middle-aged rock star seated his friends at an adjacent table before imposing himself upon us. He apologised for being unable to contain his curiosity about us, the only family of Westerners on the island.

He glowed in a lemon shirt and bright blue jacket with high lapels, cut in a style worn by teddy boys in the 1950s. His face was polished and his hair slicked by oil. We expected him to produce a guitar and belt out 'Rock Around the Clock'. Instead, to our surprise, he distributed cheap key rings bearing the inscription 'Golkar', the political party previously controlled by President Suharto, and introduced himself as its candidate for the area.

The aspiring parliamentarian shared his propaganda with us. No, there had been no corruption or cronyism under Suharto. Yes, it was all lies spread by Golkar's political enemies. Of course Suharto had not ruined the economy while filling his own coffers. No, Suharto had not practiced nepotism. Yes, Golkar would win the election, despite the slanders spread by its enemies. Yes, Golkar was the only party that could hold democracy together in the thousands of islands spread over almost 5000 kilometres of ocean that was home to over 300 ethnic groups who spoke 250 languages. Hadn't Golkar succeeded in doing just that during the 33 years of Suharto's reign? There was no question that after the election they would do it for another 30 years, and beyond. Look what had happened within the country since Suharto had stepped down: wasn't that proof enough that only Golkar had the wisdom and support to keep the country peaceful and viable?

Curiously, the Golkar candidate directed his comments at us, completely ignoring Aziz, the only person at our table eligible to vote for him. He did not even present him with a key ring. Aziz was probably relieved because Aceh Merdeka, the freedom movement, persecuted the party's members.

We wondered whether Aziz was more than a simple shipping agent. Sebang was a tiny town. Stores and restaurants with wide verandahs, relics of the 1920s, bordered the town's unpaved main street. The town was so small that everyone would have known each another, but no one greeted Aziz when he followed us in and out of stores and around the island.

He would not allow us to move around We without trailing along. He even insisted on accompanying us when we hired motorcycles to tour the island and experience some of the best snorkelling outside the Maldives. He was most perplexed when he learned we intended visiting a carnival and political rally being held on the second evening of our stay. He shadowed our every movement. Perhaps, we thought, he was reporting our activities to officials who feared we might be spying on the island; or could it be that our safety was in jeopardy and Aziz was there to guard against an incident that would result in embarrassing publicity because we were foreigners? We never discovered his motives but we enjoyed his company and never felt threatened.

The quality produce at a market in town delighted us. We stocked up on fresh eggs, green vegetables, tomatoes and a chicken, killed and plucked while we waited. It was the best produce we had seen since we left Thailand five months before.

As I waited in shade near the water's edge for Esmae and Justine to return from markets a few hours before sailing, a stooped old man motioned he wanted to sit beside me. After I introduced myself, he enquired about our home port, where we had sailed and our destination after we departed Sebang. I complimented him on his English.

'I rearn at sea. I was on boats eight years,' he revealed proudly with a broad smile that exposed toothless gums. 'Not little boats like here, but big freighters. I bin to Amerikee, Engrand, Afwica. I bin everywhere.'

'You were on an Indonesian ship?'

'No. I on Libya ship.'

'You were a soldier?' I wondered whether he had been a guerrilla in Libya. A company of about 100 men had been trained there some years before and returned to blow up police stations and military bases, escalating the conflict that had, until then, lost much of its impetus.

'Not Indonesian soldier,' he admitted slyly, as if pondering whether I could be trusted. 'I am Aceh, not Javanese.'

He left the statement hanging, as if I should draw my own conclusions from his proud admission.

'You are Muslim?'

'Of course.'

'You have been to Mecca?'

'No. Maybe I still do haj before I die. Haj cost much money. Maybe you take me in your boat?' He laughed wheezily. Like most Muslims, Indonesians save throughout their lives to fulfil the dream of making the pilgrimage to Mecca.

He lit a cigarette with trembling hands. The joints on his fingers were knotted with arthritis. I felt self-conscious when he noticed I stared at his distorted hands.

'I tell you somethin' but you not tell anyone, ah,' he said, clearing his throat. 'Suharto's soldiers are bandits.

'Look,' he thrust out a shaking hand, 'they pull off fingernails with pliers because they think me member of ASNLF (Aceh-Sumatra National Liberation Front). Me, I admit nothing. Then they take pliers and pull my nose.' He pointed to scars on his left nostril. 'Me, I admit nothing,' he repeated proudly.

'You must be very brave.'

'Me? Brave?' Again came the wheezy laugh. 'No. I terrified they shoot me like my friends. They disappear, never come back. Soldiers torture and kill them.'

Unexpectedly, he terminated the conversation and sauntered off when he saw Aziz and the women approaching.

We sailed from Sebang pondering the insanity that bred hatred so intense that it contaminated even a tropical island as tranquil as We. An island where an old man should be able to dream in peace, without fear in his heart, about making the haj before he dies. An island whose people were unique in the Indonesian archipelago and who surely had a right to once again determine their future.

CHAPTER 9

SEX, POLITICS AND
SUPERSTITION

Hank teetered on A jetty, clutching a can of beer. His rheumy eyes gazed beyond *Antares II* into jungle on the opposite side of the marina. Although it was not yet 10 o'clock in the morning, the temperature had already reached 28°C. We had been talking for five minutes but I did not invite him onto the yacht and into the shade because he was drunk.

'You want companionship?' he asked.

'What do you mean?'

'Well, Esmae is away. You've been on your own for a while. You should have someone looking after you.'

'No thanks. I'm capable of looking after myself.'

Hank was one of an increasing number of yachtsmen arriving at Rebak with Asian wives and mistresses. We suspected many had pasts that kept them from returning to their own countries. It was incongruous, for instance, that an aristocratic Englishman whose conversation and demeanour revealed he was well educated and well read preferred the dirt, heat and Western cultural sterility of Phuket to the abundance of England. He blotted out reality with marijuana, booze and other drugs. We suspected another

135

Englishman to be a paedophile fleeing British justice. A couple of former policemen may also have had something to hide; others were simply hiding from themselves. Hank was an incorrigible drunk who had made a geographic change in the hope that his life would improve. It did not.

Thailand had recently tightened regulations governing expatriates and, to avoid being expelled from the country, many made monthly trips to Malaysia to have their passports stamped with new visas before returning to Phuket. Crossing Malaysia's borders enabled expatriates to stay in Thailand another month.

Because of its close proximity, most of these transients headed to Langkawi, which provided duty-free shopping, friendly bureaucrats and good marina facilities. When they discovered Malaysia's liberal immigration laws, which allowed boats to stay indefinitely and their crews for up to six months, several elected not to return across the border and rented berths at Rebak Marina.

'It's not good for a man to be on his own. If you change your mind, let me know. Fa has a beautiful friend who would be very happy to provide companionship until Esmae comes back. You should seriously think about it. She's a good woman. A man shouldn't be on his own. '

'You're all heart, Hank. I can't see Esmae thinking it's a good idea.'

'Yeah. Well, the offer is there.'

Hank probably had an ulterior motive. Like many of the Asian women on boats at Langkawi, Fa toiled night and day to please him. As well as looking after their two young children, she cleaned, cooked and did most of the general maintenance aboard Hank's yacht. He had only to click his fingers and she would stop whatever she was doing and get him a beer.

Hank did very little, but Fa was happy to satisfy his every need because life with him was better than the poverty and hardship she had endured in Thailand. However, despite her determination to please him, she complained that she was only human and could not cope with her workload. If she had a friend nearby with little to do, she would probably arrange for her to help lessen her burden.

We had been fortunate to enjoy several years at Rebak without many other yachts there. Now, the marina was almost full with nearly 200 foreign boats tied in its jetties and hauled out of the water onto a recently built hardstand. Although cruising yachtsmen were a friendly bunch, the increased population made the place much more impersonal and prone to petty conflicts.

A division existed between the cruisers waiting out the monsoon before heading on, and yachtsmen living there with Asian women. The latter considered themselves permanent residents and were intolerant of the visitors, many of whom they regarded as cultural ignoramuses. They worried that the transients would undermine their lifestyles by upsetting both their partners and marina authorities.

There was certainly a clash of cultures. Some cruising wives despised Western men living with attractive Asians. At smorgasbords at the resort restaurant, Western women gossiped about the petite Thais who waited on their partners, queuing to select their food and delivering it to them before getting their own. The women's subservient status annoyed Justine. She endured an expatriate's wrath after suggesting to an Asian girl with whom we dined that her partner was capable of getting his own food. Aboard their boats, the Asian women prepared meals for their partner's friends but, maintaining traditions from their villages, would not dine themselves or feed their children until the men had finished eating. To Western women, this practice emphasised their subservience.

Some Western women, however, could not suppress a certain jealousy as well, because, despite their toil, sexy young Asian women were generally exquisitely groomed. Most had hourglass figures and long black hair that shone as brightly as their smiles. Conversation was difficult. Most spoke only Pidgin English and few of the transients mastered Thai, so there was little intelligent dialogue between the groups. Even the girls' partners admitted missing stimulating conversation, a void they longed to fill. Opinions about the mixed relationships plummeted even further when a middle-aged former bar girl from Phuket plied her trade around the marina while her elderly partner slept, oblivious to his mistress's nocturnal business activities.

Thais have a liberal view of sex. When Esmae challenged a Thai friend who had enjoyed a long but stormy marriage to a *farang* (Westerner) about prostitution at the marina, she responded, 'Why not? She needs money.' One English woman was so upset about the violence she believed was occurring between an elderly German cruiser and his young Thai mistress that she reported the man to Captain Ahmed, the harbourmaster at Rebak. 'He's beating her. You should hear the noise. The poor girl is screaming out in pain. You must do something about it,' she insisted.

Broaching the subject must have been an ordeal for Captain Ahmed, who was a shy and reserved person. When he raised the subject with the German, the man protested his innocence, claiming he had never, in anger, laid a hand on the woman. His mistress confirmed this. Further probing attributed the noise to the boisterousness of the sex the couple enjoyed. Everyone involved was embarrassed but the commotion did not abate.

Jimmy, a decrepit American who arrived at Rebak after living in Thailand for several years, used the availability of girls as a form of geriatric care. When he discovered his mistress had been selling her services while he slept, he shipped her back to Thailand and flew to the Philippines to search for a replacement. He returned with Sophie, a pretty teenager he had bought from Manila's slums. Her baby daughter, Mary, too young to walk, accompanied her.

Jimmy boasted he had deliberately chosen a young mother in the belief that she would be more stable than his previous mistress. The poor girl had never been out of the slums. She had little idea about how to live in sophisticated society, let alone in the restrictive confines of a yacht. When, after a few weeks, Jimmy returned to the United States for medical treatment, Sophie had difficulty coping. Her life became even more burdensome when Mary began to walk. Within days of taking her first steps, Mary was exploring all over the boat, frequently teetering on deck while peering into the water below.

Women on surrounding yachts, fearing Mary would fall overboard and drown, befriended Sophie and taught the little girl to swim. She was a bright adorable baby who won the hearts of all the women, and several of the men, on A Jetty. Sophie, slim, young and attractive, also won several hearts. She frequently partied into the early hours of the morning with young men, leaving Mary alone aboard the yacht. A couple of times the child woke and crawled into the cockpit where she sat howling for her mother until rescued by neighbours.

Sophie knew little about cleanliness. Visitors to the yacht found bits of rotting food, chicken bones, soiled nappies and other filth lying about. Unfinished meals clung to plates that had not been scraped or cleaned. After a while, a stench arose and swarms of flies and vermin plagued the boat.

Sophie despised the old American and complained about the way he treated her: 'He want me to cook for him and clean and tidy. He want oral sex every day at twelve o'clock. He dirty. He never bathe. I scared for him to come back.' Everyone she complained to felt revolted. When Jimmy did return he found his yacht in a disgusting state.

Although oblivious to the squalor in which she lived, Sophie groomed herself exquisitely. Jimmy was baffled as to how she could afford several pairs of new shoes, new outfits, a pram and a pile of toys. When he solved the riddle, the whole jetty heard his rage. Sophie had plundered several thousand dollars of foreign currency he had hidden on board. That was not the only shock awaiting him. Jimmy discovered he was responsible for hundreds of dollars of bills Sophie had accumulated at the resort's restaurant and bar while partying with her young admirers. When they argued about her debts, she began throwing his records and CDs at him. Most of them went overboard. We were all sad to see Sophie and Mary banished back to the slums of Manila.

Although many Western women condemn foreign men for exploiting Thai and Filipino women, this is not necessarily the case. Often, it is the women doing the exploiting. They are adept at taking all they can from men who eventually discover that, by living with an Asian, they are expected to care for the girl's extended family. Without exception, the men who lived with Thai women complained about the number of times money had been diverted to the girl's family, or about the relatives who had imposed themselves upon them.

While we may frown on their customs, we do not necessarily endear ourselves to Thais either, as I discovered on a trip to Hat Yai, a depressing town in Southern Thailand. Hank and I travelled there to find an engineer to repair broken engine parts. We took a ferry from Langkawi to Satun from where we had to take a minibus to Hat Yai, which is popular with Malaysian men because of the availability of prostitutes.

A squat middle-aged woman laden with parcels struggled up the aisle of the bus, chatting loudly to other passengers as she made her way to the rear of the vehicle to take the only seat available, which was beside me. Hank, who spoke Thai, sternly rebuked her and addressed other passengers. Although I did not understand the language, Hank's tone indicated he was not being pleasant.

'What was all that about?' I asked as the bus got under way.

'She was complaining that the only seat left was next to a foreigner. She said she did not want to sit with pigs. I told her to watch what she said. She was shocked I spoke her language. I said their economy is so bad they need all the help they can get and she should be pleased to see us here spending our money.'

The then prime minister of Malaysia, Dr Mahathir bin Mohamad, had a special place in his heart for Langkawi, an island he frequently visited. In the two decades he was in power, Dr Mahathir's vision lifted Malaysians' living standards as he motivated its people to propel the country into becoming a First World economy. He was so successful that we often pondered on which was the developing country, New Zealand or Malaysia.

For years, Langkawi's people languished under the spell of a curse placed on the island by Mahsuri, a 10th-century Malay princess sentenced to death for adultery. Legend says that when she was executed Mahsuri proclaimed: 'There shall be no peace or prosperity on this island for a period of seven generations.' Dr Mahathir declared the period of the curse to be over. With the prime minister taking a personal interest in its development, Langkawi became the government's main target for tourism. Developers moved in and bought tracts of land, mostly jungle or paddy fields, and built lavish resorts. Peasants used the money to make pilgrimages to Mecca. Men in Langkawi sporting white skullcaps, signifying they have undertaken a haj, are a common sight.

Dr Mahathir visited Rebak Marina several times while we were there. Each time, he was particularly interested in meeting sailing couples. On one occasion, his wife invited Esmae to bring some of the sailing women for tea with her and the wife of the prime minister of Ghana, who accompanied Dr Mahathir to the island. Esmae arranged for Rebecca Mudgway, from *Southern Voyager*, Betty Smith, from the New Zealand boat *Tillerman*, and Nancy Erley, from an American yacht *Tethys* to accompany her. The women's stories kept the prime ministers' wives spellbound. They were incredulous that Nancy sailed her boat single-handed and that the women could cook aboard their boats, navigate, undertake maintenance and sail alone with their husbands.

Dr Mahathir's brother-in-law, Dato' Haji Zainal Abidin Haji Mohammed Ali, also frequently visited Rebak. A very spiritual man, he is an architect and former Malaysian Davis Cup tennis player. We became firm friends. We never knew when Dato' Zainal would appear on visits that heralded experiencing the unexpected. They usually began with a telephone call. A couple of times he said, 'Tony, the prime minister is visiting. Would you like to join us?' Wearing my best shirt and slacks I would catch a ferry from Rebak to Langkawi where Dato' Zainal would pick me up in one of the three Mercedes he kept on the island. Often late, we would rush to the airport to join the prime minister's cavalcade.

During the 1998 Commonwealth Games, I received an invitation to join them at the shooting, which was held at Langkawi. When we arrived at the venue, security officers were concerned to find a middle-aged farang in the middle of the official party. Each time they blocked my way, Dato' Zainal uttered magic words that, like Moses parting the Red Sea, cleared a passage for us. After taking morning tea with the prime minister and his entourage, we entered shooting galleries. Participants mobbed Dr Mahathir, who used his charisma to inspire Malaysia's athletes to excel and win a record number of medals. '*Malaysia bolay!*' they cheered. 'Malaysia can do it!' We were ushered to seats behind marksmen for a rifle event. I was placed in the front row directly behind Stephen Pettersen, whom I watched win gold for New Zealand.

Dr Mahathir was receptive to ideas for improving facilities to attract yachting folk to Langkawi. One evening, during a conversation over dinner with the chairman of the company that ran the Rebak Resort, Dato' On, Esmae pointed out that an existing regulation caused inconvenience because it required sailors to leave the country every two months and then re-enter to get a fresh stamp on their passports. Dato' On suggested she should put her thoughts on paper for forwarding to the prime minister.

Esmae was sceptical about the offer, considering it little more than a hollow gesture that would be quickly forgotten after the meal. It was not so. At seven o'clock the next morning, resort staff knocked on the side of the boat and asked for the letter she had promised Dato' On. Within weeks, the policy was changed so that sailors at Rebak could renew visas every eight weeks at the local immigration office for a period of six months, after which they would have to leave and re-enter the country.

We also raised the idea of building a hardstand, over lunch one day with Dato' On. Until then they had no inkling about the advantages a hardstand could provide for their business and visiting boats. It was built and operating within three years, after I attended presentations to their bankers to show it could be run profitably.

We found Malaysians receptive to ideas, but others did not, usually because of the manner in which they presented their proposals.

Aaron, a middle-aged millionaire son of an American industrialist, believed the marina could be better run. In one letter to the owners he complained about staff incompetence. In another, he suggested the ferries transporting people between Rebak and Langkawi were dangerously overloaded; the management solved this by leaving many of us behind on jetties. The ferry captains delighted in informing us Aaron's complaint was the reason for departing without us. The convenience of taking propane bottles on ferries for refilling at Kuah was banned after Aaron wrote that the practice was dangerous.

His correspondence was referred to Captain Ahmed who was then only a few weeks into his job as harbourmaster. Ahmed was particularly upset when he saw copies of a letter questioning his competency and suggesting he should be dismissed and replaced by Aaron. We were flabbergasted at the suggestion. Aaron did not need to work; he had inherited several million dollars from his father.

When we challenged Aaron about his complaints, at one of our regular afternoon sojourns at the swimming pool, he stared at us blankly, a whisky in his hand, but refused to be drawn on the subject. Next, we heard he had written to the owners proposing the swimming pool should be closed because of the amount of algae attacking it. Each of Aaron's complaints elicited action from the resort's managers. We feared losing the use of our swimming pool, a focal point of our social lives and a necessity for relief from tropical heat.

Problems, mostly imagined, continued to grow in Aaron's mind until he recommended, preposterously, that the marina should be closed because of the amount of silting being caused by monsoon rains. Soil did wash from a red clay scar that ringed the basin where jungle had been cleared for houses and shops, but the silting was not serious and would take several years to clog the lagoon. The Malaysians, humble, gentle folk, unfamiliar with running marinas, were eager to learn from the experience of Westerners, particularly Americans; they took Aaron's complaints seriously. A number of us reassured management we saw no problem and that Aaron expressed only his own opinions.

Aaron's behaviour became even more bizarre when he extended his correspondence to the editor of Malaysia's national daily newspaper, the *New Straits Times*, whom he had met when the newspaper held a staff conference at the resort. Not wanting to become the focus of unwanted publicity, the management concluded that Aaron's behaviour was intolerable. Writing venomous letters was not his only bad habit: his rudeness frequently reduced resort staff to tears.

The pace of decision-making can be slow in Malaysia, probably because of sluggishness engendered by the tropical heat. After several weeks of discussions with lawyers, Captain Ahmed delivered a letter to Aaron, giving him a deadline by which to leave the marina. He ignored it and took his wife touring on land. Another letter was delivered on his return, giving him a few more days to prepare to leave. Aaron dismantled the boat's engine, claiming he could not set sail until it was repaired.

A few days later, I was up the mast in a bo'sun's chair taping the ends of the spreaders when four burly men in brown uniforms with gold epaulettes on their shoulders marched down A Jetty. Captain Ahmed had consulted police and immigration officials about evicting Aaron who, until then, had had difficulty accepting the seriousness of his plight. We felt sorry for his wife when they sailed from the marina a few days later: she believed everyone had turned against them.

Expatriates considered Aaron had escaped more lightly than he would have in Thailand, where they have their own peculiar ways of dealing with troublesome farangs. They claimed Thais might have drilled a small hole in his boat to let it fill with water while he was away touring, or put snakes inside to surprise him when he returned.

Aaron had damaged the good relationship between the resort management and the yacht owners. To rectify it, we held a meeting with the Malaysians and expressed our appreciation for the services provided. Dato' On attended and listened intently to suggestions about ways in which facilities could be improved. Many of the ideas were acted upon. Aaron's eviction gave Captain Ahmed a taste for power. He had little hesitation evicting other yachtsmen who upset him; in fact, he appeared to enjoy it. He even placed a curse upon a couple he expelled from the marina.

Most sailors are superstitious. We will not leave port on a Friday, for instance, because it is considered bad luck. On occasions when we have ignored the rule, we have paid a hefty price. We avoid having anything coloured green on board. We have drawn a line at not having bananas, which some consider an ill omen. We have never needed to worry about a superstition that rabbits are bad luck aboard a vessel.

One day, we were intrigued to see a yacht we had sailed with in Indonesia, *Kona Star*, tie up at Rebak Marina under the name *Santushti*. She had new owners, Tom and Cathy Hilko, from Washington State. We asked whether they were aware of the superstition about changing boat names.

Tom and Cathy explained that although they had little sailing experience, they decided to leave high-pressure corporate life, sell up and cruise. They spent four years searching for a yacht and found *Kona Star* laid up at Phuket. They decided to change the name because they were 'santushted' as soon as they saw the yacht.

Cathy explained the word was Hindu and meant satisfied or content. Because they knew very little about sailing, they sometimes wondered whether they had named the boat incorrectly: occasionally they felt anything but contented with the yacht's performance.

Having decided to change the name, Tom searched the Internet to learn how to go about the task. He discovered he had to be ruthless in removing her original name. Everything bearing the appellation *Kona Star* had to be removed, including the log, charts and even monogrammed towels. 'We couldn't quite part with the charts, though,' Tom admitted. 'They had *Kona Star* stamped all over them and we put our own stamp on them because we weren't going to throw them out.'

In a berth at Phuket's crowded Boat Lagoon marina, they self-consciously set about the ritual to introduce the yacht's new identity. They invoked the Gods of the Sea, thanking them for being good to *Kona Star* and requesting them to be as kind to *Santushti*. They mumbled their incantations and hoped no one at the marina heard their litany. They did stray from one ritual, though. It is customary to smash a bottle of champagne over a boat's bow and formally name her, but the cheapest bottle they could find cost US$90, so they threw their G&Ts at her instead.

Of course, if you build a boat yourself, a pleasure we have never experienced, you can name her whatever you like. Ralph and Connie McNeil saw similarities between the Shah who built the Taj Mahal for the love of his life and the toil they embarked upon to build their yacht. The McNeils' labour of love took them 11 years, while the Shah's lasted 20 years, involved 20,000 men and nearly bankrupted India. The McNeils were particularly impressed when they read of the Shah's deep love for his sole wife whereas his father had thousands of wives and concubines. 'When she died during the birth of the 14th child after 19 years of marriage he had the Taj built in her honour. Her private name was Arjumand but most people know her as Mumtaz Mahal,' they told us. Connie admits that Ralph is the romantic and chose the name *Arjumand* for their beloved yacht. She turned out to be a creation of great beauty, just like the Taj Mahal.

Although he had a penchant for expelling cruisers, Captain Ahmed was not as successful at ridding the marina of other unwanted guests, monkeys, whose colonies grew at an awesome rate. The monkeys provided entertainment as they cautiously stalked crabs along the water's edge, deftly tossing them in the air to avoid being nipped, but they were far from friendly and not to be trusted. Owners occasionally returned from a day in Langkawi to find the mischievous animals had invaded their unlocked boats. Charts and clothing were ripped to shreds and rice, flour and sugar tipped out of packages and scattered over floors. When approached, particularly by early morning joggers, the monkeys became vicious.

Animals can be pests at marinas. Several yachts had cats on board, some of which were kept on leashes by their enterprising owners. Incredibly, after the animals had been tethered for a few weeks, they never tried to jump off a boat when attached to a line. Dragging a leash behind them, the felines strutted about within the boat's confines, apparently unaware that if they jumped onto the jetty they could run free because the line secured to their collar was not attached to anything else. Their owners believed the practice essential for keeping the cats from jumping overboard at sea.

Not everyone was that clever. Civil war almost broke out when a cat from an American boat killed a bird in a cage aboard an expatriate's yacht. The same animal almost killed a sailor sleeping with a hatch open one sticky night. The cat jumped through the opening and landed on the man's chest. The shock almost gave him a heart attack. After we all endured the animal's unsocial behaviour throughout the monsoon season, its owners left it behind when they sailed for the Mediterranean.

They were not considered as irresponsible as a couple who sailed without their dog. Each night before sunset, the poor lonely animal sat at the marina entrance looking out to sea, awaiting their return.

They never came back. Fortunately, the crew of another yacht adopted the dog and took it with them when they left.

We found Malaysians to be very hospitable and generous. As we came to know them, they included us in their family activities, birthdays, weddings and Hari Raya, a celebration that marks the end of the Ramadan fasting period. Esmae initially had difficulty getting used to their parties, which segregated women into one room and men into another.

Occasionally, I accompanied Dato' Zainal and his friends on boys' nights out. Intriguingly they were not much different from similar occasions in the West, except that Muslims did not drink alcohol. Tea, fruit juice, soft drinks and conviviality had a similar effect. As the night progressed, tongues loosened as men relaxed and participated in karaoke. Dato' Zainal had a very good voice and crooned like Tony Bennett.

A waitress at the resort invited us to her wedding at a *kampong* (village) at Langkawi. From the beginning, the occasion did not go well. We set out in our best finery and got drenched on the ferry crossing from Rebak because the monsoon was blowing at strength. We hired a car and set out with Roy and Lesley from the yacht *Foremost*. Roy had learned to speak Malay while home in Melbourne a few months before. He assured us he knew how to get to the kampong.

Malaysian celebrations are easy to find. Dozens of cars park outside kampong houses and large marquees are erected to accommodate crowds attending feasts. Hundreds usually turn up to celebrations that continue for a couple of days.

When we arrived at a kampong surrounded by scores of cars, Roy and I set out to confirm that we were at the right wedding. When Roy thrust our crude hand-made invitation before a child playing beside a grove of palm trees she nodded coyly and replied in Malay. Satisfied, we went back to the car and got Esmae and Lesley.

Several men greeted us at the entrance to the festivities. Roy produced the invitation again and they ushered us toward a long wooden bench and signalled that we should sit down to eat. Uncertain about protocol, we discussed whether we should hand over our envelopes containing gifts of money for the bride and groom. Before we reached a decision, our hosts placed bowls containing three different curries and steamed rice on the table. There was no alcohol, only jugs of rose water and a tin jug of tap water.

Scooping food off plates with our fingers, as is the custom, we tucked into the curries, which were divine. We had to be careful which hand we used for shovelling the food from the plates to our mouths because Muslims use one hand for eating, greeting and accepting change, and another for cleaning themselves. Using the wrong hand is regarded as very bad form. While we enjoyed the feast, members of the bride's family visited the table, handing out symbols of fertility: hard-boiled eggs attached to colourful plastic flowers.

Except for women waiting on tables, Lesley and Esmae were the only females in the dining area.

'You really should be in there with the other women,' Roy teased as he ate. 'You know the rules: men in one room, sheilas in another.'

'We're not budging. We're staying here with you two,' Lesley replied.

'But you're the only women here,' I said.

'Doesn't matter. We're not budging,' she reiterated.

'Well, if you don't want to, perhaps Roy and I should join the women,' I ventured.

A man sitting beside us curtly interjected: 'Cannot!'

I was embarrassed. We had not realised he could speak English.

'The curry's wonderful,' I said truthfully, hoping to placate the man in the white skullcap.

Suddenly, there was a flurry of activity behind us: the bride and groom had arrived. They swept into the banquet followed by a team of fussing escorts carrying baskets of presents and flowers. The only Westerners there, we were as conspicuous as infidels in a mosque at prayer time. Our table stood beside the entrance, so we got a good look at the newly married couple, as they did at us. They gave us quizzical glances.

'That's not Nor Shikan!' Esmae exclaimed.

'Good God, I think we're at the wrong wedding!' Roy declared.

'Oh, I'm so embarrassed!' Lesley cried.

Roy cleared his throat loudly and suggested we should get out of there as quickly and discreetly as possible. I repeated that the curry was too good to leave and suggested the Muslims might be insulted if we suddenly fled.

'No, I think we should go *now*,' Roy insisted.

While fleeing, Roy tried, in his stumbling Malay, to explain to our hosts the magnitude of our embarrassment. They graciously assured us it did not matter and suggested we should stay. 'Thank you, but no,' Roy said. 'We have to get to the right wedding. They're expecting us.' We proffered our eggs on plastic flowers, but they insisted we keep them.

As we searched for the next wedding, Roy said he should have realised that none of them could read the invitation he thrust before them: it was written in English. Typically, they were too polite to admit incomprehension.

Farther down the road, we happened upon another wedding. This time I suggested Roy should stay in the car while I asked whether it was the celebration we sought. In broken English, the man I spoke to declared it was not the right wedding. He indicated the kampong we sought was still a few kilometres along the road 'near vely many petrols'. We took this to mean petrol tanks that Esmae vaguely recalled having seen in the area but we looked for ages before eventually stumbling upon the right place. So many cars were parked in a field outside the kampong that we could not get near it. We nimbly navigated ruts of mud and picked our way over puddles left by the monsoon, teetering precariously on slippery grass, like a troupe of overweight, middle-aged ballerinas.

Etiquette dictates that gifts of money should be given to the groom's father. Esmae and Lesley, chastened by our earlier experience, were anxious to avoid further faux pas. With all the subtlety of desperate women obtaining tickets from a tout, they pressed the envelopes containing money onto the first man to greet us. We think he was the groom's father, but we will never know.

Weddings were not the only festivities we experienced. In an attempt to make sailors feel at home, resort staff prepared sumptuous feasts to help us celebrate Christmas and Thanksgiving Day. They were grand occasions where the fare included Western and Asian delicacies.

One year, a group of North American cruisers decided to celebrate Thanksgiving on their own. Half a dozen of them sailed to the islands off which we had found the crew of the Indonesian cargo boat.

One of the most experienced sailors, an American who has been sailing the world for many years, insisted upon returning to his yacht to whip up dessert in his ice cream maker. He switched on the engine to charge batteries to compensate for the power drained by the device. He worked on his creation in the galley for some time. Suddenly, he was jolted off his feet as the sound of a crash resounded through the yacht. Dashing into the cockpit, he discovered his bow resting amidships on another boat. When he had started his engine, the boat was in gear, and while he was concentrating on his ice cream, his vessel had stealthily moved forward on its anchor until it smashed into the other yacht.

Every day while we were in Malaysia we spied yachties walking along the jetty with their little black bags, reminiscent of the business life from which we thought we had escaped. Instead of suits, they wore shorts and floral shirts. Instead of homburgs or Stetsons, they sported caps bearing the names of exotic ports. But they strode purposefully to queue in line to connect to the world through the computers clutched in their hands.

When we met them, they talked a foreign language. They were into megabytes, gigabytes, downloading, Yahoo, Bigfoot, Hotmail and surfing the net. Discussion at the bar changed too. It was not about the attributes of one autopilot compared to another, as it used to be, but about the merits of having a second computer on board. When they talked about engines, they referred not to motors on their boats, but to search engines and acoustic couplers. This is the new breed of yachting folk, those who cruise cyberspace. When they arrive at a port, they can barely contain themselves from finding the nearest cyber café to download news from home.

The Internet has revolutionised sailing. When we set out from New Zealand in 1995, we informed family and friends about our itinerary and provided them with addresses to which they could send mail. After arriving at a destination, one of our first jobs was to dash off to the designated postal drop to search for news from home. Often, mail had not arrived and followed us around the world, or ended up on somebody else's yacht for delivery when they caught us up. The Internet has changed all that and computers have become vital pieces of onboard equipment, used for communications, navigation, monitoring weather and engine performance, and a host of other activities.

Stan Honey and Jim Corenman, two Americans who sailed in the flotilla we had joined on the voyage from Australia to Malaysia, returned to the United States to set up SailMail, a communications system that enables transmission of email on high-frequency radios. Within the budgets of most sailors, it has removed much of the isolation from cruising by enabling us to keep in touch with civilisation from even the most remote locations.

In 1995 after he retired as an officer with the New Zealand Fire Service, Barney Barnard set sail with his wife Pat. They managed to navigate their steel cutter, *Rustingburg*, through the Pacific, Australia and Indonesia without a computer on board. At Rebak, they succumbed to the email bug, which swept through the cruising world like a virus. The Barnards wanted to keep in touch with family and friends through email, via ham radio, and they were not alone. Susan Mitchell, from San Diego, co-ordinated examinations at Rebak for crews with similar aspirations. The number applying to sit ham radio exams increased threefold as a result of the medium's email capability.

Was nothing sacred? I fled business to avoid the deluge of technology rolling towards me, but there was no escape. Even here, in our idyllic island paradise, it had caught up with us. We even had classes to learn about surfing the net and working a computer. Our teacher was Susan Angus, formerly in Bank of America's computer section in San Francisco. She and her partner Steve Whitmore also helped sailors select their computers.

It was not long before a cyber café was set up at a bar next to the resort's restaurant; later, it expanded into a club on the hardstand. The cyber café enabled sailors to keep an eye on what was happening at home through scanning daily newspapers and stock exchanges. It opened a new world for ordering boat parts from the United States and Europe and for obtaining technical advice. Previously, we were limited to faxes and telephone calls that were too expensive to allow us to scan catalogues and inventories.

We have found cyber cafés in the strangest of places. In Phuket, Thailand, I shared an evening with two mangy dogs that lay at my feet while Esmae sat at a bank of four computer screens to download email. While she tapped the computer keys, I tapped my toes in the sand on the floor, patiently waiting for her to catch up with the world while hoping I would not catch anything from the dogs.

The technology revolution defeated two of our main adversaries – isolation and distance. It was not long, however, before we found ourselves facing new adversaries when Osama bin Laden's acolytes attacked the Twin Towers and the Pentagon.

CHAPTER 10

NO ESCAPE FROM 9/11

As CNN replayed the scenes of the aircraft smashing into the Twin Towers, Captain Ahmed and a few of his colleagues appeared unable to contain their mirth. Like much of the world, we were incredulous as the buildings collapsed and a ballooning pall of smoke and dust tumbled down a canyon of skyscrapers, a cloud of evil enveloping the world.

Initially, shocked and numbed by the carnage, none of us knew what to expect following the attacks. While American yachties feared for the safety of loved ones in the States, our worst fear was that if war flared between Muslims and the West we would be trapped in Malaysia, an Islamic country. If we were to flee in our boats, we would have to run a gauntlet of Muslim states, no matter which route we chose. Heading east to Australia involved sailing past angry Indonesia, the world's largest Muslim nation. Going west to the Mediterranean would entail passing through the tinderbox of violence that was the Middle East. Striking out for Hong Kong or Japan meant skirting Malaysia, Borneo, Brunei and the Philippines; all had significant Muslim populations and a reputation for pirates and terrorists. That route was also prone to typhoons.

Those who observed the apparently gleeful attitude of the Malaysians viewing television replays felt disgusted and frightened. We suggested that the Muslims' response was not as sinister as it appeared because, when uncomfortable, Malaysians tend to hide their embarrassment with smiles, giggles and laughter, and we were confident nothing malicious should be taken from their reaction. Although this assumption proved correct, little could be said to placate fears.

We had arrived back in Malaysia only a day before the attacks on New York and Washington, after spending several months at home in New Zealand. We had left *Antares II* on the hardstand at Rebak Island and returned to find her sitting proud but forlorn. Varnish was peeling off the capping on her gunwales. Her bottom needed repairs and painting. A considerable amount of essential work was required before she could sail: the seacocks needed easing and greasing, the stern gland would have to be repacked, the impellers on pumps serviced, the oil changed and a multitude of forgotten and unseen problems attended to. We were awaiting delivery of two new batteries that were on a yacht currently in Indonesia. Without them, we had insufficient power to satisfy the appetite of the boat's sophisticated electronics. Given the current situation, we were not confident they would arrive. It would be impossible to make a quick exit if conditions deteriorated.

The yacht's condition was not the only complication that would hinder our departure. If we were to flee, heading west to Africa or the Mediterranean would be a battle: the south-west monsoon still had three months of life. If we decided to fight the weather to get out of Malaysia, it would wrestle us all the way. We concluded that the safest route would be to go west to Aceh, at the tip of Sumatra. From there, we would alter course to head south to Christmas Island. Although it would be a hard, gruelling voyage beating into the monsoon, it would take us clear of Indonesia's crowded islands where bin Laden enjoyed support. From Christmas Island, we could choose either to cut across to Darwin or to make a long passage to Fremantle where we would be with our son and daughter-in-law.

There was little time for dallying. In three months, cyclones spinning across the Timor Sea, which separates Asia from Australia, could close the route. With calls for jihad ringing louder, we held our breath with the rest of the world, awaiting America's response, and set about gathering intelligence on our situation.

Dato' Zainal and his wife Normah visited Langkawi a couple of days after 9/11 and invited us to dine with them. They refused to believe Muslims could be responsible for such carnage: Islam expounded love and peace, they postulated. The Koran forbade suicide and killing innocent people, such as had occurred at the World Trade Center. They suspected the culprits to be Colombian drug barons hitting back at the United States, blaming Muslims while trying to divert the Americans from curtailing their wicked trade. At the same time, they condemned America's Middle East policies as bitter poison that left iron in the souls of Muslims. While admitting concern about the adverse impact the attack would have on Muslims, they reassured us we would be safe in Malaysia, a peaceful, trouble-free country that benefited from strong leadership. The government had firm control over radical Islamic groups.

We questioned them about jihad, a holy war against infidels. We asked whether Muslims would respond to such demands, which were intensifying worldwide; even several thousand Malaysians had joined the chorus. When we pressed her about consequences of a jihad, Normah replied by drawing a well-manicured finger across her throat. This message, from one of our closest friends, was chilling.

As the world teetered on the brink over the following weeks, Dr Mahathir's opponents rallied support against the United States. PAS, the largest Malaysian opposition party, declared jihad against America and encouraged its members to go to Afghanistan. Thousands of people, brandishing placards proclaiming 'Destroy America' and chanting 'God is Great' turned out to demonstrate in

Kuala Lumpur. Police dispersed them with water cannon.

There were several other incidents that tested confidence in Malaysia. When a United States Air Force B-2 stealth bomber flew into Malaysian airspace, many saw it as a sign the country was not immune from American wrath.

Until the government revealed Malaysian students had trained in Afghanistan, some of the transient yachties had been unaware that clandestine groups of Islamic fundamentalists existed in the country. In fact, hundreds of them lived in exile only 24 kilometres away in southern Thailand. The media disclosed that several radicals had been detained under the Internal Security Act. Newspapers reported incidents of Muslims, including Malaysians, being badly treated in the United States, Britain and Australia, simply because of their nationalities, their names, their looks and their religion. Who could blame Malaysians if they felt inclined to balance the ledger by dishing out similar violence and humiliation to Westerners in their country? Was it our imaginations, or did the villagers at Kuah look at us differently these days?

The situation was worse in Indonesia. Students demonstrated in many cities, burning American flags and shouting slogans such as 'Go To Hell America!' Anti-Western propaganda cluttered the Internet. Some warned that attacks similar to those in New York would occur at the Petronas Towers, Kuala Lumpur, the world's tallest buildings.

As sabres rattled, the imminence of war forced participants in Lima 2001, an air and armaments show held at Langkawi every two years, to cancel their attendance. None of the signs inspired confidence.

Muslim leaders, particularly in Indonesia, called for calm and stressed that America would wage war on terrorism, not Muslims, but this did not dampen fervour for a jihad against the United States. Following attacks against its citizens and facilities, the United States government authorised the departure of its personnel in Indonesia.

The state of Kedah, of which Langkawi is a part, is the most devoutly Muslim province on Malaysia's west coast. While welcoming the benefits tourists bring to the local economy, many do not appreciate the number of infidels visiting their country. Some yachties were dismayed when taxi drivers declined to carry them because the passengers wanted to load cartons of beer into the back of their vehicles. The Koran forbids the consumption of alcohol. Many women in Langkawi wear headscarves, which has become a symbol of the battle for the minds of the population, a sign that the beautiful faces beneath the scarves support a fundamentalist approach to their religion.

On the way into Kuah, we often made a detour to the village of Matserart where we enjoyed a glass of black tea and crisp roti dipped in spicy curry sauce. The café owner delighted in having us dine at his establishment because we were the only Westerners frequenting the premises. A proud man, he boasted of holding a high regional office in the ruling UMNO political party. A photograph of him bowing respectfully as he clasped the hand of a benevolent Dr Mahathir adorned a prominent place near the entrance.

When we invited him to assess the mood following September 11, he vehemently condemned the United States for supporting Israel against Palestine and for the suffering that sanctions caused Iraqi Muslims.

'America, they kill my brothers. I watch CNN and I cry when I see what is happening in Palestine and Iraq. Truly, I cry,' he admitted earnestly. 'Why they do this? Why they hate Muslims? I tell you why. The Jews have bought the American president with the votes,' he claimed. 'That is why Muslims hate Americans. That is why martyrs attack America.

'You do not need to worry, my friend,' he continued. 'Malaysia is a peaceful country. Our PM, Dr Mahathir, he is a great man. He makes Malaysia peaceful. There will be no trouble here,' he reassured with conviction.

'Mahathir, he deals with the troublemakers,' he smashed his fist into his hand to demonstrate the force of the prime minister's rule. 'He uses ISA (Internal Security Act) to deal with them. He locks them up. There will be no trouble here, not like Indonesia. You're safe.'

Having reassured us, he confided that since September 11 the party's youth wing had had difficulty controlling its members. Osama bin Laden's doleful face adorned the black T-shirts UMNO Youth members wore to anti-American demonstrations. They had bought the T-shirts at Langkawi's markets for a couple of dollars. Our friend revealed that these young men had twice burnt American flags in Pantai Cenang, Langkawi's main tourist area.

Chinese traders at Kuah remembered a time when Malaysians were less tolerant: about 300 people died in ethnic violence in 1969. Since then, Dr Mahathir's government had placated Malaysians with a programme of affirmative action that, in the fields of education, employment and business, favoured them ahead of Chinese and Indians. Understandably, ethnic jealousies and resentments simmered beneath the surface.

'Be very careful of the Muslims,' a Chinese trader in Kuah warned. 'When they turn to jihad they will kill each other. Brothers will kill their sisters; sons will kill their fathers. Kill you. Kill me. A Muslim has no loyalty other than to Allah,' he spat as he drew a crooked, dirty finger across his throat exactly as Normah had a few nights before.

On the way to the ferry back to Rebak, a taxi driver reiterated his hatred of Americans, giving the same reasons as the café owner. Other yachting folk returned from Kuah with similar tales, engendering debate among Rebak's foreign inhabitants about the predicament in which we found ourselves. If militant Muslims were determined to vent their fury at the United States, Rebak Island, with a couple of hundred expensive foreign boats sitting in the marina, would be a good place to start. Assuming that fanatics would not distinguish between nationalities, we could all be at risk. The government apparently also considered us potential targets.

RIGHT Trader at the gun and goat market, Salalah, Oman.

BELOW Guide Mohammed introduces us to a frankincense tree at Salalah.

LEFT Wattie Goodwood and Aden 'boatman' Mohammed. Wattie's yacht went aground on a Red Sea reef.

BELOW Not everyone in Yemen is against the USA, as this store window in Aden demonstrates.

RIGHT A painful existence – suffering was all too common in Asia and the Middle East.

BOTTOM RIGHT Swimming in the Gulf of Aden was at times beguilingly placid, belying the threat of terrorists and pirates.

ABOVE War-torn ruins of Emperor Haile Selassie's palace at Massawa, Eritrea.

BELOW Camels awaiting their loads at El Geyf, Suakin. Once, the caravans would have numbered in their thousands.

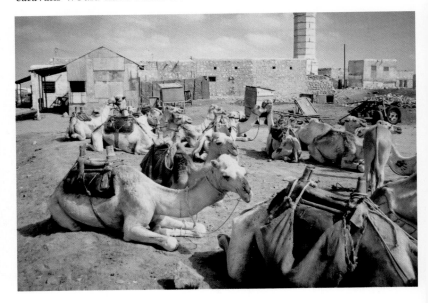

TOP Sunset in Suakin.

ABOVE Entrance to the crumbling city of Suakin. The gates are the only ancient edifice still intact.

Tony, guide Mohammed, Brec Morgan and Justin with swords purchased at Port Sudan.

One of the main forms of transport at Suakin.

A Thai garland, a good luck talisman, is still secured to *Antares'* bow as she lies at anchor off Suakin's ruins.

ABOVE Surrounded by locals at Suakin. Police had to disperse the crowd when it grew.

BELOW Mosque at El Geyf, under a lofty gaze.

A couple of dozen uniformed security force officers arrived at the resort to study maps and scrutinise the dense jungle shrouding the island's hilly contours.

Esmae and I were in a precarious situation. We considered our options. Prudence dictated we should accompany *Southern Voyager*, which was returning to Australia to be sold, so we set about preparing *Antares II* for the voyage, working feverishly in the sweltering heat. Meticulous maintenance would ensure she would remain in top condition for a passage in which we might have to sail 8000 kilometres with minimum stops. We checked our list of spare parts and, anticipating the breakdowns common on long voyages, ordered extras for the engine and generator.

By now there were only a dozen or so cruisers at the marina. Like us, most crews had left the tropics during the hottest, most humid months. Traditionally, they begin to return from October onwards to prepare to resume voyages to the Mediterranean or Africa. Our American friends concluded their best choice was to wait out the monsoon and sail to Africa. They could leave from Phuket and stop at Sri Lanka, or preferably the Maldives, if they were peaceful, before going to the Chagos archipelago, a popular anchorage where cruisers from Asia await weather to take them to Africa. They hoped that America's reopening of the US Air Force base at nearby Diego Garcia would not bar access to Chagos.

The threat of widespread American retaliation subsided as President Bush held the Taliban in his sights. We were relieved that even Muslim nations joined a worldwide coalition against terrorism. Fleetingly, the world appeared to have drawn back from a bleak precipice to glimpse the brightness of a new co-operative spirit. Sadly, it was ephemeral. Israel had peered over the precipice and found only darkness. Her might descended upon Palestine; and as gangs of Palestinian children, their courage fuelled by decades of hatred, futilely hurled stones at Israeli tanks, we glimpsed the next generation of Osama bin Laden's foot soldiers.

The *New Straits Times* disclosed a close link between the bin

Laden family and Malaysia: one of the terrorist's brothers was building an underground railway to link downtown Kuala Lumpur with its new international airport 50 kilometres away. This news provided fuel for black humour.

'You've got to look at history,' I suggested lightheartedly to Kirk Hall, an American sailor. 'Malaysia and Singapore fell to the enemy in the Second World War. The same will happen again if war breaks out here.

'Just as Westerners were rounded up to work on the Burmese railway, you'll end up working on bin Laden's railroad in KL. You can't tell me it's just coincidence that he happens to be here, building a railroad, at this particular time in history. There's a reason for everything, you know.'

I whistled the 'Colonel Bogey March', the theme tune from the classic film *The Bridge on the River Kwai*, which told the story of prisoners of war who built the notorious Burmese railway.

Lesley, who followed our banter with amusement, broke into song:

> 'Santa never made it into Darwin,
> A big wind came and blew the town away.'

Her refrain reminded us of the perils of sailing to Darwin. The song commemorated events that occurred on Christmas Eve 1974 when Cyclone Tracy demolished Darwin and 65 people died, 16 of them at sea.

'I wouldn't go to Darwin this time of year, love,' she counselled with a benevolent smile.

'Better to stay here,' Kirk advised.

Over the next couple of weeks, two factions existed: those who whistled 'Colonel Bogey' and those who sang the Santa song.

Two things became apparent as time went on: Malaysia was probably the safest of all Muslim countries and we had no hope of completing the work on *Antares II* in time to beat Australia's cyclone season. But having decided to leave, we had no desire to remain in Malaysia. The new managers running Rebak had destroyed the previous warmth and sense of family. The type of people arriving at the marina had changed, too, as Phuket's human flotsam washed into Langkawi when Thailand changed its immigration laws. We were determined to depart for either Africa or, preferably, if it appeared safe, the Mediterranean via the Red Sea.

To prepare *Antares II* for her voyage, Esmae and I made a quick trip to Singapore. While returning to Rebak Island on a friend's yacht, we met advance boats from the 2001 season's flotilla from Australia. The new arrivals were a sorry lot. We met on a rock for a barbecue at the Pulau Pisang group of islands at the southern end of the Malacca Straits, about 64 kilometres from Singapore. We huddled like penguins on an iceberg as an encroaching tide crept over the rock and eventually sent us scurrying back to boats anchored in the bay. Earlier, they had endeavoured to sail against the prevailing monsoon to the next anchorage at the Water Islands, off the ancient city of Malacca, only to be forced back by current and an unfavourable wind.

They discussed warnings on NAVTEX about pirates working the Malacca Straits, but their main concern was that they had entered a predominantly Muslim country whose opposition party had declared a jihad on the United States and urged its members to travel to Afghanistan to fight alongside the Taleban. They had picked up reports from Singapore radio that a couple of thousand pro-Afghanistan demonstrators had protested earlier that day outside the American embassy in Kuala Lumpur. On their high-frequency radios they had learned that Langkawi's two marinas had waiting lists, most of the moorings were taken and there was a considerable wait to use its hardstand. The situation would be little better in Thailand, which, they had heard, was not as hospitable towards cruisers as was Malaysia.

After 9/11, they had lived with fear and rumours about what they would encounter in Indonesia and Malaysia. Before returning to our yacht, we put on brave faces and tried to lift their spirits with reassurances about the inaccuracy of much of their information. We did not admit their concerns highlighted the insecurity we all felt.

When we returned to Rebak, Dato' Zainal invited us to dine with a businessman who had accompanied him to the resort. Other crews were horrified when we revealed the businessman was a Palestinian. A couple called at our boat and complained: 'God, a Palestinian is the last person we need here when we're going to the Middle East. He might be taking details of our boats. Can't you dissuade your friend from bringing such people here?'

Their attitude astounded us. Dato' Zainal had more right to be at the resort than any of us and would never do anything to jeopardise our safety. Bigotry and ignorance are insidious cankers. Even though the sailors had lived among Muslims for some time, they clung to preconceived notions that had travelled with them from afar. Unfortunately, the two who complained to us were not alone.

Travel does not broaden all minds. Some who journey the world are too tarnished with prejudice to be enriched by the cultural diversity that surrounds them. Instead of embracing differences, they complain about them – food, music, art, religion and living conditions. Privileged enough to free themselves from the shackles of ignorance, they return home more enslaved than when they set out.

Malaysians hold values for which many in the West are nostalgic. They respect their elders, who command prestigious positions within their extended families, maintaining their influence until they are so feeble their children care for them. They look after their sick and give tithes to the poor. At Hari Raya, a celebration marking the end of Ramadhan, the Muslim month of fasting, they visit each other's homes, admitting transgressions and humbly seeking forgiveness. Praying five times a day is not a burden. It is a pity that Muslims are feared because of the distorted views of a comparative few. We were not immune, however. We still feared the consequences of calls for jihad.

Concerns deepened when Australian, British, New Zealand and United States governments issued travel alerts to deter their citizens from entering countries we were flirting with visiting. Even Thailand was not safe. One travel alert revealed that on 5 October 2001 police across the border at Hat Yai picked up six illegal aliens carrying suspicious devices that could be used with explosives. Those arrested were from Iran, Iraq and Afghanistan. Authorities urged vigilance when visiting Thailand and warned against calling at most of the countries en route to the Mediterranean.

Fears abated as international forces drove the Taliban from Kabul. A growing number of sailors quietly predicted that, despite travel alerts, the Red Sea route to the Mediterranean might be safe after all. The chances of sailing there increased with news of seven German warships steaming through the Suez Canal to protect sea lanes.

We took heart from the optimism generated by other cruisers and contacted Justine, who was working in London, to tell her *Antares II* could be sailing to the Mediterranean in January 2002. She had insisted on joining us for the voyage, which she believed would provide memories of a lifetime. We hoped they would be good.

Antares II's return to the water was far from auspicious. As we slowly motored across the short distance from the hardstand to a marina berth, a fuel blockage stopped the engine. The yacht drifted forward towards the jetty where friends waited with lines.

When we were almost close enough to hurl a line to the jetty, a breeze caught the yacht's bow and changed the direction in which we headed. The lines we tossed dropped into the water a few metres short. We tried to drop anchor. It jammed. As we drifted, disabled, towards other boats tied in berths, Roy launched a dinghy and nudged us in the direction of a ferry wharf as their captains rushed to move their vessels before we collided.

Wind caught *Antares II* again as Roy tried to hold us off the wharf and the yacht's 29 tonnes crushed the dinghy against a pile. Roy popped out of the craft like a pea expelled from a pod and disappeared under the wharf. The dinghy's outboard screamed as its progress halted. *Antares II* bounced off the wharf and the dinghy set off in pursuit of its helmsman.

We feared for Roy's safety. A few years before, Paul Lee, skipper of *Leeway*, a ketch from Picton, was seriously injured when he fell from his dinghy at Rok Nok, a Thai maritime park about halfway between Langkawi and Phuket. Out of control, the boat sped toward Paul as he thrashed about in the water. He dived, but could not go deep enough and the propeller ripped through his head. The circling craft hit him twice more before other sailors dragged him out of the water, blood streaming from deep gashes in his head and an arm.

We worried that Roy might receive similar injuries, but fortunately his dinghy slammed into rocks beside the wharf before it could reach him and he floated to the surface unscathed.

After bleeding the fuel, the engine spat into life and *Antares II* crept into her berth. We had received yet another lesson about how easily she could humble us when we least expected it.

She did it again a few weeks later, after we smugly boasted to *Southern Voyager* and other friends tuned to high-frequency radios that we had completed a fast overnight passage from Langkawi to Phuket. Well aware of hazards lurking in Asian waters, we had remained particularly vigilant when sailing at night. We worked in three-hour shifts during which one of us kept watch while the other slept. As usual, we had to avoid hundreds of fishing boats and kilometres of nets floating beneath the surface. Fishing vessels of all sizes worked in the darkness, laying snares attached to thick cables, and metal and bamboo stakes that could foul a propeller and damage a boat.

Fishermen went about their business with scant regard for approaching vessels. Some sailed in pairs and trawled huge nets between them; to go up the middle of them would be disastrous. Others worked alone, towing a net behind; to cross too close could cause a calamity. Because many ignored international conventions about lighting their vessels, considerable concentration and a large degree of guesswork were required to determine a safe course and distance.

On a couple of occasions, the fishing fleets were so large that circumnavigating them was impossible. We experienced only two unnerving incidents where collisions could have occurred had we been careless. We sailed so close that we saw figures with bare yellow chests working their lines, pulling squid from ponds of light. At dawn, our sails ballooning under a following wind, we congratulated ourselves that we had successfully manoeuvred through the fleets without incident. We altered course and headed for Phuket's Boat Lagoon marina to pick up Justine.

The gentle dawn breeze dissipated while, over the radio, we told friends of our safe arrival. We turned *Antares II* into light air to drop the mainsail. Immediately after we started the motor, it died and would not start. The propeller was fouled. I dived under the boat and discovered tentacles of a huge fishing net streaming from the rudder and tangled around the propeller. We had obviously dragged it for some time.

Esmae and I took turns diving under the boat, trying to cut it free. Although the engine had barely turned over, the net had compacted into a solid mass around the propeller shaft. Using a sharp knife, we managed to hack through dozens of nylon strands but we could stay under the water on snorkel for only a few seconds at a time and soon grew tired. Our diving tanks were stowed in the lazarette to be filled with air at Phuket.

Fortunately, we were only a few kilometres from the marina. We called for help and a couple of divers from Boat Lagoon arrived with hacksaws and wire cutters. They freed the net within minutes and we anchored nearby to await the next morning's tide to navigate tricky shoals that led to the marina.

Had we persisted in doing it ourselves, we would have eventually freed the propeller, but we were discouraged by memories of the last time I had worked beneath *Antares II* in Asian waters. Within days of arriving at Rebak Island, following the harrowing storm in the Indian Ocean on the way back from the Maldives, an ambulance had rushed me to the Langkawi hospital. Severe chest pains indicated a possible heart attack, but doctors concluded I was suffering from pleurisy that had developed from pneumonia I endured during the rough ride across the Indian Ocean on the way to Malaysia. They believed the pneumonia had developed from a chest infection I had picked up while diving under *Antares II* at Cochin to free the plastic bag from the inlet.

The approach into Boat Lagoon is dreadful, full of shallows that can be negotiated only on a high tide. Having a deep keel, we had little room for errors. We grounded three times as we made our way past sandy spits and mangrove swamps that border the narrow channel. Sometimes, boats require assistance to get off shoals, but the tide always lifted us free.

We had arranged for small repairs to be made at the marina and were impressed at the way everything was done. No sooner had we guided *Antares II* into a tight berth, than the first of the artisans came aboard. For the next three days we were never alone. Carpenters, refrigeration engineers, mechanics and electricians climbed over the yacht, tweaking things here and there, perfecting her for coping with a demanding cruise into the unknown. Everything was completed on time and, with Justine aboard, we left on schedule on a rising tide.

Antares II is equipped with state-of-the-art electronics, including forward scanning sonar, to accurately assess depths, but none of it was much good on the way out of Boat Lagoon. We seemed to graze every shelf in the channel. At one shoal, we sat impatiently revving the engine, trying to help nature move the boat. Neither Neptune nor *Antares II* would be hurried. We eased out of the mud only when they were ready.

A wizened old man in a primitive dugout drifted past as we sat, self-consciously, on a mud bank. Unable to speak English, he pointed irritably to the side of the channel that contained deeper water. When we drifted free, he waved confidently toward the direction we should motor. He pulled a tree branch from inside the dugout and prodded the water beneath him, indicating its depth. We ploughed through the seabed with the depth sounder in some places showing only two metres of water under us. We are aground at 2.3 metres, so we must have made tracks in the mud most of the way from Boat Lagoon.

Finally escaping into deep water, we set a course for one of our favourite places, the eccentric, fractured islands of Phang Nga Bay. Of all the unexpected delights encountered in Thailand, few compare to spellbinding discoveries that lie above and below her shores. Those who do not venture beyond the land do not experience the best Thailand has to offer.

Phang Nga remains a mystery, even to geologists. A bewildering number of islands protrude hundreds of metres above the sea. Frequently shrouded in morning mist and shimmering in afternoon haze, the labyrinth of phantom peaks harbours dark secrets of epochs far beyond the coming of Mohammed, Christ, the Buddha or dinosaurs. Occasionally, they tantalise with a glimpse of their ancestry: rocks formed from molluscs, crustaceans and corals captured at the time the land emerged into the sunlight, rock paintings scratched on smooth surfaces by anonymous artists who left shells and stone tools on cave floors when they fled more than 3000 years ago, long before Thais swept down from the north.

Some see signs that Phang Nga was once a vast coral reef, to which Langkawi's monoliths, 200 kilometres away, were attached. Others believe it to have been a swampy basin, absorbing the run-off from the huge continent housing Thailand, Laos, Vietnam and southern China. We remained ignorant about the tectonic forces that sculpted this dramatic, mysterious wilderness in whose shallow waters *Antares II* sailed.

We anchored beneath a solitary spectacular plug of rock rising 300 metres above us, glistening like topaz in the harsh sunlight. We explored the imposing hongs (caves within islands) in our dinghy. Colossal stalactites, delicately fashioned over many millennia, cling to exterior and interior walls of caves whose ceilings have collapsed. Fishermen have attached lines to fluted overhangs to secure their noisy longteows (traditional boats) for shelter from monsoon rain and a merciless sun. We bartered for fresh fish, crab and prawns, occasionally with cash, sometimes with beers or cigarettes. On some of the larger islands, reed lines stake a route along which daring men teeter precariously while groping to collect birds' nests. Guano from the roosts become condiments that command prices for which the rock climbers consider it worth the risk of scaling vertical cliffs hundreds of metres above the sea.

We kept to sea level. We squeezed the dinghy through keyhole passages and, without a flashlight to illuminate our way, bumped against slimy walls invisible in the darkness. Many hongs conceal their secrets by restricting access to the brief minutes between tides. A few open into breathtaking chambers in which trapped water forms emerald lagoons. We paddled around, enchanted by nature's handiwork. Other hongs, where water surges out with the tide, can be explored only in flood. Some, which have not yet lost their ceilings, are caves in which bats are disturbed into frenzied activity by beams from intruders' torches.

We sailed in search of solitude, far from the boisterous tourist haunts of Phi Phi Don and Krabi. Our pilgrimage took us to the golden pebble beach of Koh Roi, which, because of its isolation, is visited only by a few sailors and fishing folk.

From the sea, Koh Roi is not Phang Nga Bay's most imposing island. Its treasures are concealed behind bleak walls, penetrable only at half tide through a hidden archway carved by the sea. Entering the inner sanctum, we caught our breath in awe. A primaeval swampy garden surrounded us – an ominous forest of tangled mangroves that has taken root on a mound, a remnant of a ceiling that enclosed the cave aeons ago. The forest shares its detritus with ferns, flowers, vines and delicate mushrooms that cling like orchids to tree trunks. Large red ants scurry busily, determined to beat the tide.

Fractured vertical walls, which completely enclose the garden, rise to clouds where eagles soar. High on cliff faces, beyond the reach of intruders, tentacles of hardy cycads, perhaps thousands of years old, spiral down like elephant trunks that have snatched a feed of ferns. Chandeliers of stalactites dangle nearby. The sound of pistol crabs snapping their claws competes with gas bubbles exploding from the heat of the sun, like stones dropping at intervals into a pond.

Esmae left to barter with fishermen who had arrived in the bay. Justine, sitting in water at the beach to keep cool, was reading a book. Alone, I contemplated the tide's ebb and flow. Ours were the only footprints that defiled the white sand. When embraced by the tide, all trace of our intrusion would vanish; the hong would again be pristine. But part of us, unlike our footprints, would always remain within Koh Roi's craggy walls.

CHAPTER 11

DOLPHINS IN THE MOONLIGHT

Explosions resounded around the idyllic bay as the clattering anchor chain rose from the seabed. *Antares II* was about to set out for the Bay of Bengal, on her way to the Mediterranean. Fire crackers, tied to her bowsprit, detonated and created a pall of smoke, a sign, we hoped, of evil spirits fleeing. It cleared to reveal another talisman, a yellow monk's garland, secured to the rail. As we headed away from Ao Chalong, a harbour in which foreign yachts check in and out of Thailand, Esmae distributed silver coins for the crew to hurl into the sea in the hope that Neptune would protect us during the voyage ahead.

Memories of our foray into the Bay of Bengal three years before – the first cyclone recorded in the area during February for 22 years, and a six-day storm with 50-knot winds – made us apprehensive about our new adventure, even though indications were favourable. The monsoon had arrived early and was blowing steadily, providing good wind and fair weather. Those who had already departed had enjoyed their passages.

This time, however, Esmae and Justine took no chances. Thais are superstitious people. Fishermen seek the Buddha's protection

173

by having a monk's garland attached to the bow of their vessels. Esmae proclaimed that if it was good for them, it was good for us, and bought a tacky yellow plastic wreath to secure to the bowsprit. The string of bangers was Justine's contribution. I suggested that a silent prayer would have sufficed.

A logical explanation existed for the atrocious weather we had endured on our previous foray into the Bay of Bengal. Shortly after we returned to Malaysia, the *New Straits Times* reported that the US National Science Foundation had found a dense brown haze of pollution hovering above the Indian Ocean, in which the Bay of Bengal lies. The cloud, which covered an area almost the size of the United States, was so dense that it had altered the climate and brought acid rain. 'That explains how our drinking water got contaminated when I filled the tanks with rain,' I concluded.

The north-east monsoon had carried the pollution cloud over the Indian Ocean during the northern hemisphere winter. When the monsoon changed direction, winds blew it back the other way. 'So that's what happened,' I ventured. 'A dirty big cloud, *dirty* being the operative word, sat above us, drifted with us when we headed toward Sri Lanka and then came with us months later when we returned to Malaysia. We had the bad luck to get it both ways.'

'Precisely!' Esmae conceded. 'Bad luck! The garland and the coins will ensure we don't have any more.'

After returning from Phang Nga Bay, we had swung on anchor off a reef at Ban Nit, a beautiful white beach opposite Ao Chalong, which is not a particularly pleasant harbour. In contrast, Ban Nit's shores are lined with coconut palms under which half-naked men construct ambitious bamboo fish traps, large enough to house cars. Hoards of translucent white ghost crabs scurry nimbly along the shining sand. A jumble of well-manicured mansions and expensive holiday resorts share this prime real estate, only a short drive from the centre of Phuket, with untidy shanties and crude prawn farms. Part of Asia's allure is its illogical and unpredictable disorder.

Here, we had awaited arrival of Justine's fiancé, Justin Rae, who would also crew on the voyage to the Mediterranean. The delay put us at the back of the fleet, of which the first boats had departed before Christmas. We would not leave until the end of January 2002, and we worried we may have left our run too late because, over the last couple of days, the trade winds had lost a little consistency to unseasonable weather. Thailand's English daily newspaper, the *Bangkok Post*, reported that plummeting temperatures in the northern hill country had claimed an elderly woman's life when the mercury fell to 15°C. Usually, it is in the high 30s. Unfortunately, Phuket experienced nothing like those comfortable temperatures and we continued to endure the sweltering heat.

Esmae, whose adventurous spirit and humorous haggling had previously always won admiration from Thai stall keepers, detected a changed attitude toward us in Phuket's markets. She believed it was a result of anti-Western sentiment that simmered beneath the surface because of attacks against Afghanistan. Fortunately, we did not encounter any open hostility, although we heard that Muslims had attacked a sailor near a marina at the top of Phuket Island.

Governments continued to discourage us from travelling through the Middle East. Warnings were issued for all the countries on our route: Yemen, Somalia, Djibouti, Eritrea, Sudan and Egypt. Only Oman, our first Arabian port, appeared to be safe. The timing was not good. Only four months had elapsed since the attacks on New York and Washington. The hunt for Osama bin Laden and members of his terror group, al Qaeda, was relentless. Coalition forces in Afghanistan, led by the United States, pursued the Taliban, the cabal that had ruled the country, by mercilessly pounding the countryside and towns with bombs. Seething hatred in Israel inflamed violence to which Palestinians responded with suicide bombings that killed and maimed Jews, who retaliated with sickening brutality. In Iraq innocent people suffered the deprivation of sanctions that disgusted most Muslims. On top of all this, pirates along our route were plundering ships.

Insurance companies considered the Middle East to be one of

the world's most dangerous places and had only recently, reluctantly, reinstated cover. They warned, however, that an attack by terrorists or entry to a war zone would invalidate their protection. We wondered how, in these waters, they could distinguish between a terrorist and a pirate. In this region, especially in these circumstances, wars might erupt anytime during our four-month odyssey, and we would be unable to escape quickly.

Although the situation looked grim, the consensus among the cruising fraternity was that, with the build-up of coalition warships in the Middle East, 2002 could be the safest year in which to sail there. If we waited another 12 months, the situation could be even more perilous.

While we awaited Justin's arrival, we set about provisioning with supplies essential for an 8000-kilometre voyage. Because there would be little entertainment during our long journey, meals aboard *Antares II* gained special significance. Ignorant about the availability of supplies en route, Esmae compiled a detailed list of the provisions she considered essential. In anticipation of delays through unforeseen circumstances, such as wars or going aground, she bought quantities capable of lasting eight months. There was enough to cater for an army. It was as if *we* were going to war.

When I queried her list, she reprimanded me. 'Provisioning is my job, keeping the boat going is yours. I don't query your list of spares, so don't question my lists of essentials. You'll complain if we run out of food. Our first stop is the Maldives and you know we can't get much there. We can't be sure about supplies in the Middle East. They could be very expensive compared to here, so I'm getting all our essentials before we leave Phuket. We know the quality is good here.'

She set about her task with purpose. On a computer, she calculated how much each of us would eat and drink, then added extra in case of delays. She took her computer lists to primitive village markets and modern supermarkets and we stocked up with 10 kilograms of washing powder; 10 bottles of dishwashing liquids; dozens of bottles of Dettol, bleach, Napisan, Jif, toilet/floor/window cleaners, anti-bacterial spray and other cleaners and polishes; masses of dishcloths, scourers and rubber gloves; 10 dozen eggs; 20 kilograms of wholemeal flour and 35 kilograms of bread flour; 20 dozen assorted soft drinks, 10 bottles of assorted cordials, 10 dozen beers, four dozen assorted wines and bottles of spirits; 1000 English Breakfast tea bags, 500 assorted flavoured teabags, Milo, Horlicks and 15 kilograms of coffee; 12 large tins of margarine; 10 litres of olive oil; 10 kilograms each of jasmine and basmati rice; two kilograms each of salt, peppercorns and assorted sugars; three dozen tins each of spinach, baby potatoes, peas, soya, baked beans, barbecue and red beans, whole tomatoes, tomato purée, mushrooms and coconut milk; two dozen jars of jam, assorted honeys, Marmite and Vegemite; lockers full of sauces, spices, spreads, mayonnaises and vinegars; 12 dozen cans of mussels, oysters, crab meat, tuna, sardines and anchovies; snack bars, nibbles, two dozen assorted packets of crackers and biscuits, chocolates, boiled sweets and so on.

In our freezers Esmae squeezed 20 kilograms of rib eye steaks, three pork roasts, 20 pork spare ribs, six legs of lamb, 100 lamb chops; 10 kilograms each of beef, chicken and pork mince; 10 kilograms of chicken breasts, livers and duck fillets, plus other assorted meats and sausages. A couple of large smoked Norwegian salmon, bought at an unimaginably cheap price, were also stashed in the freezer. Assorted cheeses – we lost count of the packets of Parmesan, Romano and other hard cheeses and brie – were wedged between the cuts of meat in the freezer.

After Justin arrived, we stocked up with fresh vegetables: a sack each of potatoes, onions and garlic; 10 cabbages, pumpkins and lettuces; large bags of carrots, cucumbers, gherkins, radishes; red, green and yellow chillies; water chestnuts; white and black fungus; three dozen tomatoes; green peppers; purple and green aubergines; celery; fresh bunches of mint, parsley, coriander and basil.

Justine, who was in charge of selecting fruit, bought a magnificent range of oranges, limes, pawpaws, mangoes, pomelos (large grapefruit), watermelons, bunches of green bananas (they were meant to ripen progressively over the voyage but all became edible at the same time) and an assortment of other fruits, the names of which we were unsure.

Justine and Justin ('the Js') marvelled at Esmae's ability to shop at Thai markets. Like a local, she stood in front of mountains of aromatic green and red curry pastes, sampling morsels as she haggled over prices while ensuring she got the best quality. Not even the sight of an occasional fat rat wandering beneath her distracted Esmae from her mission.

Each bag of produce was loaded into our dinghy for delivery to the yacht, which lay at anchor in deep water 500 metres from shore, beyond a fringing reef. Getting there presented a challenge. Low tide exposed the reef and left us grounded on coralline shallows, unable to manoeuvre the heavily laden dinghy into deep water. At high tide, we had to find a channel through which to navigate around sharp rock outcrops. We made numerous trips.

Storing and preserving all the perishables for the voyage was an art in itself. Fruit and vegetables were dunked in a bucket of water mixed with chlorine to kill ants, cockroaches and other undesirables that, hidden in the crease of a leaf, could creep aboard to breed a plague. To avoid growing mould, they were dried before being stored either in plastic containers lined with paper towels or in green plastic bags that manufacturers boasted extended a vegetable's life. I regarded this claim with the same disdain I held for the monk's garland, but it did seem to work.

Scores of carrots, garlic and gherkins were prepared and pickled for snacks to be enjoyed with a drink at the end of a day. Herbs were split into three lots, one for the fresh fridge bag, one for the freezer and one hung to dry. Tomatoes had to be graded: some for the fridge, some wrapped individually in newspaper and stored in a dark place; others were placed onto egg trays, each piece separated by a paper towel because, if their skins touched, they would perish more quickly. Eggs were coated in paraffin wax to preserve their life. Tinned food was emptied from huge cartons, sorted, and the date recorded on each item to alert us to the possibility of it spoiling and laying the crew low with illness.

While I complained about the work involved, Esmae went about the task with the anticipation of an artiste, imagining the masterpieces her toil would ultimately create. The effort proved worthwhile, as the voyage became a gourmet's delight. Competitions for creativity occupied many hours with Esmae, Justin and Justine, all of whom are as good with a pan as they are with seamanship.

At a pharmacy supermarket in Phuket, from which we could buy drugs available only with a doctor's prescription in most Western countries, we replenished our medicine chest at a fraction of the cost we would pay elsewhere. We bought a 12-month supply of vitamins, naturopathic remedies and electrolyte drinks, bandages, suturing packs, syringes, Aspro and various grades of painkillers, ointments and creams for tropical infections, burns, itches and abrasions, antibiotics, anti-inflammatory pills and pills for HRT, malaria, diarrhoea and dysentery; 10 dozen face masks for coping with the Red Sea dust; six tins of prickly heat powder and dozens of rolls of paper towels.

Esmae and I are graduates of courses that give us sufficient knowledge to handle accidents and illness at sea. Because the only assistance we can expect from a doctor is advice over a radio we have trained for all manner of emergency procedures, from giving simple injections to performing amputations. Fortunately, we have had to do little apart from the occasional suture. The only operation performed has been to extract a fishing hook from Esmae's arm.

We have found that knowledge alone can be sufficient to induce the miracle of healing. While we were cruising the Timor Sea with David and Jeannie Wolfenden, from Auckland, and their son Mark, the boat suddenly lurched over and Jeannie fell from the top of the companionway stairs and crashed her head against the side of the navigation table. Blood spurted over the floor. She lay on a berth in the saloon groaning, a darkening stain of blood spreading across the towel in which her head was wrapped. After inspecting the wound, I suggested it should be stitched. Jeannie immediately bounded from the bunk, assuring us she felt better. She was confident the wound would quickly heal, which it did. We were amazed. The gash had appeared deep. I remain uncertain whether Jeannie recovered because I made a wrong diagnosis, or because of the thought of my unsteady hands piercing her scalp with a needle.

We also stocked up with 100 rolls of toilet paper and personal items like razors, shaving soap, shampoos, conditioners and colours, contact lens solutions, eye baths, tissues, suntan cream, saltwater soap, body lotions, tampons, nail polishes, facial scrubs, a large range of essential oils for aromatherapy treatments and mosquito sprays.

With all the extra weight on board, it was little wonder we moved slowly when the smoke from the fireworks cleared and we searched for wind to fill our sails to take us into the Andaman Sea and on to the Bay of Bengal.

The first day, everything looked promising for a good trip. Justin caught a large Spanish mackerel, which we cooked on the barbecue for dinner. The next day, he pulled up a huge wahoo that we cut into steaks and stowed in the freezer. Esmae worried that, at this rate, we would not eat much of the meat she had bought. She need not have been concerned: we did not land another fish all the way to Oman.

After a couple of days of fluky breezes, in which we managed only slow progress, the trade wind arrived. It blew from behind at 12 to 24 knots, propelling us at 11–12 knots across the Andaman Sea to the Nicobar Islands and through the Sombrero Channel, our last sight of land before Sri Lanka, five days away.

Although we learned on the radio that boats behind us encountered gales, large swells and adverse currents, our weather was good. With a strong current pushing us steadily through the channel, we barbecued pork spare ribs at the back of the boat. Another evening, Esmae pan-fried duck fillets in orange and garlic, served on a bed of rice with stir-fried vegetables. For lunch, we dined on banana bread and mango and fish salad. We were enjoying life at sea. It was a complete contrast to our last voyage here, when it was too rough to hold down food and we survived on dry bread and water.

At dusk, we marvelled at spectacular sunsets. Later, a full moon lit our way, making the ocean less lonely, and the clouds that swept in after sunset less threatening. As we neared the coast of Sri Lanka, we had a couple of close encounters with ships. One, an LPG tanker, passed within 400 metres at breakneck speed. Another, a huge container vessel, loomed out of rain like a ghost in the middle of one of the few squalls we encountered. Otherwise, the journey remained uneventful.

Remembering our previous visit to Sri Lanka, we decided to skirt the island, diligently keeping watch in busy shipping lanes 48 kilometres off the coast where dozens of freighters and tankers headed to India, Singapore, Malaysia and Thailand. At Dondra Head, the southernmost tip of Sri Lanka, we altered course for the Maldives. Three days later, we arrived at Ulleguma, a tiny atoll threatened with extinction under rising water if global warming continues. A few kilometres from the island, a large turtle lifted its head to give us a contemptuous glance as we sailed past. It was the nicest greeting we could wish for. We dropped anchor on 7 February 2002, 12 days after leaving Phuket.

'So, what do you think about our superstitions now?' Esmae asked as we relaxed and enjoyed the view of the palm-lined white beach beyond the turquoise water of the fringing reef. The monk's garland hung limply on the bowsprit.

There is not much to do at Ulleguma, where 400 people live in poverty. Their dwellings, separated by broad avenues, are built of coral. Each morning, women sweep the wide sandy streets separating their rows of houses. The litter is hidden in high piles behind nearby coconut palms.

We spent our time there resting, making repairs and stitching the mainsail, which had torn on the way across. The Js snorkelled with locals and brought back a large groper and octopus which, after vigorous pounding, Justin served Maldivian style with small pickled fish and a vegetable stew. Boats preceding us reported encountering a low-pressure system with winds of over 30 knots. We waited for it to pass by. After three days relaxing when all our chores were completed, we felt rejuvenated as we set sail for the Arabian Sea and our first Arab port, Oman.

The 15-knot trade wind remained loyal, caressing our starboard side as we sailed a broad reach at six to seven knots. Unfortunately, it brought an unpleasant swell that smacked us amidships and rolled us about in our bunks. Although uncomfortable, it was nothing to fear. Whitecaps skipped across its waves, as joyful as we were to be riding the north-east monsoon, revelling in the freedom and speed it unleashed. We altered course and sailed much of the way goosewing, with our sails poled out to gain maximum benefit from the wind. When the breeze fell below 10 knots, we hoisted a multi-purpose sail that ballooned like a blue, green and yellow spinnaker. To gain extra speed, we set a mizzen staysail, which looked like a little brother to the colourful gossamer billowing off the bow. Such sailing is invigorating; we scudded into memories that will be pleasurable for life. We gybed back and forth across the rhumb line to Salalah, Oman, careful not to stray too far west for fear of pirates roaming beyond the shores of Socotra. We were cautious sailors. At twilight, we reduced the size of the mainsail by one reef, dropped the mizzen and attended to her sheets with the care we would extend when tucking a child into bed.

Most nights the sky brimmed with glittering constellations. It did not matter that the moon had gone. Sometimes a pale glimmer of phosphorescence illuminated the ocean as *Antares'* hull sliced through millions of microscopic creatures that glowed dimly in the darkness when disturbed. The ocean appeared to have stored moonbeams to welcome us as it rose and fell in gentle slumber. Some patches gleamed like large pools, as if backlit from deep within the abyss. In daylight, had they not been invisible, such light could have been mistaken for coral reefs reflecting sunlight.

Night watches were special to all of us. With four on board, we each did a stint of three hours alone in the cockpit. Our number allowed us the luxury of enjoying long sleeps between watches. Smaller crews envied us as they complained about receiving insufficient rest.

While sailing to the Maldives, I stood watch from six until nine. Because of time changes, I did from seven until ten between Ulleguma and Oman. Esmae relieved me for three hours, and then Justin took over, followed by Justine. I returned to complete the watch through dawn. They were times of solitude, times to cherish.

One night alien movement off our port intruded upon my reverie. A pool, illuminating the colour of emeralds, drifted across the ocean's dark canopy and disintegrated into glowing foam. Another puddle of light appeared on black water nearby, then another, and another. Sequins of light bejewelled the darkness with the brilliance of an opening peacock's tail. A deep sigh startled me. A splash followed. A luminous cocoon, followed by a streaking tail similar to a meteorite, peeled away from the yacht. Dolphins! Never before, in all our time at sea, had we experienced anything like this.

I summoned the others, who arrived slowly, agitated at being roused from their slumber, expecting an emergency.

'Dolphins!' I cried excitedly. 'Look at the dolphins!'

The crew's mood quickly changed. They were bewitched by the ballet around us. A bewildering number of glowing streaks punctuated the darkness. *Antares II* joined in the theatre. As she charged purposefully towards Arabia, under ballooning sails, sparkling, illuminated foam swirled from her sides. Delicately, it etched her bow wave's tumbling curves, peaks and crevices with the vivid detail of a spectrograph.

Cautiously, we inched toward the bowsprit to watch the dolphins cavort. The phosphorescence was so bright it painted the sails a pallid green. Glowing forms swooped like lasers towards the bobstays under the bowsprit. A couple of large dolphins, travelling at speed from opposite directions, propelled themselves towards the bow simultaneously, rising from the water as if to rub their backs on the rods. Somehow, they avoided colliding with the hull or each other, and careered ahead like streaks of plasma. They peeled off and others shot in to take their places. We applauded their agility, whooping and yelling our appreciation. They gambolled on the surface and, when breaching, they snorted and sighed as if in greeting. Other dolphins arrived. Swathed in cold green luminosity, they leapt from the water, which exploded with their re-entry, shattering the darkness with shards of light.

Suddenly, they were gone. The crew returned to their bunks. Even *Antares'* mood became sullen and the glow she emitted from her sides lost much of its candescence.

I shook the reef from the sail, hoisted the mizzen and broadened the sheets to gain speed as the night became still.

CHAPTER 12

SECRET CODES AND
STEALTH IN THE NIGHT

Mohammed's bulbous big toe remains indelibly etched in my mind, a bit like the fossilised imprints Muslims claim are hooves of the Prophet's camel indented in a rock face in downtown Salalah, Oman's second largest city. Mohammed's biggest digit protruded from a size 11 foot, beneath long white robes that, despite the city's dust, he managed to keep impeccably clean. A large man, he displayed a tightrope walker's agility as he tiptoed across the plastic tablecloth, nimbly negotiating around dishes of rice, dhal, curried chicken, fish and limp salad. On reaching his destination he collapsed into a pile of pillows on the floor, sighed heavily and sat attentively, like an uncorked genie, awaiting instruction.

Mohammed had taken us to one of Salalah's better restaurants as part of a tour of the district. Around him, 13 sailors sat cross-legged.

'Those camels, where do they come from?' Con Rollas, an Australian, enquired unexpectedly.

'Why, of course, they are from Oman,' Mohammed proclaimed authoritatively. 'Where else would they be from? Oman camels are best in the world.'

'There's certainly enough of them,' an American interjected. 'They're all over the place.'

There was no denying that. Camels had appeared everywhere we visited. They loitered about Salalah with the insouciance displayed by cows in India, and roamed wherever they wished. Mohammed had stopped his van several times in deference to wild camels strolling across a road. We had passed camel trains laden with burdens ranging from kindling for village fires to heavy bales containing dates and other cargoes.

'In Oman, we love our camels,' Mohammed confessed, wiping a grain of rice from his black beard. 'They are man's best friend.'

'They're smaller than Australian camels,' Con observed. 'I'm surprised, because I thought they'd be much bigger than ours.'

'What? You have camels in Australia?' Mohammed was incredulous. 'You don't have camels in Australia.'

'Oh, yes we do. We have camels in the outback. We shoot them because they're pests,' Con revealed insensitively. 'We even export some of them to the Middle East. I reckon you've got some of our camels here in Oman.'

'Never! This cannot be true. Oman camels are best in whole of Arabia, best in whole world. Camels are pests? You send to us! I think you make joke with me.'

'No, no, I'm dinkum,' Con persisted. 'Your camels aren't as big as Australian camels. They don't look as strong. I reckon ours are better because they've roamed the Australian desert for 300 years. Yours aren't as tough because they've been held in captivity.'

Mohammed shifted irritably on the floor. Pointing a large dirty finger across the food he exploded: 'Oman camels are very best. Oman camels give milk and meat. They are very fast, best racing camels in whole of Arabia. Australian camels best? Huh! Not true, I never hear this before.'

Mohammed shovelled a handful of rice into his mouth and chewed noisily on a piece of chicken.

'What would you pay for a camel?' Con asked.

'Ha! Much more than for Australian camel. Oman camel cost more than Rolls Royce. How many camels in Australia needed for buying wife?' Mohammed challenged, as if the answer would resolve the dispute.

Perplexed, Con admitted he had no idea.

'Ha! In Oman 25 camels are needed to buy wife. I think you not tell me because in Australia only 10 camels needed to get wife.' Mohammed was triumphant.

'Only 10 camels? I thought I was worth a lot more than that,' Cheryl Rollas protested.

'Nah, I didn't even pay that much,' Con admitted.

Cheryl dug him in the ribs and Mohammed adjusted his turban and smiled wickedly, savouring his victory.

'I make joke. I make joke,' Mohammed explained, generous in victory. 'I not mean to make offence.'

There was not much to explore around Salalah. The countryside was as desolate as a lunar landscape, a hot barren dust bowl strewn with rocks and stones, too harsh for all but the hardiest of weeds to survive. Only sparse withered remnants of scrawny vegetation existed, desperately clinging to the last vestiges of life until the south-west monsoon arrived with rejuvenating rains.

'You come back when monsoon here,' Mohammed suggested, 'and you see different land. Wadis all in flood. We see waterfalls. Many birds come because everything green. Beautiful wild flowers everywhere. Many, many people from Muscat come here for holiday when monsoon time.'

Unfortunately, there was no sign of this happening when we ventured out on our excursion. The only life evident in the desert was scores of camels and herds of goats being driven by nomadic Bedouin tribesmen.

Even desert dwellers accustomed to the drabness of a barren landscape crave greenery. They found it at some of Salalah's seven traffic islands, which were well irrigated and covered with lush grass. The islands became oases on which men, oblivious to the noise and fumes of passing traffic, chatted and smoked, enjoying the texture, coolness and colour of the grass.

Although we occasionally saw children on traffic islands, no women were present. Omani women were hardly ever seen. As Mohammed explained, they remained in their houses during the day and, if their husbands permitted, ventured outside in the evening. Even in supermarkets, it was men who generally shopped for the family groceries. On the few occasions we did spy Muslim women, we did not glimpse much of them. A mask or veil hid their faces, shawls covered their heads and billowing black gowns concealed their bodies as they scurried in shadows like spectres avoiding daylight. Foreign male glances bring shame, not satisfaction as in the West. If our gaze lingered too long, their husbands would take offence and we could be challenged. Because even the skin of their hands is sacred, they wore gloves. Only their eyes, which they usually kept fixed straight ahead, were exposed. As we had discovered in Malaysia, some women, realising their eyes spoke a tantalising language, became adroit at using them.

In Oman's markets, masked young women dared to play a forbidden game behind their husbands' backs. As we admired gems of frankincense displayed in bottles on the ground on which they sat, the sultry opals behind slits in their masks held our eyes with magnetic power. Well aware of their allure, they captured our attention and determinedly held our gaze until we became self-conscious about staring and broke the spell. In victory, their look turned to silent sneers of contempt.

Before lunch, we had driven through the desert to ancient sun-baked mountains to visit the tomb of Job, a man revered in three religions, Judaism, Christianity and Islam. The biblical figure's remains are claimed to lie in a long grave in a mausoleum to which scores of pilgrims trudge each day. It is ironic that, even in death, the poor man is deprived respite from the afflictions God cast upon him: thousands of curious tourists disturb his eternal slumber. If it is his tomb, Job must have been a very large man because his grave is 3 metres long. A fossilised imprint of a giant's foot, claimed to be Job's, is embedded in rock outside the mausoleum.

The people of Oman are renowned for their generosity and friendliness. We were warned that if our eyes lingered too long upon something they possessed, it would be presented to us as a gift. Justine learned the truth of this near Job's tomb. She could not restrain her gaze from wandering to a pita bread lunch a group of Omani Indians enjoyed as they sat in the shade. Sure enough, a plump man dressed in white robes offered her a whole piece, which we proceeded to share among our group. It was delicious.

The people in Oman even stopped their cars to offer us rides when they saw us walking. They did not harbour ulterior motives, wanting nothing more than conversation and knowledge of our nationalities and our impressions of their city.

As the Js left an Internet café, during a visit to Salalah, they asked where they might buy a meal. A man, who they learned was an army major, overheard their conversation and offered to take them to a restaurant. A little apprehensive, they accompanied him and were rewarded with a splendid lunch of curried fish and chicken. He insisted on paying for the meal and then drove them back to to the yacht at Port Raysut, about 10 kilometres from Salalah. He sought nothing in return.

After our lunch, Mohammed took us deep into the desert to the site of archaeological excavations of a lost city, which could be the remains of a civilisation that inhabited the area as long ago as 5000 BC. This Atlantis of the desert was discovered after satellites equipped with space imaging radar peered beneath the sand and exposed roads and rivers that had been hidden for many millennia. Archaeologists dug away dirt to uncover an octagonal castle with walls and towers 10 metres high. Close by, they uncovered hundreds of blackened fire pits that had been left by traders visiting the settlement to buy dates, frankincense and other aromatics that were as valuable to the ancient world as gold is today. Although the site has been extensively excavated, the city's origins remain a mystery. Some believe it to be the mythical lost city of the *Arabian Nights*.

Because Salalah was enjoying a four-day holiday when Mohammed took us sightseeing, the site, its information office and museum were all closed, but this did not deter Mohammed. He found a hole in a wire security fence constructed to keep trespassers and scavengers away, and ushered us into the ancient world's rubble. We trekked along rutted terraces beside wrinkled walls and parapets of yellow stone and brick bleached by the sun more than 7000 years ago. Sunken caverns, bathhouses, rooms and halls, and teetering walls and towers rose from the excavations. This had, most definitely, been an impressive place.

Atop a mound that had hidden the fortification for thousands of years, we gazed upon a haven where the desert's golden sands surrounded sparkling blue water. Wind and sea have forged the harbour into a lagoon today, its entrance clogged by a sandbar that prevents even the shallowest skiff from breaching its entrance. Once, ancient craft carried frankincense and other prized aromatics, such as myrrh and balsam, from the port to destinations along the Arabian coast. As the centuries progressed and technology advanced, mariners from as far as India and East Africa arrived and departed this trading port in boats constructed from reeds and hides. Seafarers from here, in turn, opened the earliest trade routes. From the buried city, treasures of pearls, ostrich feathers, muslins and silks, traded for Arabian incense, were loaded onto camels that carried them inland, thousands of kilometres across the desert.

'Traders come here long time ago from India, China, Greece and Rome to get frankincense. Queen of Sheba come here to get frankincense for King Solomon,' Mohammed said earnestly. 'Some think, maybe this her palace.

'See inscription,' he invited, pointing to rows of hieroglyphics an unknown scholar had carved on smooth stone tablets. 'Nobody knows what it says. Many people try to read it but nobody smart enough.

'Some say this is city of Iram. Holy Koran tells of Iram. It was a beautiful place made by the ruler, Shaddad Bin Ad, as imitation of Paradise. Holy Koran says the people here became corrupted by delights of the flesh. To punish them, Allah sent a great wind that buried the city beneath the desert sands.'

The source of Arabia's early wealth, the frankincense tree, is a singularly unattractive shrub, blackened by the desert sun. Its resin is tapped to dry into beads the size of teardrops. Possessing aromatic qualities, these were a treasure so valuable that many rulers, including Alexander the Great, plotted invasion to possess them.

The ancient civilisation had obviously chosen the castle's location for its strategic advantages. Not only did it overlook a beautiful harbour, it was constructed on a bluff that provided sweeping views of both sea and land. On the side overlooking the sea, steep cliffs plummeted to a fertile estuary that would have been cultivated with crops and date palms. Enemies would have found it difficult to storm the fortress from the surrounding land, then lush and roamed by buffalo, rhinoceros, ostrich, gazelle, oryx, lion and cheetah.

The site is so strategically important that we were surprised the current reigning sultan, His Majesty Sultan Qaboos bin Said, had not built a palace nearby. He has three estates at Salalah, each larger than anything in Britain. They sprawl across the desert, ringed with high security fences containing guardhouses manned by armed sentries. Why he needs three is a mystery because he also has palaces at the capital, Muscat, 1000 kilometres away, and he visits Salalah only a couple of times a year for two or three months to attend to the needs of the people. They write to him requesting housing or other essentials and, if inclined, he will provide them.

The passion with which Mohammed spoke about his sovereign surprised us. In some countries, the sultan's immense wealth, compared with the poverty of his subjects, would cause deep resentment. On the contrary, Mohammed extolled his virtues. 'My king is very good man. He helps the people and gives them what they need. If we need house, we ask king for house and he gives it to us. He is very good man. I am pleased to have him as my king.'

During Sultan Qaboos bin Said's reign, impressive advances have occurred. When he seized power from his father in a coup in 1970, the region of Dofar, of which Salalah is the administrative capital, had only one school. Now there are 150, in keeping with a pledge made at his coronation that he would banish ignorance and replace it with knowledge and education. Similar improvements have occurred with hospitals, clinics and the province's general infrastructure.

Mohammed was also pleased the sultan had brought peace to the area by ending fighting with neighbouring Yemen and Saudi Arabia with whom Oman had quarrelled over oil-bearing land.

Salalah's wealth and the quality of its produce surprised us. Although the city's shops are unattractive externally, inside they are as exciting as Aladdin's cave, displaying all manner of exotic goods, both local and imported, at reasonable prices. The tomatoes, which we bought for the next leg of our voyage, rank among the best in the world, and other fruit and produce is of a similar quality. Mountains of delicious plump dates adorn the counters of most shops and markets.

At the end of a passage, many of us crave food unavailable during the voyage. For more than a month, Geoff Mann, an Australian crewing aboard an American yacht, *Celerity*, had had an overwhelming desire for ice cream. As he wandered around Salalah, he was overjoyed to discover that a supermarket with an incongruous name, Lulus, stocked an array of imported goods, including the sweet for which he lusted. As he salivated, he pondered the challenges he faced getting it to *Celerity*. The first was the heat, a sizzling 38°C that, he claimed, melted even a cold shoulder quicker than he could say 'ice cube'. The second was a 20-minute taxi ride to the yacht at Port Raysut. Third, the only air conditioning in many taxis was an open window.

Geoff coerced a crew member from another boat to flag down

several taxis until he found one with air conditioning. While his friend held the taxi, Geoff dashed into the store, bought a two-litre carton of ice cream and bounded into the car with the exuberance of a footballer heading for a touchdown. After boarding *Celerity*, he checked the ice cream was still firm. Satisfied, he placed it in the yacht's freezer with the care and satisfaction reserved for a hard-won trophy.

Half an hour later Alan Walls, the yacht's owner, returned to the boat with a mechanic to remove the starter motor, thereby immo-bilising the engine that was necessary for recharging the freezer. Geoff, who had already gorged himself on ice cream while shop-ping in Salalah, almost wept when he learned he would have to either eat the two litres immediately, or dump it. Unable to bear the loss of the delicacy after all his efforts, he consumed it all.

Mechanical problems were not isolated to Alan's yacht. Most of us arrived in the Sultanate of Oman with one problem or another. After all, we had sailed 5000 kilometres from Thailand, with only short stops at Sri Lanka and/or the Maldives, so our vessels had been placed under considerable strain. A Norwegian boat, *Stormvogen*, had a major leak, but all *Antares II* had to deal with was the main engine's raw water pump, which needed new parts that we had in store. It was a reasonably easy repair. We had a more serious issue with our mainsail. Like many yachts had experienced, the mainsail had torn in several places during the voyage from Thailand. No sail makers worked at the port or at Salalah, so Esmae resigned herself to stitching the heavy cloth with her sewing machine, a tortuous job with a large sail.

A day after our arrival at Port Raysut, Esmae was on the yacht enjoying coffee with Cheryl Rollas when armed security men demanded she lower a large New Zealand flag fluttering at the stern. Surprised by the request, she reluctantly agreed but contin-ued her tête-à-tête with Cheryl. The armed men returned a few minutes later and demanded she lower the flag immediately. Seeing the gun aimed at her, she obliged straight away.

We remain mystified as to why they insisted we take down the flag. At first we thought we may have breached etiquette by flying a flag larger than those adorning the port authority buildings, but when a French frigate arrived a couple of days later it was flying an ensign much larger than ours and apparently received no such demands. Another Kiwi yacht flying a flag the same size as ours had no trouble either. We took particular pride in our flag because, fearing consequences of 9/11 and the war in Afghanistan, few American boats flew flags. Some displayed Canadian flags instead of the Stars and Stripes.

This fear was one of several symptoms of paranoia evident as foreboding spread like a drop of diesel on the sea. At the time of the flag incident, Esmae had three bed sheets drying on a line on the bow. When she took them down, she found four holes, resembling bullet holes, in the fabric and worried that, during our absence from the yacht, the sheets may have been used for target practice. There seemed to be no other explanation.

While at the harbour, we learned that Brazilian pirates had murdered legendary New Zealand yachtsman Sir Peter Blake while his yacht *Seamaster* lay at anchor on the Amazon River. The news had a sobering effect on everyone. Here we were, in the most dangerous waters in the world, about to sail into an area notorious for terrorists and pirates. Sir Peter's death made us face up to our own mortality.

When we eventually departed from Port Raysut, we would re-enter the Arabian Sea and sail into the Gulf of Aden, a stretch of water only 220 kilometres wide in places, bordered by Yemen on one side and Somalia on the other. Somalia was in a state of anarchy that not even United States forces had been able to sort out. Shipping was warned to give it wide berth. Yemen was not much better. The country is Osama bin Laden's spiritual home, the place of his ancestors. It has strong links with his al Qaeda network and local tribesmen were believed to be harbouring terrorists on the run from Afghanistan. A couple of years before, as the USS *Cole* refuelled at Aden, al Qaeda blew a hole in her side, killing 17 crew.

A year before our arrival at Oman, pirates had attacked three yachts, *Mi Marra*, *Ocean Swan* and *Shady Lady*, as they sailed in company 16 kilometres off the Yemen coast. A machine gun had strafed *Ocean Swan*'s sails and rigging. The marauders removed everything of value: radios, GPS, depth sounder, tins of food, money, cameras and even a solar panel. The attack was not an isolated event. Since 1998, at least 13 incidents of piracy had been reported in the gulf. Terror was not confined to the sea. Over recent times, several Westerners had been kidnapped and held for ransom.

On the opposite shore, off Somalia, the International Maritime Bureau warned ships to keep at least 80 and preferably 160 kilometres from the coast. They urged that use of radios, particularly VHF, should be kept to a minimum. Ships unlucky enough to develop engine trouble after straying too close to Somalia were certain to be boarded by armed gangs.

Gunboats patrolling the area in search of terrorists emphasised the dangers lurking at sea. German and American warships, while unseen, were known to be in the waters. A British navy ship, packed with electronic surveillance equipment, had called at Port Raysut a few days before our arrival. The captain entertained yacht crews aboard his ship and discouraged them from entering Yemen. He recommended sailing directly to Eritrea, 2000 kilometres away.

Crews from two French yachts spent considerable time with officers from the warship flying their country's flag. Gossip was rife that, over several bottles of wine, they had elicited a promise that the frigate would shadow them when they sailed the Gulf of Aden. Everyone envied them. Even the warships themselves presented a threat. The United States Navy announced it was operating at a heightened state of readiness and taking additional defensive precautions against terrorists. Simply put, if we failed to identify ourselves when near an American warship, we risked being blown out of the water.

Fears of piracy and terrorism dominated lengthy discussions about the security of the route ahead. Before departing for the Gulf of Aden, crews turned the port's Oasis Bar, one of the few places licensed to sell alcohol, into a war room in which they discussed strategies for safely sailing their routes. Alcohol fuelling paranoia, they devised secret codes for contacting each other on radios when at sea. Co-ordinates on charts, where yachts would alter course or meet, were agreed. They were given coded references that would enable navigators to report their distance from waypoints without divulging exact locations.

Rather than risk sailing alone, most yachts set out in convoys. When listening to their radio conversations at sea, we learned that programmes agreed after a few drinks at the Oasis Bar became a source of resentment at sea. As yachts wrestled with wind and currents, and confidence increased, agreements about courses and speeds were broken. Some yachts, fearful of the night, hid in the dark by sailing without lights. Others sneaked out of Port Raysut under the cover of darkness, unlit, fearful that unfriendly eyes spied on them and would report their departure to pirates waiting at sea.

When it was our turn to leave, after enjoying a quantity of food and alcohol aboard *Celerity*, we agreed to sail with four other yachts: *Celerity*, *Yior Yia*, crewed by Con and Cheryl Rollas, *Stormvogen*, and *Nôtre Dame*, crewed by a British couple with two young children. We pledged to support each other, promising that we would sail or motor at no less than 4.5 knots, keep within a mile of each other at all times, help if a boat experienced mechanical difficulties and provide assistance if one of us was attacked.

When we departed Port Raysut, we had no idea where our next port might be. We were undecided whether to sail directly to Eritrea, or to break the voyage at Aden or Djibouti, both six days away. The reception received when yachts ahead reached these ports would determine our destination.

CHAPTER 13

GUNS IN THE GULF

Late in the afternoon of 28 February 2002, motoring in convoy with the other yachts, we sailed from Oman, the wealthiest country we would see until we reached the Mediterranean. Just on dusk, as we rounded the fairway buoy, the tin can with screws inside clattered impatiently, alerting us to fish hooked on lines we trawled on both sides of the boat. Justin caught four fish that evening and swore he must have already reached Mecca. We fell into a routine where he caught fish in the late afternoon and I caught them during my dawn watch, peculiarly, as regularly as clockwork between 0630 and 0700.

Wistfully, we tried to peer through a haze that shrouded Yemen's parched, imposing vermilion mountains whose dust filtered the sun's brilliance, making it an immense orange orb, which emitted spectacular colours as it sank into Rub al-Khali, the 'Empty Quarter' beyond the cliffs. There, for half the year, when the temperature reaches 50°C in the shade, if any can be found, it is too hot for even the most hardy to survive. Even the sons of Noah, the Bedouins, rarely venture into the centre of the world's most forbidding arid land during the hot summer months.

Not everything beyond the slanting slopes that tumbled towards the sea was inhospitable. The peaks concealed a vast land of contradictions: a forbidding wilderness roamed by poetical Bedouins, who are both masters and victims of the desert; a harsh land whose people the Prophet Mohammed described as possessing 'the kindest and gentlest hearts of all'; a hostile wasteland in which evil's dark shadow falls on ancient rocks that shelter al Qaeda's ruthless disciples; a desert studded with intriguing architecture, relics of another age; an ancient kingdom that some believe was ruled by the Queen of Sheba in the 10th century BC.

We kept well away from it all, but out at sea the desert's fragrance filled our nostrils. We sailed 90 kilometres off the Yemen coast, hoping we were far enough away from land to avoid trouble. To our left, we occasionally glimpsed the dark round hills of Somalia. Although 128 kilometres away, they looked too close for comfort. Despite the danger, we enjoyed the warmth and gentleness of the cruise. We dined on seared kingfish, marinated in Japanese sauces with soba noodles and stir-fried vegetables, washed down with a crisp sauvignon blanc.

We motored in convoy on glassy seas, *Yior Yia* leading, followed by *Celerity*, then us, *Nôtre Dame* and *Stormvogen* at the rear. Our companions' navigation lights reflected the promise of our pledges. Their glow was all that betrayed the remoteness of the night. Illuminated on our port and starboard sides, and stern, they kept our secrets, disclosing information only about the direction in which we travelled. They revealed nothing of our size or the type of boats determinedly holding a line behind one another. The mere fact of travelling like a string of beads in the darkness may have been a deterrent to anyone plotting trouble because they could not tell who we were or how many were aboard. We could have been yachts, smugglers, gunrunners or fishing boats. To a warship lurking unlit in the night, our slow progress across their radar could have been mistaken for an enemy flotilla belligerently heading towards a target.

Thwack! Thwack! Thwack! We rushed into the cockpit to identify the cause of the commotion shattering our tranquillity. A dark silhouette of a helicopter, a solitary red light flashing from its belly, hovered over *Nôtre Dame*. It strafed the sea with a spotlight before checking out the rest of us. Its crew ignored our attempts at radio contact. Satisfied we were not al Qaeda, it disappeared into the night. It was comforting to know that if summoned, help could reach us quickly.

When the north-east monsoon's wind arrived, we poled out and scudded along the Gulf, the breeze patting our stern at a constant 10 to 16 knots. We revelled in the sensations of speed and freedom, until the wind died and we switched on the motor again. By mid-afternoon, it had usually dropped away completely. Shortly before dusk on our second night out, we joined *Yior Yia*'s crew and swam in the crystal-clear indigo water while waiting for the other yachts to arrive. We could not believe we were bathing in the Gulf of Aden, which was so still it reflected our boats like a mirror. It was 300 metres deep and just the right temperature to refreshingly wash away perspiration from the 38°C heat. After enjoying sundowners, we barbecued fresh tuna kebabs for dinner before closing ranks to traverse the night.

We had entered the Gulf's most dangerous area, off Al Mukalla, a quaint fishing port sitting in an amphitheatre of cliffs crammed with ancient terraced houses, bleached as white as old bones, that rise from the shore on sea-hugging slopes. Its beauty masks sinister secrets: it was from here that pirates had set out to attack the yachts the previous season. We were keen to anchor off the town, but were deterred by its unsavoury reputation.

At dawn, we watched apprehensively as several buris, dugout canoes 6 metres long and powered by outboard motors, sped from Al Mukalla in the direction of Somalia. We alerted each other on our radios. Holding a good breeze, *Antares II* had strayed from the rhumb line during the night and was closer to shore than the others. We became a target for three buris, each with five men aboard, as they maintained a course towards us. Both *Nôtre Dame* and *Stormvogen* headed in our direction and, probably fearing the three of us were armed, the buris turned away. 'It was probably only a group of fishermen curious to see who we were,' Esmae suggested later, when thanking the two crews. 'However, I must admit it was unnerving and I'm glad you guys were there.'

Cheryl admitted to indulging in a novel form of security aboard *Yior Yia*. Each time a buri approached, she rushed below, changed her clothes and hat and strutted about the deck. When Con asked the reason for the fashion parade, Cheryl explained, 'I reckon if pirates think they see a different person walking round the decks, they'll figure there are more people than just us on board.'

The breeze set in for our passage along the second half of the Gulf. *Antares II* revelled in wind that, according to the anemometer, measured 14 knots as it came from behind and drove us at a steady 9 knots. Soon, we were far ahead of our companions. We reduced sail to harness her and to enable the others to catch us, but *Antares II* behaved like a disobedient child and ignored our commands. Even with the mainsail double reefed and the genoa partially furled, she stubbornly refused to travel at below 6 knots. The more we slowed, the more she misbehaved, rolling severely in a following sea whipped up by the wind. The motion became slightly uncomfortable, making us all restless, and Esmae complained of feeling nauseous. Because of our agreement before departing Oman, we were obliged to wallow in the building seas until the others caught up, three hours later.

We had sailed all the way from Malaysia to Oman on our own, our only contact with other yachts being via radio. Sailing in convoy with others involved compromises with speed and freedom we did not relish. However, we reflected on the incident with the buris and agreed the inconvenience may have been worth it.

The ports of Djibouti and Aden reflect rivalry that has existed between France and Great Britain over centuries. Djibouti, tucked into Africa between Ethiopia and Somalia, is a French naval base.

From here, since colonial times, France has watched over shipping from India, Africa and Suez. About 230 kilometres across the Gulf, Britain exercised the same influence from Aden. Our decision was whether to enter one of these harbours or continue on to Eritrea with *Celerity*, *Nôtre Dame* and *Stormvogen*.

Reports from yachts at Djibouti were discouraging. The port was dirty, expensive, swarming with beggars and desperate people who boarded boats to steal anything they could lay hands on. Despite the bombing of the USS *Cole* and its links with terrorists, Aden sounded the better of the two. *Yior Yia* also intended calling there.

Aden loomed in the dawn like an island adrift from the rest of Arabia, pummelled by tumbling seas. Sharp pinnacles, like crooked finials on a coronet, protruded from its rim. Buris, making their way to fishing grounds, struggled through a violent swell that flung their shallow hulls from the water. The occupants laughed and waved merrily, oblivious to the danger of their recklessness. Bleak, brooding mountains, created by extinct volcanoes and chiselled by the monsoon, towered ominously over our route to the port. No joy danced on the cliffs, not a tree, a flower, or a blade of grass. As we neared the harbour, we saw drab shale shacks clinging like barnacles to the steep mountainsides, up which residents climbed to reach their prime real estate: there was no road, only tracks.

The towering mountains made the approach to Aden imposing, fitting for a port that has, several times in its chequered history, ranked among the world's finest. Now, though, it is in a state of decay, which became obvious as we sailed past rusting hulks of wrecks as sad as stranded whales. We picked our way around the derelicts, following a channel where, in an era long gone, tugs had towed the great Cunard, P&O and Chandris liners, which had called at Aden to bunker. We anchored off the Prince of Wales Pier which, belying its regal name, was a hotchpotch of ramshackle historic buildings and an uncompleted new terminal. A clock-tower on a hill above the pier stood like a bookmark at a page in history. A bomb had smashed through the clock face after the first shots of civil war in 1994. Scars from bullets and shrapnel disfigured surrounding buildings. Below, from a mosque, a muezzin's discordant nasal voice, a sound we always found exotically welcoming, summoned the faithful to prayer.

Immediately we stepped ashore from our dinghy, a pint-sized man with slack jowls stopped us. 'My name is Mohammed,' he announced, inevitably. 'I am a boat man. You need anything, I can get. Anything. I tell you best restaurants, get fuel, arrange tours.'

From a yellow plastic carry bag bearing a logo for Kodak film, Mohammed produced a large scrapbook and proudly turned pages of testimonials written by yachtsmen who had preceded us. They commended him as an agent who could perform miracles ranging from assisting a stranger through Yemen's intricate bureaucracy and tangled commercial structure, to finding a bargain at a market.

'I been doing it for 50 years and make many many good friends,' he confided, his sad eyes pleading to be employed. 'Come, we go to immigration and customs. You have gift, maybe? Cigarettes or money? It will help.'

The immigration official was not satisfied with cigarettes. He pointed at Esmae's T-shirt, adorned with our ship's logo, and demanded she return with two, 'one for me and one for my friend, who is asleep in the back'.

Allowing Mohammed to assist us through arrival formalities evidently established an inseparable bond between us because we could not get rid of him. Despite being only about 1.5 metres tall, he had the tenacity of a bulldog and pounced on us every time we alighted from our dinghy. No fee for his services was mentioned but we felt he viewed us as walking dollars that would eventually fall into his hands. Zealously, he ensured none of his competitors had an opportunity to feast upon his prey.

Each time we left the port, we had to pass a slovenly uniformed man sitting on a bench outside a little neo-Gothic building. An automatic assault rifle rested on his lap. Yemenis, like Omanis, who wander everywhere toting guns, consider weapons to be an extension of themselves. There are 60 million guns, mainly Kalashnikovs, in Yemen, a country of 20 million people. Arms markets sell grenades for as little as $20. It is little wonder Yemenis often take the law into their own hands.

As we were about to venture into the world beyond the sentry, Mohammed looked up at us through rheumy eyes, pointed beyond the gate and whispered conspiratorially, 'When you go out, don't talk to anyone. Don't go with anyone. It is danger.' His warning was probably designed to discourage us from befriending any of the scores of touts wandering around Aden, but his advice did little to allay our fears and we approached the town with trepidation. Aden is a gateway to the country from which Osama bin Laden's family originates; villagers openly admired the terrorist leader and America claimed many Yemenis sheltered his men. On occasion, Yemeni armed tribesmen have abducted foreigners as hostages until the Yemen government builds a new school, a hospital or some other urgently needed amenity. There had been about 100 kidnappings since 1991: 16 Western tourists were kidnapped in 1998 and four of them were killed. In December 2001, the US State Department had authorised the voluntary departure of non-emergency personnel and the families of all embassy staff. A travel alert urged visitors to maintain a high level of vigilance. Like *Celerity*, most American yachts avoided the port.

Con had not wanted to miss Aden. He had called there as a child when his family emigrated from Greece to Australia in the 1950s. Nostalgia drew him to Aden, a stop on a pilgrimage of gratitude for his parents' courage and vision in seeking a land of better opportunities. Returning in *Yior Yia*, which is Greek for Georgia, Con's mother's name, reflected the family's triumph. But when we ventured outside the perimeter of the port, Con could not believe the extent of Aden's deterioration. He remembered streets teeming with excited tourists from passenger liners, spending money at emporiums stocked with postcards, silks, jewels, gold, tobacco, alcohol and gadgets. Then, Aden was the greatest port in the world, after New York. Now, shunned by travellers, it is barren, neglected and filthy. Stores in which tight-fisted European migrants had once haggled with voluble Arab and Jewish merchants were boarded up, their façades covered in grime. Faded names of their glory days, as indistinct as distant dreams, still adorned some buildings.

Many dynasties have contributed to Aden's mercantile history. The beginnings of its trade are a mystery, but it is possible early man came from Africa to barter shells and animal trophies. Medieval merchants from India, Egypt and Ethiopia traded there and, in the 15th century, China's Grand Eunuch, Zheng He, called at Aden. Because of its strategic position, many of Europe's powers coveted it. After the discovery of the Cape route to India, it was fought over by Portuguese, Dutch and French. The British took Aden in 1836 as a coaling station for the new steamships on the Suez–Bombay run.

We strolled along uneven narrow roads beneath double-storey warehouses, whose top floors contained spacious rundown living quarters in which curious women and their shy daughters peeked from shadows behind lattice screens. Apart from housework, there was little else for them to do, except for watching television, the source of most of their information. Those fortunate to work outside their homes cannot be employed between 6 p.m. and 6 a.m.

Islam is Yemen's national religion and the source of all legislation. Accordingly, women must hide their bodies, including face and hands, from men's eyes. It is a personal preference as to whether they wear a full black cloak or a coloured one. Parents arrange marriages from which men are able to divorce for any reason. It is much more difficult for women to escape from a husband. But attitudes appeared much more relaxed than in Oman. We saw several women on the streets, often dressed in gay cloaks and not wearing headscarves, let alone veils. Youths in rusty old cars pestered young girls in school uniforms consisting of headscarves and long dresses. The students grimly avoided the boys' eyes.

The extent of Aden's filth, which rolled along unpaved streets like tumbleweed, overwhelmed us. Mountains of refuse were concealed behind fences that obscured vacant lots; elsewhere, it piled high at street corners. Roaming goats climbed atop the garbage heaps and grazed randomly while, oblivious to the squalor, gangs of noisy children played among it. They surrounded us with warm smiles and snotty noses, some extending grubby cupped hands. 'Hello, Mister Man, welcome to Yemen. Where are you from?'

Aden's refuse problem appears to have existed for centuries. In the 1890s, the British uncovered a cluster of ancient reservoirs at nearby Crater, Aden's original settlement. (As its name indicates, the town is built on the crater of an extinct volcano.) Although the rock tanks are believed to date beyond the beginning of Islam, few people, until the British found them, knew of their existence: they had been hidden beneath a deluge of garbage. Now cleared, it is estimated the cisterns could hold 20 million tonnes of water.

The contrasts between our first Arab port and Aden were stark. Oman had been orderly and clean; Aden was chaotic and filthy. People appeared to have lost their spirit. We wondered whether it had anything to do with the gentle narcotic, qat, that most Yemenis chew in the afternoons.

Daily social life in Yemen revolves around afternoon qat parties that last about three or four hours. In anticipation of the events, most houses have a room, scattered with cushions or mattresses, which is set aside exclusively for such occasions. Any man can attend. He has only to arrive with a bundle of leaves, purchased from the local market, from the smooth-barked qat tree. Lounging on mattresses, participants chew the leaves, occasionally rinsing their mouths with water and spitting the contents into containers on the floor.

Many Yemeni men, like Mohammed our boatman, have slack jowls from chewing and storing the leaves in their cheeks: a bulging cheek full of qat is a difficult technique to master and is considered worthy of admiration. The leaves produce mood swings and intense conversation but little action, exhausting men's talents and sapping their vitality.

In a country with few telephones and poor communications, qat parties are vital for disseminating and digesting news. When rumours abound about an important event, men rush to qat parties to confirm the truth and discuss implications. The occasions are also forums for political activity. Politicians, lawyers and bureaucrats listen to grievances and deliver judgments at such events.

Although a majority of Yemeni men, and an increasing number of women who attend segregated parties, accept qat as an essential ingredient of life, a minority are concerned about its sociological and economic implications. Much of Yemen's scarce productive land has been converted to qat cultivation, which is more lucrative than coffee and other export crops. The attempts of former prime minister Muhsin al-Aini to end the practice were vigorously opposed and led to his being ousted from office. In Saudi Arabia, qat is considered so socially and economically debilitating that penalties for chewing it are more severe than those for drinking alcohol.

When refuelling *Antares II* with diesel in the middle of an afternoon, I expressed surprise the service was available, because I had expected everyone to be at a qat party. The office worker responded, 'Qat is very bad. It is ruining my country.'

The first person we encountered on qat was a moneychanger. His left cheek bulged grotesquely and he chewed and dribbled while serving us with the lethargy of somebody under the influence of a narcotic. We thought he was stoned on marijuana.

'What are you eating?' I could not contain my curiosity.

'Qat,' he admitted, the bulge in his mouth hindering an attempted smile. 'It is very good. All men have qat.' He thrust his arm in the international sign for virility. 'Here, you try,' he offered, producing three crisp green leaves from under the counter.

The leaves tasted bitter, gritty and unpalatable: qat would be an acquired taste.

'How much do you chew a day?' I asked.

'A lot,' he conceded, obviously unwilling to be drawn on the subject.

'Is it expensive?'

'It cost me about $60 a day,' he revealed.

Surveys show that people spend up to 40 per cent of their income on qat, a sum few can afford, judging by the amount of poverty in Yemen.

Aden's bleak landscape also hides an interesting biblical history. Cain, the son of Adam, is said to have worshipped fire here and it is claimed his brother Abel is buried on Jabel Hadid, the extinct volcano's highest peak. The Prophet Mohammed had special words for Aden: it would provide a sign of the approach of Doomsday when fire with molten lava devours everything in its path. The prophecy has not deterred thousands of people cramming into ramshackle dwellings on the extinct volcano's crater.

The warmth and generosity of the people of Aden was humbling and more than compensated for the squalor of their surroundings. We never felt threatened as we roamed the streets and the only reference to terrorism was on a shop window proclaiming: 'Terrorism Is Pariah'. When drawn on the subject of bin Laden and terrorism, Yemenis denounced the violence which, they said, was not the way of Islam. To a man, however, they condemned the United States for supporting Israel at the expense of Palestinians.

One morning, I enjoyed a conversation in the moneychanger's shop with the qat-chewer's father, who revealed he had taken over the business from his former employer, a Jew who had migrated to Israel. They still corresponded, even though the old man berated Israel for its treatment of Palestinians. An old beggar, leaning on a staff, shuffled into the store. Without either hesitation or ceremony, the trader pulled a note from his moneybox and handed it to the pauper who, before sauntering away, muffled incantations about Allah.

'Why did you do that?' I asked.

'Gift from Allah,' he explained simply.

'You do it every day?'

'Every day.'

Same man?'

'No, no, different people.'

Islam expects Muslims to contribute up to 15 per cent of their income to the poor. In challenge to the prejudices of many Westerners, the spirituality of the people we met in Muslim countries constantly impressed us.

So many beggars roamed the streets it was impossible to satisfy the pleas of them all. After experiencing the poverty of Indonesia, Thailand, India and Sri Lanka, we thought we would be immune to their rags, their doleful pleading eyes and outstretched hands, but we never got used to them, particularly the children. They made us feel guilty about our own good fortune and, shamefully, we found it difficult to react well to them.

I fear I offended one poor man in a restaurant where I enjoyed a wonderful chicken lunch. The man, his clothes soiled like those of a labourer on a building site, arrived and sat opposite us when we were halfway through our meal. His face was troubled and he stared at us as we tucked into succulent chicken and pita bread baked in fiery ovens. I took his interest in us as a sign that he wanted to communicate. Several times, I smiled and gave him the thumbs up, a crude attempt to breach the language barrier with signs that indicated how much I enjoyed the food. He diverted his eyes, dipped bread into a bowl of liquid and returned to gaze in our direction. His staring was annoying. I could not identify the look in his eyes.

Only as we left our table did the reality of the situation dawn when I discovered that he was dipping dry bread into a bowl of water. He was too poor to buy anything better. Ashamed, I realised how, through ignorance and insensitivity, I had taunted him. I suggested to my companions that I should return and buy him a proper meal or give him money, but they considered the damage was done and such an approach might only result in further humiliation for both of us.

My shame intensified that evening when I dined with other sailors at a primitive dirty restaurant crowded with noisy men. (Women from yachts were the only females we ever saw eating out.) Waiters, young men in soiled shirts and trousers, fussed over us, relieving us of fresh fish and crabs we had bought off a dusty track outside that, at night, was converted into a wet market. They ushered us to rickety long benches where we squeezed in beside men in turbans and white robes. Diners immediately engaged us in conversation and insisted we share their food while we waited for our own. They expected nothing in return.

'Do you work?' I enquired of a bearded man after he insisted I share his spicy crab.

'I am welder,' he announced proudly.

After talking about his trade, I ventured, 'Are you married?'

'Have two wives, three childrens.'

'Two wives, too many,' I joked, 'give you stereophonic nagging.'

He glanced at me quizzically and explained, punching the air with his fist for emphasis, 'No problem. I beat them. They give no trouble.'

Bemused that I had not identified such a simple solution, he muttered something in Arabic to his companions who smiled and nodded knowingly. We had gained an impression from conversations with other men that brutality is accepted as part of a woman's lot in life.

The waiters returned and placed newspaper over the table on which they slammed steaming pita breads, seared whole fish with flesh charcoaled in flaming ovens, whole crabs drowned in red chilli sauce, plates of rice and tin bowls of condiments. There was no cutlery. With eight other cruisers, we ripped into the food with our hands, enjoying a feast that we talked about for days.

I motioned the welder to share our food. He declined with a shake of his head and announced, 'I go to my wives and childrens.'

CHAPTER 14

THE PRICE OF WAR

The barograph plummeted six points the day we departed Aden for the Red Sea, a sudden drop that elsewhere would be a harbinger of bad weather. In other ports, after such a plunge, we would have stayed at the anchorage until the mercury settled, but this time we regarded it as a good omen. Sailors who had preceded us suggested a falling barometer foretold of weather suitable for sailing the waterway, which is one of the world's most challenging.

Predicting climate in the Red Sea is unlike anywhere else we have sailed. Forecasts are scarce and usually inaccurate. Forces in the Mediterranean, more than 2400 kilometres away, determine Red Sea weather. Erratic winds blow through the region as if in a funnel, bordered by East Africa on one side and Arabia on the other. Without warning, within minutes, a gentle breeze becomes a gale that whips a mellow sea into a fury. The wind drops just as suddenly. Without notice, it can change direction and blow so strongly it builds the sea into steep square waves that stall a boat, making headway impossible. Sometimes, yachts hide inside a marsa, a bay that is like a reef, for days, even weeks, before conditions improve enough for them to move on again.

211

We sailed in the company of *Yior Yia*. A New Zealand yacht, *Cariad*, was due to depart with us but the skipper, Wattie Goodwood, changed his mind at the last minute. We set sail at 1400 hours, on 9 March 2002, a time precisely calculated to enable us to enter the neck of the funnel, the Straits of Bab el Mandeb (alarmingly translated as the Gates of Sorrow), at slack tide the next morning. Although we had confidence in the advice of sailors experienced in the region, we admitted to niggling doubts. The falling barometer added to our apprehension.

We were heartened that *Celerity* and *Nôtre Dame* had reported an enjoyable, trouble-free passage and we hoped to be as fortunate. Originally, we had intended making only day hops most of the way to Massawa, Eritrea, 700 kilometres away. Because of rumours about dangers at some anchorages, I had trudged from the port to ask the harbourmaster at Aden about havens where we might stop. He was horrified at the suggestion and encouraged us not to break our voyage, warning that we could be boarded.

With a 10-knot breeze across our stern, we poled out and sailed at a comfortable six knots. It was good to be back at sea. Through the night we saw, far away on our port side, lights of ships that had come from Europe, through the Suez Canal and into the Red Sea to the Gulf of Aden, in which we still sailed. We glided in the dark with our sails stretched out on opposite sides, embracing the monsoon's warm breath that caressed us more gently than we had dared to dream. We hoped it would remain benevolent, as a navigation light on Perim Island indicated we were approaching the Small Strait, one of two entrances into the neck of the funnel through which winds and sea could howl. We chose to keep away from shipping lanes that, we were surprised to discover later, were not as busy as we had expected. Our pilot book suggested the Small Strait should be used only in an emergency and it recommended keeping a wide berth of the island, which is a restricted military base. An alternative route was through the Large Strait, to the left of Perim Island, which contained busy shipping lanes.

Our entrance into the Red Sea was spectacular. A brilliant dawn splashed Yemen. The sky filled with pink, orange and gold, which lifted our spirits and wiped away any need for sorrows as we sailed through Bab el Mandeb in perfect weather.

We were too early for slack tide. A 3-knot current propelled us forward as the Indian Ocean squeezed through the narrow neck that joins the Gulf of Aden to the Red Sea. Only 46 kilometres wide, it is a constricted space for the ocean's ebb and flow to funnel as it replenishes and fertilises a trench 2300 kilometres long, 350 kilometres at its widest point, and an average depth of only 490 metres. The current swept us past Perim Island's lofty cliffs and the dwellings from which soldiers spied on us. It swept us into the Red Sea with fish, turtles and plankton that, like us, rode the great ocean.

A dozen buris darted about the Small Strait, trawling to catch fish grazing on the tide. The can on our starboard side clattered. It had announced a fish so big that by the time I reached the line it had gone limp because the catch had snapped the thick wire trace.

Suddenly, we stopped. Our sails hung limp, without a breeze. We could not believe we had lost our wind in this treacherous strait whose name alone is enough to conjure fear in sailors' minds. We dropped our sails, motored across the shipping lanes towards Eritrea's shores, and set a course toward Massawa. We congratulated ourselves that we were through the worst of it.

Leaving on a falling barometer was definitely the right decision. *Cariad* left 24 hours later and was hammered as she entered Bab el Mandeb. A few days later, the crew of a German registered catamaran, *Bohey*, was evacuated after losing a mast in a 50-knot gale north of the notorious straits. A German naval ship patrolling the waters for terrorists answered their call for help and lifted them off their boat by helicopter.

Eritrea is one of the world's poorest countries: the average annual income is only US$170. For decades it has been dogged by drought, famine and war. The hardships are reflected in the life expectancy: men only 49 years and women 52 years. We were mystified that Eritrea's people should starve when it was apparent the Red Sea contains an abundance of food. We caught so many fish we could not justify continuing with our sport. Surprisingly, no fishing boats appeared; our two yachts were the only craft riding the currents.

However, there were plenty of birds. Some 3000 million migrate across Arabia twice a year, and thousands use the Red Sea as a corridor to avoid Arabia's arid hinterland. Huge flocks stalked the sea. As they swooped above the flashing bodies of schools of little fish being forced to the surface by larger predators, the birds glided so gracefully a music score could have been set to their motion. Masses of them dived in feeding frenzies, trying to pilfer a meal before it was devoured by schools of tuna, wahoo and other predators that leapt from a war zone seething with excitement.

Our passage to Eritrea was wonderful. We sailed all the way wing and wing on winds of 12–28 knots, not stopping until we reached Shumma, which protrudes above the sea from behind a reef about 50 kilometres from Massawa. It was a fitting stop for our first Red Sea anchorage. We revived ourselves by swimming over the reef and barbecuing whole fish for dinner. While exploring the small island, which has been abandoned to wild camels and goats, we stubbed our toes on military relics, mementoes from the Second World War. Then, Mussolini had controlled Eritrea, which he characterised as the heart of the new empire.

Wars have constantly plagued Eritrea. Three decades of fighting for independence, which was attained in 1993, claimed 150,000 lives, a further 100,000 people were disabled or orphaned and about a quarter of the population fled the country. Eritrea's economy and infrastructure were destroyed. On entering the port of Massawa, once the largest and safest harbour on Africa's east coast, we saw why Eritreans could not feed themselves from the sea. Dozens of boats, their backs broken during the siege of Massawa, littered the harbour's shores like shoals of rotting fish.

War's horrific price is evident throughout the port, around which is built an intriguing Moorish town. Its dusty alleys conceal charming double-storey buildings with carved wooden doors, shutters and balconies – trophies left behind by Turks, Egyptians and Italians who occupied Massawa during their lust for Africa. Strolling the alleys at night, we found locals sleeping outside their houses on litters, the only way to escape the oppressive heat.

Whitewashed palaces that once embodied the might of Italy and the Emperor Haile Selassie are crumbling ruins. Bombs and mortars have disfigured the broad domes and tall archways and parapets that symbolised their glory and power. The Red Sea Hotel, once the venue for grand colonial balls and jolly parties, is a sorry sight, also a victim of war's remorseless hangover. Weary men and women sat in the shade at the port's railway station, obviously aware no train would arrive because, further up the line, many kilometres of track had disappeared. During the struggle for independence, freedom fighters ripped up the rails to use as girders for fortifying bunkers.

The Eritreans are still distrustful. Jittery armed guards check passes of those entering the port. Posters portraying the bravery of Eritrea's freedom fighters adorn the walls of government offices. One poster depicted a tall warrior with an Afro hairstyle and a man's muscles on a woman's ebony body. She was poised to hurl a hand grenade. Her eyes were wild, her lips sneered defiance and her teeth were clenched in determination. A corpse lay at her feet. The caption read: 'Eritrea 1961–1989. Quarter of a Century of Armed Struggle for Liberation, Democracy, Peace and Progress.'

Women played a major part in Eritrea's struggle. Today, their beautiful young daughters have a struggle of their own as they wrestle with making a living. The only way many survive is by becoming 'business girls' who sell their exquisitely groomed bodies to sailors in the port's bars, restaurants and disco. There is little other opportunity for work.

Eritrea is a backpackers' paradise awaiting discovery. Prices for meals and accommodation were cheaper than in Asia. Massawa, the main port on the country's 1200-kilometre coastline, is a gateway to some of the 354 islands that bejewel the Red Sea. We felt fortunate to call there before the rest of the world discovers it.

Restaurants provide ethnic and Italian fare. Our favourite was in an empty car park on which, after dark, tables were set. Music of our generation boomed from outdoor speakers and there was a fine selection of delicious seafood at very reasonable prices. The speciality was succulent tiger prawns. We were not impressed with ethnic spongy sour bread that looked like a soggy bath mat, and smelled and tasted just as bad. We ripped it apart and dipped handfuls into spicy purée of chickpeas and other vegetables, but the spices did not conceal the bread's unpalatable texture or flavour. The restaurant was owned by a short, plump young man with a warm smile who was said to have stowed away on a ship to Britain as a teenager, worked diligently and saved his money until he could return to Massawa to open his own establishment.

Even though we enjoyed the food, it was still Third World and not to everyone's liking. An Australian schoolteacher embarrassed us when he loudly complained to the owner about the state of the toilets, which were filthy, the speed of service, which was slow, and the amount of oil in the French fries, which were soggy.

'You'll never survive if you don't learn to go with the flow,' I suggested after his rude outburst.

'I don't care,' he responded, 'I expect better service when I pay for something.'

'But look how little you're paying,' I reminded him. 'You're not paying enough to expect good service.'

'It's not just the service. The food was bloody awful anyway and the beer was warm. If they're providing a service, they should provide *good* service.'

'What do you expect if you go for French fries and burgers? They don't know how to cook that crap. Eat what they eat, it's much better.'

The teacher earnestly proclaimed his ambition to rectify short-comings in the developing countries he visited. It was an impossible goal over which he became so agitated that we feared a heart attack. His attitude embarrassed the rest of us. We assured the restaurateur, who was intimidated by the Australian's outburst, how much we enjoyed his food.

Before leaving Eritrea, we trekked to the capital, Asmara, 2500 metres above sea level, where the temperature was a delightful 26°C, which seemed pleasantly cool after the oppressive heat at sea level. The Js had made the five-hour bus journey a couple of days before us. Their trip was a revelation. People suffering motion sickness vomited, goats accompanying passengers gave off a rank smell and a man sitting next to them occupied a window seat that Justin had booked. As Justin contemplated suggesting the passenger should move, the man rose and removed a belt from around his waist. Two hand grenades hung from it. Justin chose not to quibble.

The overladen bus struggled around steep, narrow hairpin bends on mountains with open sides that plunged to valley floors 250 metres below. People have roamed these mountains since arriving from Egypt's Nile Valley 5000 years ago. Once green and fertile, the slopes and valleys are now an arid lunar landscape through which dry riverbeds meander.

Italy's influence has lasted much longer than its occupation. Refined old gentlemen, retired freedom fighters, promenaded along Asmara's main boulevard, Liberty Avenue, resplendent in Italian suits and cocked hats. Others lounged under umbrellas at bars, sidewalk cafés and patisseries. As they spied on beautiful people passing by, they sipped wine and coffee and ate delicate pastries filled with custard and cream.

Cariad arrived in port after we returned from touring. She had battled high winds and heavy seas that forced her to shelter off islands for several days. A 50-knot sandstorm had covered the yacht with grit. *Cariad* had taken double our time to reach Massawa. We reflected on the difference a day could make when at sea.

We were about to leave Massawa when the unexpected happened: it rained for the first time since we had sailed from the Maldives. It was little more than a mist that settled over the boat and sent wrinkles of red mud meandering down the decks as water mingled with the desert dust coating the yacht. The dirt got into everything and covered *Antares II* from the top of the mast to the bottom of the bilges. Washing it off proved futile because water only changed its colour and highlighted its presence. We resigned ourselves to living this way until we reached the Mediterranean where we hoped to find a jetty with a high-pressure hose.

Although a sand cloud had shrouded the coast most of the way from Oman, our first real encounter with dust had not occurred until we arrived at Massawa. As soon as we tied alongside the frontier town's wharf a spiralling breeze carried a cloud of thick dust towards us, coating everything in its path. Ashore, trucks unloading ships sprayed grime over us as we walked to present our passports to immigration. The streets in the town were coated in dirt and the slightest breeze flung it in our mouths and eyes.

Strong wind followed the drizzle and locked a fleet of 12 departing boats in the harbour for three days. We consoled ourselves that it was better to wait out the gales inside the port. The winds dropped on the evening of Thursday, 21 March. Despite our impatience to set sail, all the yachts resisted the temptation to lift their anchors the following day because it is deemed bad luck to leave port on a Friday. Most sailors respect the superstition. At 6 a.m. on Saturday, 23 March, we motored to the wharf opposite the immigration office. Officials clamoured over the yacht, opening cupboards and inspecting the engine room in search of refugees.

We left Eritrea believing that, if it is sensibly governed and the flames of war do not rekindle, the country has good prospects, particularly with tourism. But it faces many challenges. Although its people are industrious, it has lost many of its best to other nations. The war appears to have robbed Eritrea of its intelligentsia. Sadly, we found no literature, no art, no written record of its history.

CHAPTER 15

GHOSTS OF SUAKIN

Dolphins tumbled like quicksilver in water that looked as clear and pure as the air we breathed. Only a bouquet of bubbles cascading from the waterline below *Antares*'s bow told of the barrier that separated sea from sky. Never had we seen dolphins like this. They hung beside us as vivid as dirigibles suspended in the indigo of space.

Previously, dolphins had courted us in oceans rich with nutrients that clouded the sea and hampered our vision, allowing only a partial glimpse of their frolicking near the surface. Here, the Red Sea's deserts keep the sea clear. There are few rivers to transport silt and few cities to spew pollutants into the waterway. In these pristine waters, we were mesmerised by every detail of their silky, agile bodies as they rolled and zigzagged around us, leading us toward Sudan's ancient port of Suakin, halfway up the Red Sea.

This was not the first time we had marvelled at the clarity of the water here. Only a few hours, before we had sailed from Talla Talla Saghir, one of 30 islands that comprise the Suakin archipelago, where we had anchored for a couple of nights. There, the water was clearer than anything in which we had previously swum. Like many of the islands and hideaways in the Red Sea, Talla Talla Saghir is little more than a lonely sand dune protruding a few metres above the ocean. It is just high enough to protect yachts and fishing boats from vicious northerly gales.

Exploring the island was reminiscent of a bizarre scene from *Alice in Wonderland*. It is a topsy-turvy place, a reef that has been thrust above the ocean. Although strolling on land, we actually trod upon a brittle ancient seabed, wandering over a tangle of dead corals and fossils, long worms and shells that have interwoven to form the featureless mound. It is barren, except for an occasional hardy shrub and clumps of spiky grass that cling like porcupines to pockets of sand trapped in clusters in a coral graveyard.

This desolate and isolated place provides a safe breeding ground for hundreds of hawksbill turtles. For centuries, they have returned to the island to lumber from the water at a secluded sandy corner and dig nests in which they deposit dozens of eggs. The shell housing the hawksbill is so beautiful that ancient civilisations prized it. Cleopatra's throne was decorated with scutes that may have been gathered in the Suakin archipelago.

A spectacular fringing reef surrounds the island's shores before its cliffs plunge deep into the sea. Here, hidden beneath a watery veil, lies unique beauty, an exotic and dramatic garden teeming with friendly fish. We imagined ourselves inside an aquatic amphitheatre watching a spectacular performance. Blue fan corals, as large as tables, shaded enormous clams. Tentacles on colonies of delicate anemones swayed gently in the current. Troupes of fish paraded around vibrant corals – red jewel fish, intimidating barracuda, damselfish, butterfly fish and emperor angel fish, to mention only a few.

More than 1600 kilometres of coral reefs, a stark contrast to the drabness of the deserts, adorn the Red Sea, but few are more magnificent than those off Suakin. One of the best underwater sites in the world, it is full of surprises. In shallows graze dugongs, shy hippopotami of the sea, which are verging on extinction. Over a dozen species of shark maintain a patrol. Shadows fall over colourful coral as manta rays glide by. Parrotfish peck at algae that would otherwise suffocate a reef. Scraping coral is not their only interesting attribute. Like damselfish, gropers and wrasses, a dominant parrotfish miraculously transforms from a female to a male when the shoal's existing male disappears.

Once a major trading centre, Suakin is now a forlorn little port. As we entered the harbour, we received a mixed reception. Heavy artillery at the entrance pointed ominously towards us, and through binoculars we watched a soldier spying on us through a telescope. Our fears were allayed by dozens of white-robed Sudanese who waved and shouted greetings from a bank on the opposite side, a promise of the continuing hospitality we had enjoyed throughout our voyage. We passed a pier alongside which a small passenger liner took on pilgrims on their way to Mecca.

Then before us stood the sight we had come to see: the skeleton of a crumbling ghost town built by the blistered hands of slaves of the Egyptian and Ottoman empires. They created a place as beautiful as Venice with coral gathered from surrounding reefs. Now, teetering on an island shaped like a giant lily pad floating on a blue pond, rimmed by the desert's white stands, the town's bleached buildings lay in ruins. Quays to which sailing ships had tied had rotted away long ago. Wealthy merchants had loaded the vessels with cargoes of spices, ivory, turtle shell, gold, cotton, ceramics – and slaves.

For centuries Suakin was pivotal to Sudan's slave trade. From this East African port, wretched men and women were sold to masters in Cairo, Medina, Constantinople and antiquity's other great capitals. Shamefully, the trade still existed at the end of the 20th century when victims of a bloody civil war, which had ripped the country apart for two decades, were sold into servitude.

The decaying town is only one of many tombstones of a harbour whose history dates beyond the 10th century BC when Pharaoh Rameses III used it as a trading port. Since the rise of Islam, it has often been a haven for warring Muslims. Over millennia Ancient

Egyptians, the Ptolemies, Greeks, Romans, Arabs, Turks and Portuguese have sacked it. Winston Churchill served there as a young lieutenant with the 4th Hussars when the British Expeditionary Force used Suakin as headquarters in a battle against troops led by the slave trader Osman Digna in the late 19th century. This was the first war in which white colonials went to the aid of the Mother Country. The government of New South Wales sent an infantry battalion and an artillery battery, some of whom had previously fought in the New Zealand Wars.

With Justin on the bow spotting coral heads that could rip a hole in our side, we gingerly navigated a tight passage past Suakin's ruins. After we passed the rubble of once grand houses, the ancient customs building, the old Eastern Telegraph building and the columns of the once imposing Egyptian National Bank, we entered a crescent-shaped lagoon in which only one other yacht lay at anchor.

'Well, it's good to see you. Have you spoken to the port authority?' Jean Nicca, skipper of the Californian yacht *Peregrine*, asked on the radio.

'Yes,' Esmae responded. 'They told us not to leave the boat before an agent arrives to clear us in.'

'Oh yeah? They told me that 24 goddamn hours ago and I've still seen no one. I keep calling them on the radio to find out what's going on, but they don't answer. They just don't give a damn.'

Jean made several disparaging remarks about Sudanese efficiency. Fearing the bureaucrats would take offence if they overheard, we suggested that since our boats were anchored within shouting distance of each other, we should continue the conversation across the water.

A few hours later, another American boat, *Otter*, crewed single-handed by Connecticut sailor Breccon (Brec) Morgan, arrived. Shortly, an agent, yet another Mohammed, radioed and requested a ride to our yachts because he was without a boat of his own. He apologised for the delay and turned out to be a wonderful guide. Waiting for a gale that raged outside the port to abate, we stayed at Suakin for five days. During this time, we were the only yachts in the harbour.

Mohammed told us that 40 yachts had called at Suakin the previous season. Three years before that, 150 boats had visited. The three of us anchored in the bay made the total for 2002 only six and there were not too many vessels behind us. Government travel alerts warning citizens not to visit Sudan had kept most sailors away from a port that became a highlight of our voyage. A fear of terrorism was not the sole reason for the boycott. The Sudanese government had added to the port's unpopularity by increasing harbour charges. Crews on tight budgets decided they could not afford the US$120 the government demanded from yachts calling there.

Conditions on the mainland, at El Geyf, were almost as primitive and squalid as those on the island. The town was a slum, its buildings little better than sheep pens and stockyards. Much of the village was constructed from coral, some of it pilfered from the island's rubble, and any other materials its inhabitants could get their hands on. Some walls and fences were made of rusting 40-gallon drums, emptied of oil and pesticides, and cut and beaten flat. Wooden structures, their planks uneven and rotten, tilted precariously. Chasms of decay gaped from houses of crumbling coral. The streets, full of donkeys and camels, were unpaved and ankle-deep in dust.

A steady procession of Bedouins rode camels into town and tethered them in a square behind ramshackle buildings. While awaiting their burdens, the camels crouched on the ground among rubble, coughed, spat, farted and ate from sacks tied around their necks. Once, colourful caravans of up to 1000 camels had departed from here for the Sudanese interior with cargoes of sugar, soap, candles, rice, spices and incense.

Donkeys were the main form of transport within the town. They carried people, milk, fuel, water, wood, large trays of pita bread and all manner of vegetables. Wandering these alleys, we had to remain vigilant to avoid the donkey carts, whose drivers would have knocked us down if we inadvertently strolled in front of them. Goats scratched their necks on the sides of stone buildings and roamed the streets, picking at whatever they could find. The number of animals meant we had to be careful where we trod.

Generators provide the town's electricity, and cooking was done on charcoal. The sweet fragrance of incense, which is used to ward off swarms of flies, pervaded the air, pleasantly filling our nostrils with an aroma of unexpected freshness amid the squalor. There was neither sanitation nor flowing water. The market sold an abundance of fresh fruit and vegetables, along with sheep and goat meat on which swarms of flies feasted. We had to arrive early to buy bread before flies settled on it too.

Sadly, the people were among the poorest we had met. Every child thrust a hand toward us and begged for money. The adults were subtler and their needs were different. A toothless old man blocked our way, dribbled, grunted and pointed to his one-lensed spectacles, asking whether we could give him a new set. A man with grotesquely swollen legs pointed at them while his friend enquired in faltering English whether we had any medicine that could cure his elephantiasis. Every Sudanese male appeared to carry a dagger under his robe and many wore swords. Men, too proud to beg, ripped their weapons from their girths and offered to sell them to us.

Bedouin women thrust beads and needlework before us. A colourful sequined veil covered the face of a woman with whom Esmae negotiated the purchase of a piece of intricate African beadwork. Language was not a barrier as the woman spoke with her eyes. They hardened when she talked price, danced when she talked quality, softened and shared women's secrets when she was friendly.

About 40 people gathered as the two women negotiated. Suddenly, three trucks of police arrived and, using loud hailers and whistles, dispersed the spectators.

'They weren't doing any harm, we weren't in any danger,' Esmae explained to a policeman holding an automatic rifle. 'I was only trying to buy something from her.'

'How much you pay her?' the policeman demanded.

'We hadn't agreed on a price,' Esmae admitted, suspecting he was about to demand a percentage from the deal.

'What you want to pay?' he insisted.

'I offered her eight American dollars.'

'That is a fortune for a poor person here,' the officer said harshly. 'We not here to protect you. We come to protect her because she will be attacked by robbers if they know she has such large money.'

The woman found Esmae later and surreptitiously the beadwork and dollars changed hands. Admiring her purchase back on the yacht, Esmae pondered over the design. At first glimpse, in the village, it had appeared exotically African. Beadwork designs traditionally portray mythological scenes, or animals, or images as primitive as rock paintings in a hidden cave. But scrutiny revealed the art of a new generation. It depicted luxuries about which the poor people of Sudan could only fantasise: etched in delicate multi-coloured glass beads, three mobile phones were embroidered into a white background.

Brec, from *Otter*, also had a narrow escape when dozens of men surrounded him and expressed interest in a sword he had purchased. Locals were amused that an American had a sword. The men took turns at snatching it, raising it above their heads and quivering it in the air to test the quality of its blade.

Brec is an artist and curious about other cultures. Surrounded by about 40 men, he endeavoured to engage them in conversation and asked about the tribal scarring on a man's face. (In many African tribes the parents slash children's faces to draw flies away from their eyes.) The man, obviously upset by the reference to his disfigurement, pulled his dagger and, shouting, advanced toward Brec. The man's friends intervened and Brec took off.

Although Esmae and Justine were the only Western women at the port, they never felt threatened, despite the men's intimidating stares. We learned later that a woman tourist had been murdered at Suakin the year before.

The plague of flies did not deter us from trying local food in shacks that served as restaurants. The most popular meal was a type of omelette cooked in the dust outdoors in a black greasy pan on a wood-fired stove. The chef ground garlic and chillies in a mortar and pestle and tossed them into a simmering purée of sautéed onions and tomatoes. When it was stewed, he broke eggs into it, slightly scrambled the mixture, and then added feta cheese. Before serving, he drizzled it with freshly ground cumin seeds and chilli. I was not courageous enough to try it, but from all accounts it was delicious. So was a bean dish called fool, a type of porridge, which the chef cooked in a metal gourd and served with tea to which he added spices, probably to disguise the taste of the local water. Some of our party paid a price for their adventurous palates when their stomachs protested about the experience.

In the evenings, a building open to the sea became a zawia, a praying space at which 20 men supplicated before Allah. When prayers finished, it transformed into an entertainment centre in which many more men and boys crowded to watch television. The programmes over, they lay on mats on the floor and slept.

There is little fresh water in Suakin. Muslims, who the Koran instructs must wash themselves in running water before praying, used the bay for their ablutions. Men scrubbed themselves vigorously in the sea at the beginning and the end of each day. Fully clothed women used another part of the lagoon, far away from men's gazes. Playful children splashed about most of the time.

A prison, surrounded by a high wire fence close to the water's edge, appeared to be the town's largest and most permanent building. We never saw anyone in its grounds, and at night a solitary light flickered furtively from a window. We wondered what secrets lurked behind its bleak walls. Sudan's human rights record is appalling. Its prisons have been condemned for overcrowding and brutality, and for providing inmates with insufficient nutrition and health care.

Prayers at the beginning and the end of the day provoked a bizarre chorus from braying donkeys and grunting camels roaming Suakin's ruins as they competed with the muezzins' monotone calls to the faithful. In its glory days, 600 buildings, each two or three storeys high, had crammed onto the island, even though it measures only about 400 metres in diameter. Apart from a couple of squatters living among the ruins, camels, goats and donkeys are now its only inhabitants. The eerie moonlight and animal babble enhanced its haunted atmosphere. All the crews who visited the ruins felt a presence lurking in the ancient soil.

A causeway, built by the British in 1877, joins the mainland to the island, which is entered through impressive gates, one of the few structures that has survived intact. The doomed town is as sad as London after the Blitz, or Berlin after the Soviet advance. Minarets of the island's two mosques remain intact and proudly tower above the rubble of houses, warehouses, shops and government buildings. As we walked its irregular, narrow lanes, we occasionally glimpsed the dignity of its past in the few remnants still standing – a carved door framed by an elaborate decorative hood, the denticulated parapet from a once grand mansion. Farther on, a shuttered window clung to a balcony that protruded, like a junk's sail, from a wall to catch even the gentlest of zephyrs and provide relief from oppressive heat. Through empty arched doorways, we glimpsed the sparkle of the turquoise sea.

We squeezed through heavy metal gates, as tall as those of a medieval castle, and found ourselves on a large open yard surrounded by high walls studded by iron-barred windows. We wondered whether this was where slaves had waited to board boats that would take them to unknown destinations and undetermined fates.

Two cannon stood on either side of the main administration building, which was one of the few still standing reasonably intact.

A plaque inside recorded that the Turks built it in 1884. A curved stone staircase took us to balconies on the second floor, from which jutted casement windows constructed of Java teak. Adorned with intricate lattice shutters and fretwork, they stood as a monument to past opulence. We found Brec, sitting cross-legged like a lepre-chaun, sketching among the shadows of the Egyptian National Bank's tall columns and arches.

Suakin's decay began almost immediately slaves pulled coral from the sea for Egyptian masons to hew for the skilled craftsmen who created the town. Exposing the coral to the extremities of a desert climate encouraged it to crumble. Coated with a mortar fin-ish, it could have survived, had it been maintained. The buildings fell into total disrepair when Port Sudan, 60 kilometres away, opened early in the 20th century and enticed away the merchants who had lived on the island. Suakin was decaying even when Churchill was stationed there. In his classic book *The River War*, Churchill described it as 'a dreary place … a nearer view reveals a melancholy squalor … tumbled down and neglected houses … the soil exhales an odour of stagnation and decay'.

Too hot and dusty during the day and too cold at night, without greenery or fresh water and with only men, camels and donkeys for company, Suakin would have been a challenging and unpleasant base for a soldier apprehensively awaiting a battle. For us, it was one of the most stimulating ports of the voyage, firing our imagi-nations and demonstrating nature's delicate balance and the destruction man can cause through ignorance and neglect.

We learned similar lessons at El Geyf where society is so deli-cately poised, because its people are as poor as the desert soils on which they dwell, that the paltry sum of US$8 is enough to shatter it, just as mobile telephones have polluted old dreams. Despite the poverty and the deprivations they have suffered from civil war and famine, the Sudanese displayed the pride, dignity, calm spirituality and warm hospitality we experienced in many African countries.

Before farewelling Suakin, we took a bus to Port Sudan where we bought swords and daggers, fought off flies to eat some of the best fried chicken we have ever had, and jostled through crowds of curious people in the city's large souk (market). We counted our blessings as we sped through the desert past huge tent cities in which thousands of Bedouins and refugees from the civil war live in worse poverty than those at El Geyf. Tornadoes twisting across the desert sucked up sand and hurled it at the tents.

Jean Nicca sat behind us on the way back to El Geyf, talking loudly to a crewman beside him about Islam: what a closed religion it was, how we were not welcome at Mecca and how he could not tolerate religions that practised secrecy and exclusion.

'Hey, Tony,' he leaned over the back of my seat and tapped my shoulder, 'what do they call us?'

'What do you mean? What do who call us?'

'You know, the Muslims. I've just forgotten. What is it they call us?'

About 30 people, mostly men with daggers concealed under their cloaks, were crammed into the bus. Some, I knew, understood English.

'You mean infidels?'

'Yeah, that's right, infidels. I don't like being called an infidel. I don't like people like that, who don't want me in their mosques or in Mecca. That secrecy isn't healthy.'

Mohammed, who had accompanied us to Port Sudan, overheard the conversation from his seat at the front of the bus. He stood up and glanced about anxiously. In a desperate attempt to change the conversation, I drew Jean's attention to a rusting freighter straddling a reef opposite the highway. It worked.

Several people reminded us that in 1998 America had attacked a Sudanese chemical factory that Washington suspected produced VX nerve gas with technical assistance from Baghdad. Afterwards, investigations found the factory produced nothing more than veterinary antibiotics. How could such a mistake be made? The mighty United States is not threatened by people as poor as these.

They did not deserve to be bullied by the president of a super-power placating a population who had demanded retaliation for attacks on American embassies in East Africa two weeks earlier.

CHAPTER 16

TOWARDS NEW ADVENTURES

Silver bubbles rose like a string of crystal beads from a dome encrusted with coral. The Js' silhouettes disappeared underneath the reef. The tapping of parrotfish scraping algae off the rock was the only sound.

We dived on a mound of manmade reef that had claimed a structure shaped like a flying saucer, which had settled on the seabed many years ago. Before being covered in coral, it had been a garage for a diving saucer, a small submersible vessel used by legendary French explorer Jacques Cousteau during experiments in 1963 when he created an underwater habitat on the Shaab Rumi reef, 18 kilometres off the Sudanese coast. Here, Cousteau and his divers had lived underwater observing the behaviour of sharks, manta rays and shoals of fish that inhabit the reef. He chose Shaab Rumi because of its clarity, the vividness of its flourishing coral and the diversity of its marine life.

Con, from *Yior Yia*, who is built like an Arab stallion, free-dived past me to the garage 10 metres below. The Js were still inside the dome. They had removed their regulators and breathed warm fetid air trapped under the garage roof. Apart from a plaque on the seabed honouring a diver who had died during the experiments, the garage is all that is left of Cousteau's visit. It has become part of the reef.

Cousteau and four others had lived in a dwelling that stood on the seabed on stilts. Called Starfish House, it resembled an alien space station. They stayed there for a month, breathing air fed through an umbilical cord attached to compressors aboard Cousteau's motor yacht *Calypso*, anchored above them. They explored the reef by aqualung, which Cousteau had invented, the diving saucer and a vessel resembling a hot-air balloon that descended into deep water. After completing their research, they hauled Starfish House from the sea, but left the diving saucer's garage for scientists curious about the colonisation of an artificial reef in an area about which comparatively little was known.

We appreciated Cousteau's foresight. It was a great dive. The coral was even grander and more colourful and the fish as plentiful and as friendly as at Talla Talla Saghir.

Because the reef's lagoon provides poor anchorage in a gale, we stayed there only a few hours before heading out of its narrow entrance and setting a course towards Khor Shinab, a spectacular hideaway on the Sudanese coast. Cautiously, with the sun in our eyes, we searched for the channel leading into deep water. A few years earlier, a boat with 23 Nigerian Muslim pilgrims aboard had missed the entrance and hit the reef. None survived the shark attack that followed. *Yior Yia*, made of steel, went out first and we tried to follow her wake but a wind chopped up the water and made trailing her difficult.

We considered ourselves fortunate. Suakin marks a boundary at which boats enter the toughest part of a Red Sea passage. From here, winds blow relentlessly from the north, often at 50 knots, hurling before them sand from the desert, making it almost impossible for boats to progress. So far, we had seen none of it.

Keeping close to the Sudanese coast, we had experienced good sailing and enjoyed our first glimpse of the desert that had previously concealed its beauty behind a shroud of dust. A chain of bald, tawny mountains, devoid of grass and trees, rose from the coast a few kilometres from the sea. For centuries, their walls have resisted squadrons of sand-bearing gales that sculpted them into majestic, smooth shapes upon which soft mutating light played, its shadows kneading the slopes like putty. Many who had made the journey before us complained about the coast's barren monotony, but we were spellbound by a Pharaonic land.

The mainland was not all that titillated our imaginations. Before heading to Shaab Rumi, we passed several rusting shipwrecks. Entering the reefs and marsas, the peculiar raised seabeds that surround the Red Sea coast, is a precarious exercise. Like Shaab Rumi, they are frequently so tight that getting *Antares II* into them was like putting a model boat through the neck of a bottle.

Khor Shinab was one of those. As we approached, we scanned water breaking over the coast's fringing reef, searching for an entrance through the coral. Inside lay a huge lagoon enveloped by high hills, protection from a gale that had unexpectedly sprung up at 0200 hours. A forest of whitecaps crashing over the coral camouflaged the reef.

We faced a precarious situation. With the gale's fury raging around us, we were eager to enter the tranquillity of sheltered waters. Finding a narrow entrance can take ages and creates impatience and frustration upon which feasts one of our greatest foes: recklessness. We had to remain patient, disciplined, ultra-cautious and alert to being tricked by false appearances. We could not rely on charts and other information because, at some places, we had discovered them to be inaccurate by up to two kilometres. A navigation miscalculation would put *Antares II* onto the coral.

Unexpectedly, when we were almost on top of the reef, we spied an opening only a few boat lengths wide. Beyond it, the water changed from the sea's tempestuous sapphire blue to the welcoming emerald green of a lagoon. With the Js up front spotting for coral heads, I wrestled with the helm, fighting the wind and current for control. We surfed toward the entrance, the sea's force taking command by snatching away the rudder's rigidity, making the wheel feel limp in my hands, until the yacht sat heavily upon the waves again and the rudder dug into the sea. Towering water crashed over reefs on either side of us.

The coral ran a considerable distance along the entrance. Midway through it, an alarm screamed, warning that the engine, which had been under strain for 12 hours since the weather changed, was overheating. Motoring at high revs, we had bashed into huge seas that slowed our progress to one knot. Until now, the engine had performed faultlessly. With reefs on either side, and the sea and wind pushing us toward coral on our port, the prospect of the engine quitting was unnerving. Fortunately, under reduced power, it settled down and gave no further worry.

Suddenly, we saw our talisman was gone. The gale had snatched from our bowsprit the garland of yellow plastic flowers Esmae had tied there when we left Thailand a little more than three months before. Although at the time I had scoffed at the Buddhist superstition, I had to admit we had enjoyed over 6500 kilometres of near perfect cruising.

'The windlass is stuffed,' Justin called from the bow, when we were safely inside the lagoon and about to drop the anchor. 'It's the same old problem. The electric motor is turning but no chain is coming out.'

'Christ, it would have to happen in a gale. And what a place for it to happen! Look how little room we've got to manoeuvre,' I said when I joined him, leaving Esmae on the helm.

She had turned *Antares II* into the gale to enable us to anchor. While the lagoon meandered on either side of us like a river, shadows of coral lurked beneath water the in front of and behind us. It was not an ideal place to shelter, but our anchor had always held previously and we were confident we could secure the yacht to ride out the blow. Our plan was to nudge up to the reef lying off our bow, drop the anchor and let the wind carry us back until the pick caught on a rock or dug into sand to hold us firm. Only half a dozen boat lengths separated the reefs on either side of us. When laying an anchor in the gale roaring over the marsa's low banks, there would be no room for mistakes. Luckily, although we were still exposed to the wind, dunes surrounding the lagoon blocked a swell from building by deflecting the gale above the water.

Esmae continued to circle the boat in the narrow neck for almost an hour while Justin and I tried to fix the windlass. Defeated, we decided to motor further into the marsa to find shallower water and a wider area in which the boat could swing. Because the winch had let us down, we expected to have only one chance at dropping the anchor.

On entering the bulbous expanse of a cul-de-sac, we came across three other yachts sheltering in the bay. We unwound the clutch on the windlass to let the chain spill out. It did not budge. As Esmae struggled to hold *Antares II* into the gale, we pulled 40 metres of chain from the well and laid it on deck. We attached a line to it at the 20-metre mark, secured it to a cleat and let the chain run into the sea.

'Let's hope the pick catches on something solid enough to hold us,' Justin wished aloud. If it did not hold, we would have to pull up the heavy chain by hand, an exhausting, time-consuming task.

Even with Esmae maintaining forward thrust with the engine, the wind pushed us back at an alarming rate. Justine maintained a lookout from the stern to ensure we did not land on the reef on the other side of the lagoon. Suddenly, the chain tugged taut and the boat slewed slightly to port in protest that it could not maintain its momentum.

'The anchor's caught!' Justin shouted, relieved.

It held us safely for three days until the gale abated and we could continue our voyage.

Justin spent a good part of his birthday working on the windlass. He was familiar with the problem because of the regularity with which it occurred: a sheer pin that connected shafts from the electric motor and the gears had fallen out. The windlass had been installed only three years earlier and it had certainly never been overtaxed during that time. It was the most unreliable piece of equipment aboard the yacht.

We did not mind waiting at Khor Shinab. It is a dramatic, fawn, lunar landscape composed of rugged hills, sharp peaks, steep gorges and plateaus. Neither a bush nor a blade of grass clung to its sterile soils. As we sat upon a turquoise sea spattered with whitecaps kicked up by the gale, we could have been in a crater on the moon. Occasionally, as if to reassure us we were still earth-bound, a camel raised its head above a sand dune.

Ashore, exploring the bewildering landscape, we found terraces and balconies of shells, fossils and crystalline rock, once covered by the sea. Beyond these strata, and the sand dunes and knolls surrounding us, lay dusty gentle planes upon which the sun shimmered in a watery mirage. Farther away, past the plateau and barely visible through a haze, rose huge round mountains. Beyond them, and beyond our view, meandered the mighty Nile River.

Finally, the gale subsided and we hauled the anchor and headed for sea. As we motored between the embankments on either side of us, we paused before a timeless biblical scene. In the distance, near the exit, a solitary figure, swathed in white robes, strode leisurely along a bank above the lagoon. Occasionally he placed the staff he was carrying behind his neck, wrapping his arms around it as though shouldering the crossbeam of a crucifix. We shattered the tranquillity by waving and shouting greetings but he ignored our intrusion and continued to stride purposefully along the tawny wilderness, his white robes stark against a cloudless blue sky.

Unfortunately, we had left Khor Shinab a day too soon. Although the wind was down, the seas still ran high. We managed to motor only about 30 kilometres before giving up and heading for an anchorage at Marsa Wasi where we waited for the sea to settle. While there, we learned that a French yacht with two children aboard had gone aground on a reef ahead of us and was being pounded by the sea. Fortunately, all aboard had survived.

Their plight highlighted the challenges we faced as we slowly plugged our way up the Red Sea, travelling only 20 kilometres one day before being forced to run to shelter from yet another gale, making 35 kilometres another day. Usually, in such conditions, we would sail a minimum of 170 kilometres in 24 hours. After tucking in behind a marsa, we often waited days for the weather to improve sufficiently for us to continue our journey. The delays did not bother us. We spent the time reading books, watching DVDs we had bought in Asia and enjoying meals with *Yior Yia*'s crew.

Accurate weather forecasts were vital but impossible to find. We scanned radio networks maintained by yachts ahead and behind us but few had accurate information. Some relied on predictions they downloaded from the Internet when they were in port. Others subscribed to commercial services that sent forecasts via shipboard email. Some, like us, had software programs, satellite communications and facsimile receivers to gather forecasts. None succeeded in receiving accurate information in the Red Sea.

Our fortunes improved after an Australian cruising friend, Bernard (Bin) Anderson, skipper of the deep-sea launch *Dracamarus*, which had motored from Australia to Spain the year we lost our dinghy, offered to provide us with weather forecasts via shipboard email. Bin logged into information supplied by the University of Athens, which proved to be impressively accurate. Early each morning he transmitted his analysis for us to download via SailMail. We depended on Bin's forecasts all the way from Sudan and up through the Gulf of Suez, where, daily, we sheltered at anchorages after making only a few kilometres of progress. His information was so accurate that, if he foretold of a weather change occurring at 1500 hours, we were confident it would happen. Many other yachts cruising the Red Sea depended on his messages, which Esmae relayed to the fleet by a radio network Brec organised every day. We were grateful to Bin, whose generosity made our voyage one of the better ones.

The Red Sea weather could change within minutes and without warning. Several times, we enjoyed robust sailing only to find our sails suddenly flogging because, inexplicably, they had no wind. Peering behind, we saw water churning in a gale until it reached an invisible line beyond which it was almost glassy calm. We searched the horizon for buttresses of land that could dramatically change the weather pattern but there were none because we were sailing far off the coast. It was bizarre and unpredictable.

We entered an area with the intimidating name of Foul Bay, one of the most notorious parts of the Red Sea, a place where most of the yachts that had sailed before us experienced bad weather. Devoid of wind, we motored at five knots and heard on an early morning radio broadcast that yachts 60 kilometres ahead had encountered strong wind. Because the sea was like glass, we were optimistic we could make good headway toward our closest safe anchorage at Ras Banas, about 60 kilometres away, before the change arrived.

About an hour after the radio broadcast, however, we saw a line of breaking water ahead of us. Everything on our side of it remained calm. We checked the chart for a reef, but found nothing. Immediately we sailed over the line the wind rose from five to 15 knots. We dropped a reef in the main, hauled down the staysail and reefed the working jib. The breeze continued building until it gusted at 30 knots coming, of course, from the direction in which we headed. We reefed the main again.

Making way became frustrating and tedious. The sea rose steeply until it reached three metres and attacked us with short-spaced, square waves with curling crests from which white foam crashed. At first, *Antares II* revelled in it. Her weight and length enabled her to cut through the sea's fury. Occasionally, though, a wave stopped her in her tracks as if she had hit a brick wall. As the gale intensified, she continued to struggle and the waves confronting her began to win; at times, they even pushed her backwards. Our morale ebbed and we talked about alternative anchorages, but there were none. The sea appeared determined to keep us from our destination and we considered sitting out the gale in the middle of the Red Sea under bare poles.

We talked to a yacht already anchored at Ras Banas and received bad news. The skipper advised that, because of the number of coral heads he had encountered close to the reef, we should not enter in bad light. We were confused. Everything we had read indicated Ras Banas was an easy anchorage free of obstacles. If we proceeded, we would arrive in darkness because we could make only 2 knots of speed, which meant it would take us another 10 hours to reach our destination.

Yior Yia arrived at Ras Banas three hours later and assured us our original information was correct: there were no obstacles and we would lay it easily in the dark. They signed off the radio, promising to leave a light on for us to use as a beacon to guide us into the anchorage. We tacked out towards Saudi Arabia to get a better wind angle and, under staysail and with two reefs in the main, laid a better course. Although it was tight, we lifted our speed to 6 knots and managed to drop our anchor shortly before dark without incurring any obstructions.

We sat there for three days listening to wind roaring through the rigging. It was too rough to venture ashore in our dinghy, so out came the movies and books again. Ras Banas was our first Egyptian landfall. Usually, we would venture ashore to explore a new country. However, after noticing a warning in the pilot book that live mines littered the beach, we decided to remain aboard.

On the radio, we followed the progress of a couple of yachts as they fought the gale. They had little success and made no headway at all. Their only accomplishment was to put strain on their gear, spill their energy and fray their nerves. Elsewhere, the conditions would not have been a problem, but here, a wind of only 20 knots whips up such horrible seas that progress is extremely difficult.

Brec was anxious to reach an anchorage in Egypt because he was scheduled to meet his wife in Cairo. On several occasions, he fought his way up the Red Sea in gales, each time questioning whether the little progress he made was worth the effort and risk. Jean also took his chances out there because, he admitted, he had heard so many horror stories about sailing the Red Sea that he wanted to get through it as quickly as possible.

We made the same mistake again. When the wind abated, we were too anxious to get under way and left Ras Banas a day earlier than we should. Away from our shelter, the wind blew on our nose at 12 to 15 knots and the sea remained high.

We stopped at a reef called Fury Shoal for a spot of diving and snorkelling. An American boat, *Reunion*, had anchored there several days before and radioed that, because of the water's clarity, we should not pass it by. Despite its name, Fury Shoal had a reputation for being a safe anchorage where we could shelter if the sea did not calm. The diving was as good as *Reunion* had promised. Dozens of large clams littered the seabed and life flourished among tall coral columns and deep canyons.

By the time we finished exploring the reef, the sea outside appeared to be settling and we set off for the Egyptian port of entry, Safaga. Again, we were mistaken. Between seven that evening and four the following morning, we covered only 2.2 nautical miles each hour, and it took us 57 litres of diesel to do it. At that rate, we would run out of fuel before we reached port. We radioed *Yior Yia* that we intended calling into Marsa Alam, a difficult reef to navigate, but one at which we could buy fuel.

Several large charter launches swung on anchor inside the lagoon, awaiting tourists booked for diving excursions. The town on the edge of the marsa was a weird, desolate little place. Apart from the dive boats, it comprised some squat, square huts, a few shops and a strip of highway. Nothing on land would entice visitors. Egyptians living there were as desolate as the landscape. The Js went into the local village, where Egyptian men groped Justine and made lewd suggestions as she shopped. Not even the produce was particularly good. The Js bought some dreadful pita bread and some wonderful oranges and honeydew melons. We bought 400 litres of fuel, for US25 cents a litre, and lugged it out to the boat in jerry cans in our dinghy.

When we arrived, police confiscated our passports, explaining they would be returned on departure. The Js experienced Egyptian corruption for the first time when they requested the documents a few hours before we were due to sail. Officials refused to return them. Heated discussion ensued. A group of Swedish sailors, who were also anchored in the lagoon, arrived and helped resolve the problem. When also denied their documents, the argument became even louder. While they distracted the police, Justin opened a drawer and fled with the passports.

Despite the difficulties, the stop was worthwhile because it delayed us long enough to enjoy better weather. During the continuation of the passage to Safaga, we motored at five knots on a glassy sea without a breeze. It was certainly preferable to the gales.

From Safaga, the Js travelled to Luxor to explore the Valley of the Kings, where pharaohs are buried. Esmae and I, who had seen them on a previous visit to Egypt, decided to stay and enjoy luxurious facilities available at holiday resorts ashore. The Js lost themselves in antiquity as they rode donkeys at dawn across old workers' trails atop the valley. With the sun rising over parched hills, they found it easy to imagine themselves following desolate, historic tracks, only to have the spell shattered when touts selling water and trinkets appeared from nowhere. The Js blamed the water they bought for stomach problems that followed. They suspect that, even though the bottles were sealed, the touts had filled them from a poisoned supply.

The 400 kilometres from Safaga to Port Suez were the most difficult of the voyage as we encountered one gale after another. Fortunately, by following Bin Anderson's advice, we were seldom caught in them for very long. Weather was not our only concern as we approached Port Suez. Our instruction book warned that the course could be peppered with several abandoned and unlit oil rigs and increased shipping.

Throughout the night, after leaving Safaga, we sailed among blazing amber flames of gas fires atop oil rigs that lit the sky with a glow as intense as that of a large city. Convoys of huge dark ships from the Suez Canal passed within 500 metres of us. There was no chance of a rest during our watches. At 0200 hours, I popped my head out of a hatch above my cabin and saw Justin studiously staring abeam, his head surrounded by the flames of gas burning on dozens of oil rigs. It was surreal, like a scene from a movie.

The next morning, Bin's email predicted more gales and sand-storms, which would be among the worst weather he had forecast for us. We could not believe it because, unexpectedly, we were again sailing with our poles out with the wind at our back, which was unusual for this time of the year in the Red Sea. Again, we got greedy and tried to steal a few more kilometres because Port Suez was now only a little over 60 kilometres away.

With the entrance to the Suez Canal so close, we elected to continue sailing up the western side of the Gulf in the hope of reaching Port Suez that day. We passed our nearest shelter, Marsa Thelemet, at which the skipper on another yacht advised we could anchor. We felt better about our decision when a Canadian yacht, *Sky*, aborted an attempt to enter the anchorage; in a southerly, it was open to the sea, making the entrance too rough to penetrate.

An hour later, the wind suddenly dropped. We knew what it meant and hauled in the sails. Within seconds of reefing, the wind howled in from the north. Half an hour later the gale had set in, and we could make little forward progress. Concluding that the water would be calmer on the eastern side of the channel, we decided to cross the shipping lanes and shelter beneath the Sinai Peninsula. It meant slogging north for another 20 kilometres but it would put us closer to Port Suez. Unfortunately, we did not find the improved conditions we sought. For 48 hours we sheltered behind a spit off a bleak town at Damaran Abu Meish as the wind raged around us at up to 30 knots. We were much more comfortable than yachts only 30 kilometres to our south: they endured sandstorms of up to 50 knots.

After two days, we slogged to Ras Sudr, a desolate oil town 14 kilometres further up the coast. Although it was an uncomfortable passage, we did not mind as we had inched a little closer to Port Suez. While anchored there, we heard that a British yacht had crashed onto the reef outside Marsa Thelemet while trying to find shelter from the gale. It was sobering news because we had listened to the skipper on the radio not long before. A few hours later, we heard that another French yacht had also gone aground on a reef. We listened to Wattie aboard *Cariad* seeking weather information as he fought his way through Fury Bay toward Ras Banas, just as we had done. The Red Sea was living up to its reputation as one of the world's most difficult sailing grounds.

Two days later, at 0100 on 28 May, I awoke to feel the yacht's movement had changed. *Antares II* was bobbing about on a gentle sea, confused because the wind had disappeared.

'C'mon, let's go.' I roused the crew from their bunks. 'This time we might make it to Port Suez.'

We lifted anchor and headed to sea, only to have the wind return immediately we reached the end of the spit behind which we had sheltered. Fortunately, although the gale still raged, the sea, sheltered by the land, behaved and we made Port Suez safely. It had taken us five days to travel the 400 kilometres from Safaga. As it turned out, ours was one of the faster passages: several other yachts waited another 11 days before escaping from the gale.

With *Yior Yia* anchored alongside us, we surveyed the wrecks littering the entrance to Port Suez. Waiting to be called to enter the canal, we watched dozens of merchant ships of all shapes and sizes vanish into the jowls of the city, which appeared to be devouring them. When it was our turn, we motored past the wrecks and dozens of ferries and cargo vessels awaiting work. At first, the entrance to the canal was difficult to find, because it cut between buildings and mosques built on either side of it.

'Just look at that. We're in the Suez Canal!' Esmae exclaimed excitedly.

'God, it doesn't look much better than the entrance to Boat Lagoon Marina at Phuket,' I announced, disappointed by the navigation poles and sand dunes that lay ahead. 'Are you sure we're in the right place?'

Despite the lack of grandeur, however, we all felt a sense of accomplishment and excitement. After a short distance, we turned off the canal to tie up at the Port Suez Yacht Club's spider's web moorings, which are similar to those at Sri Lanka. Entranced, we watched ships ranging from passenger liners and supertankers to small freighters entering and departing the canal, only a few metres from our berth.

Port Suez is a little like Cochin, India. Attractive colonial houses, their gardens struggling in the arid conditions, nestle behind trees that shade the streets. The greenery was a novel sight because we had seen neither trees nor grass for thousands of kilometres.

As is the case with many former colonial towns, little seems to have been done to improve old Port Suez since the ignominious withdrawal of the British in 1956, almost 100 years after the first sod was turned to dig the waterway. Evidence of another aspect of the country's turbulent history is apparent in many buildings riddled by bullet holes from the Israeli-Egyptian Six Day War, fought over 30 years before. We explored the town and bought some of the best olives and strawberries we have had anywhere. We would have liked to have stayed longer, but we feared we could be trapped by weather and our visas had almost expired.

We entered the Suez Canal at 0900 the next morning under the guidance of a pilot, which is mandatory when transiting the 160-kilometre waterway. His name, of course, was Mohammed. Other yachts had warned us to expect the worst from pilots, who have a reputation for groping women, chain-smoking, demanding food, gifts and buckshee – money. In the past, some women had been so traumatised by the experience they locked themselves in cabins for the whole passage.

Mohammed was not like that at all; in fact, he could not have been nicer. Seeing the pilot book lying on the chart table, he enquired about its comments on Suez Canal pilots.

'I am very sorry for this,' he said earnestly after we read its contents. 'It is older men who caused these problems. Since then, they have been replaced with younger men like me, and we not like that. We have job to do and we want to be very professional. We do not create any problems.'

Mohammed was very conscientious. He took the helm and refused to leave his station during most of the eight-hour passage to Ismailia, a city halfway along the canal where we would have to stay before continuing our transit. The only exceptions were to go to the toilet, eat lunch, which he gulped down in five minutes, and to say afternoon prayers.

We were surprised when he requested a bowl of water at 1600 hours. 'Please, it must be clean water, not dirty water from canal,' he insisted. He invited me to take the helm. Then, before going to the bow, where he faced Mecca and prayed, he vigorously scrubbed his hands, face and feet. He explained later that, like all good Muslims, he prayed five times a day.

Like Port Suez, Ismailia is a charming little place in which strong British and French influences prevail. The harbour provided an abundance of fresh water, so we spent two days cleaning *Antares II* from top to bottom. The Js even went to the top of the masts and hosed down dirt caked there. We scrubbed decks and sails and made repairs and the boat regained some of her old sparkle.

We used Ismailia as a base for touring and restocking provisions. After cleaning the boat, we travelled by train to Alexandria, a five-hour trip through interesting countryside. I felt we had cheated when we received our first glimpse of the Mediterranean from a hotel balcony at Alexandria, a city looking as if it is built of ivory glowing in the sun beside a sparkling, crescent-shaped harbour.

Con and I made a pilgrimage to El Alamein, 64 kilometres away, a graveyard for 5000 British and Commonwealth soldiers killed during the famous battle against the Germans' advance during the Second World War. It is hard to believe that so many young lives were wasted in this unprepossessing place. Today, thousands of modern condominiums and holiday resorts line the highway leading to the battlefield.

The Js scuba dived on a sunken city that has only recently been discovered. It is so precious that an archaeologist had to accompany them to ensure they did not disturb the marble columns, sphinxes, urns and vases lying on the seabed. Nearby, they dived on a German bomber shot down during the war.

After a couple of days exploring, we took a train to Cairo, a big, dirty, hot city full of Egyptians determined to part tourists from their money. We visited the Pyramids, the museum and the Muslim quarter.

'Haere mai,' a voice called behind me in the markets.

A tall, thin, stooped elderly man stood grinning at us. I suspected him to be a Maori on holiday who had noticed my New Zealand America's Cup cap.

'Kia ora,' he said, smiling broadly.

'Kia ora,' I offered. 'Are you a Kiwi?'

'Yes, I am honorary New Zealand.'

He prattled off a string of Maori sentences I could not comprehend.

'What do you mean, an *honorary* New Zealander?'

'I know many New Zealanders. When they come to Cairo they look me up. They are my very good friends. I help them find many bargains here in the souk.'

Our guard immediately went up. Touts insisting we buy perfumes, watches and fabrics had pestered us throughout Cairo.

'Come with me, I take you to cheapest places,' he offered, crowning the invitation with another string of Maori.

'Where did you learn to speak Maori?' I asked, impressed with his command of the language.

'I work with New Zealand troops during the war, Maori Battalion. They all know me. Come, I take you for shay (tea) at shop.'

'No thank you, we just want to stroll around on our own.'

'You cannot. You Kiwis, you must come with me to shop for shay and perfumes. You need not buy.'

We had heard that before and remained adamant we would not accompany him. As we walked away, a tirade of abuse, none of it in Maori, followed us.

Security in Egypt was very tight. At Ismailia, we were unable to leave our yacht without reporting to immigration and police who, each time, inspected our passports. There were more uniformed and armed police than tourists, who have stayed away since terrorists gunned down a group of visitors in Cairo some years ago. The police were so security conscious that they even used mirrors to search underneath cars for bombs.

By the time we got back to Ismailia, we were sick of the hassles and anxious to continue our journey along the Suez Canal to Port Said, our last stop before entering the Mediterranean.

We decided to depart on 10 May – a *Friday*.

'It'll be okay,' I rationalised, trying to allay fears about the superstition. 'We're not leaving port for a new voyage, but continuing our previous passage along the Suez Canal. Therefore, the superstition about leaving port on a Friday doesn't apply.'

How wrong I was.

The first problem was the pilot, a middle-aged man; we liked neither his appearance nor his manner. While climbing aboard, he 'fell' on Justine, thrusting his hands at her breasts to steady himself. He leered lustfully at the women who were so intimidated they avoided him throughout the journey. Esmae spent her time in the galley, roasting a leg of goat she had bought at a market at Ismailia. Shopping alone, she had been lucky to get the beast back to the boat. After a butcher chopped the carcass into portions, Esmae put the meat in her backpack. As she walked back to the port with the goat on her back and bags of fruit in each hand, a bag broke and apples and oranges spilled into the dust. Squatting, she gathered the fruit off the ground. When she rose to resume her journey, she found she could not move. The weight on her back was so heavy she did not have the strength to straighten her legs.

'Can you help me up?' she pleaded to a passing woman who ignored her, obviously not expecting to find anyone trapped in such a position.

A couple of women in Muslim dress approached. Suspecting they would not understand English, she used sign language to indicate her difficulty. Fortunately, they obliged and lifted her up and she continued her journey.

While Esmae prepared dinner, the pilot made demands. He wanted food and cigarettes, which he smoked all the way to Port Said. He complained we travelled too slowly and he wanted to return to Ismailia early. He urged me to raise our sails to increase our boat speed. Reluctantly, with Esmae condemning my judgment, I did. No sooner had we unfurled our genoa, than a sandstorm hit us. The furling cable snapped as we wound in the sail, which flogged wildly in the 35-knot gale. We fought to drop it as the pilot wrestled for control of the boat in the narrow canal.

The sandstorm produced a white-out that obscured our view of the desert and coated the boat in dust. The Js were devastated: the hard work they had undertaken cleaning *Antares II* was undone.

My disappointment lay in being unable to see the desert. Many cruisers regard the transit through the Suez Canal as a boring, tedious passage, but I found the first leg of the transit fascinating. Unlike deserts in Australia and South Africa, the Egyptian desert is gentle and feminine. While the Australian outback boasts masculine, virile colours, here the sands are tinged with pastels: pink, white, beige/brown, yellow and orange. Soft white light, filtered by dust, veils the horizon, which gently merges with the blueness of space. Nothing is green.

Sadly, this time, none of that was visible. We had to keep washing the sand off our windows so we could see ahead. Grit got into our mouths, our hair, and every nook and cranny on the yacht.

While in the sandstorm, we heard on the radio that *Cariad* was aground on a reef. Fortunately, Wattie and Jill were unharmed. *Cariad* was the fifth yacht of the 2002 flotilla to be lost, which could well be some kind of macabre record. Fortunately, no one died. The loss of *Cariad* affected us particularly: her crew was from our hometown, Kerikeri, they had been aboard *Antares II* and, at Aden, Justin had helped Wattie repair a leaking stern gland. They had shared the meal with us at Aden when we ate at a very basic fish restaurant where the seared food was slapped onto newspaper that acted as a tablecloth and we ripped the plump flesh from the bones with our hands. Wattie and Jill had brought knives and forks, and tucked into the feast in a more civilised fashion. They had been due to leave Aden with us, but they had changed their minds.

While Wattie was battling to retrieve his boat from the reef, we were having our own problems. Mid-afternoon, as we motored into the sandstorm, an alarm sounded to warn the engine was over-heating. From then on, we made slow headway as we nursed the engine and battled the gale at low revs.

When eventually we arrived at Port Said, we dropped anchor among a group of fishing boats inside a breakwater that protects the harbour from the Mediterranean. Driven by the gale, the sea exploded over the rock wall sheltering us as we bucked about on metre-high waves.

Undeterred by the rough conditions that made *Antares II* lurch dangerously, Justine dived under the hull and poked a screwdriver up the engine's water intake to clear an obstruction that caused the alarm to sound every time we tried to increase power. Out fell dozens of white shrimp-like creatures that had blocked the hole and prevented the engine from sucking sea water to cool the motor.

I had just finished cleaning the obstruction from the engine's raw water strainer when we heard a commotion outside. In the dark, we could barely identify the silhouette of a pilot boat standing off our beam.

'Cap-i-tain, you must go,' the pilot announced gruffly through a megaphone.

I protested that it was dark and the gale made it dangerous to move.

'If you stay, you remain at your *peril*,' he warned, his nonchalant tone at odds with his message.

Despite his chilling words, we did not relish having to haul up the anchor in the dark and search for a new shelter in the gale. We were inclined to plead we were disabled and could not leave because our water pump was broken. When we saw the huge dark shape of a container ship inching toward us, we understood. All the fishing boats surrounding us were anxiously hauling their anchors and fleeing.

The gale still raging, we headed back to the Port Said Yacht Club in the middle of the harbour. We were about to drop our anchor when the windlass failed again. For the next two hours, we circled outside the yacht club in one of the world's busiest ports as Justin worked in the cramped anchor well to replace the shattered sheer pin. When it was fixed, it took three attempts before the anchor held. Throughout the voyage, Justin had thought our superstition about leaving port on a Friday was another of our eccentricities. Now he too is a believer.

By dawn, the gale had abated. We lifted our anchor at 0900 hours, headed into the Mediterranean's blue waters and sailed close-hauled to Cyprus in a steady 15-knot breeze.

As Egypt's shores disappeared behind us, we reflected on the voyage. We had set out with considerable trepidation, fearful of meeting pirates, Islamic fundamentalists and, perhaps, even terrorists. Instead, we had encountered wonderful, friendly people who, in varying degrees, wanted nothing more for themselves than we wanted: peace and a chance to find a little prosperity and the benefits it provides. What threatened us were factors that have waylaid and wrecked ships for centuries: our vessel's seaworthiness, our seamanship, the elements and our physical and psychological strength.

The religious fervour we witnessed in Muslim countries impressed us. Their devotion to their religion is undoubtedly genuine, not a result of peer or political pressure. We had been moved by the sight of Muslims praying in the most unexpected of places. At Eritrea, crews on fishing boats anchored beside us assembled on deck at prayer times. Prayer mats were rolled out amid the ruins of Suakin. In a restaurant at Ismailia, a waiter supplicated on a prayer mat between tables while we dined. Taxi drivers in Egypt and Oman drove to the taped accompaniment of muezzins chanting from the Koran. Men pulled books containing verses of the Koran from their pockets for recitation at railway stations and other public places. In the train to Alexandria, we observed people in the countryside praying on their knees among crops.

We were impressed by the kindness, sincerity, friendliness and faith of the Muslims we met. We felt safe in all the Muslim countries in which we travelled, even those our government had warned us to avoid. We felt safer, in fact, than we feel in parts of Britain, New Zealand, Australia and the United States.

On a couple of occasions, the honesty of individuals impressed us. Once, a man who had served us in a halal butchery pursued us down a street shouting incomprehensibly. I worried that I must have offended him. When he finally caught up with us, he thrust money onto us, explaining we had paid too much for the meat we had bought. On another occasion, Esmae left her handbag hanging on a hook in a women's toilet cubicle at Kuala Lumpur's International Airport. Fearing she had lost her passport, credit cards, jewellery and cash, she returned to find a couple of excited Muslim women rushing toward her: 'Madam! Madam! You forgot your bag.' Nothing inside had been disturbed.

As well as their devotion to Islam, another deep belief united the Muslims we met in nine countries where the religion is a significant inspirational force. In each, we heard the same message: condemnation of America for helping Israel to oppress Palestine.

In 2000, scenes of young boys hurling rocks at Israeli tanks filled the world's television screens; the pictures were still playing in Muslim countries two years later. They had been incorporated into popular music. In Egypt, a video of a dirge that became top of the pops played continuously in cafés and restaurants. The images that accompanied the female Arabic voice were compelling. They showed boys throwing stones at Israeli tanks like David taking on Goliath. The film then moved on to an infamous video clip capturing the last seconds of the life of traumatised 12-year-old Mohammed al-Dura, cowering with his father beneath a rock wall while Israeli gunfire burst around them on 30 September 2000. It was one of the most poignant scenes from the conflict. Throughout the Muslim world the boy has become a symbol of terror, just as the Twin Towers are to Americans, Hiroshima is to the peace movement, or the *Rainbow Warrior* is to New Zealanders. Although bullets killed al-Dura, he remains an inspiration for Palestinians to continue the struggle.

Muslim feelings towards the United States were reminiscent of dissent I had discovered three decades before in Johannesburg, South Africa. As a journalist on the *Johannesburg Star*, I had accompanied Winnie Mandela to Soweto after she had successfully appealed against a conviction under the Terrorism Act. As we drove through the African township, children acknowledged her by raising their fists in salutes but their parents' eyes avoided her. It was obvious from where revolution's flames would ignite. Today, a similar atmosphere exists in Muslim countries where sparks of bitterness simmer within a new generation. It is incongruous that the West, and America in particular, ignores the views, threats and opportunities of more than one billion of the world's people.

Sailing towards Cyprus, we experienced a sense of freedom as *Antares II* revelled in the brisk conditions. It felt as if a tether that had constrained her all the way from Sudan had snapped. She cantered on a new ocean in search of new adventures.

EPILOGUE

Buddhists consider life as fragile as a dewdrop on a blade of grass. The significance of the proverb was evident in the devastation that followed the catastrophic earthquake off Sumatra, Indonesia, on 26 December 2004. As I write this, in the final stages of preparing the book for publication, the death toll is creeping over 150,000. Nature has plundered all the Asian countries that comprised our playground – Malaysia, Indonesia, Thailand, Sri Lanka and India. None escaped its might.

Via the Internet we have tracked the fate of friends and their families. Our beloved Rebak Marina is no more, taken by the sea. At Sri Lanka, our friend Marlin lost his mother and a sister when monster waves obliterated the harbour city of Galle.

Another friend, Dato' Zainal, and his wife Normah watched the waves coming towards them as they ate breakfast at a Phuket hotel. Thankfully, they were safely evacuated.

Fortunately, all our yachting friends survived, as did their boats, although some were damaged.

Thirty tourists swimming in an emerald lagoon inside one of Thailand's imposing hongs, one of our favourites, disappeared in the tsunami. The island of We, at the tip of Aceh, was close to the earthquake's epicentre. Information is scarce, but I fear it was devastated. Many Thai acquaintances died at Phi Phi, Krabi and Patong.

The experiences we enjoyed in villages dotted along Asia's coasts are unlikely to be repeated because many of the settlements and their people have disappeared, washed away by the tsunami's giant waves.

As is happening all around the globe, we feel for the victims. Our hearts go out to them and we recognise our own fragility when measured against such cataclysmic forces.

GLOSSARY

abaft the beam	the rear quarter of a yacht	cockpit	place where crew may sit or stand
aft	towards the stern		
autopilot	electronic equipment that automatically steers a boat	desalinator	equipment for converting salt water to fresh water
backstay	a stay supporting a mast	dhoni	large motorboat in Maldives and Indonesia
beam	portion at a boat's centre line		
bemo	minivan used for public transport in Indonesia	EPIRB	Emergency Position Indicating Radio Beacon which transmits signals on distress frequency
berth	place where a vessel can lie, or a person can sleep		
bilge	rounded part of a boat where the bottom curves up to the sides	farang	foreigner, Westerner
		forestay	a stay running from the mast to the bowsprit
bobstays	metal rods holding the bowsprit to the stem, to counter the upward pull of the forestay	gaff	instrument with hook on its end for hoisting fish aboard a boat
boom	spar to which the foot of a sail is attached	genoa	large headsail
bo'sun's chair	chair on which crew is hoisted aloft to work on rigging, etc.	goosewing	sailing with a headsail poled out to capture wind on the opposite side to the mainsail
bow	forward part of a vessel		
bowsprit	platform fastened to the bow	GPS	Global Positioning System, which receives navigation information from satellites
bow wave	wave system generated by a boat moving through water		
buri	Yemeni dugout canoe	guardrail	safety line fitted around the boat to stop crew falling overboard
capping	wooden strip around the top of a gunwale	gunwales	upper edge of the side of a boat
cleat	fitting with two horns around which rope is secured	gybe	to change direction by turning the stern through the wind
close-hauled	sailing on a bearing close to the eye of the wind	hardstand	area on which boats are stored out of water

helm	vessel's steering wheel	seacock	device that operates like a stopcock to prevent water entering the hull through inlets
keel	backbone running under the boat		
ketch	boat with two masts, the forward being the taller	sextant	navigation instrument with which angles are measured using heavenly bodies or other identifiable objects
kris	Malaysian/Indonesian knife		
latitude	position measured in degrees, minutes and seconds north and south of the equator	shackle	a link for connecting ropes and wires
		sheets	ropes, lines or wire rope attached to sails
lazarette	small stowage compartment at the stern	slack tide	period when tide is turning and current is at its slowest
lifeline	(or guardrail), fits around sides of boat to stop crew falling overboard	souk	market
		sounder	equipment measuring distance to seabed
longitude	position measured in degrees, minutes and seconds east and west of meridian that passes through Greenwich, London	spar	general term for supports, stays, etc. aboard a boat
		spreaders	struts attached to either side of the mast to spread the sideways angle of shrouds
		stanchion	post through which lifelines (guardrails) run
mainsail	principal sail	starboard	right-hand side of a vessel, when looking towards the bow
mizzen	small sail set on the mizzen-mast of a ketch		
mizzenmast	the smaller after mast of a ketch or yawl	staysail	sail set on a stay
muezzin	official in a mosque who calls the faithful to prayer	stem	the forward member that is attached to the keel, or where laminates overlap
		stern	the back part of a vessel
NAVTEX	onboard message system	stern gland	packing round the propeller shaft where it passes through the hull, or where the shaft joins
painter	line for towing or making fast a dinghy		
poled out	with sails out on opposite sides to fill with wind coming from the stern	stern wave	waves at the rear of boat generated by the vessel moving through water
port	left-hand side of a vessel, when looking toward the bow	tack	to change direction with the bow passing through the eye of the wind
prahus	large Indonesian motorboat		
		tender	dinghy for transporting crew
reef (verb)	to reduce the area of sail	tuktuk	three-wheel bus in Thailand
rhumb line	a line between two points on the earth's surface	track	the path between one position and another
rupiah	Indonesian currency		
		warps	rope
SailMail	email via high frequency radio	windlass	device used to raise the anchor
saloon	main cabin	working jib	sails for close-hauled sailing
sea anchor	a device streamed from the bow or stern to hold a vessel into the wind or sea and to slow her	yawl	yacht, similar to a ketch, having two masts